"I'm thrilled to see the public[..] because it fills a real gap in th[..] uniquely qualified to write suc[..] [..] for the various lifesaving and life-preserving technologies that have been developed over the last half-century, they raise taxing ethical questions that Christians in previous eras never had to grapple with. As a seminary professor who teaches a required ethics course, I've discovered that students find end-of-life issues especially challenging to navigate, often leaning on gut instincts or vague appeals to divine providence rather than on careful and consistent biblical reasoning. From now on, I will direct those students to Dr. Davis's excellent and comprehensive treatment, which expertly combines biblical principles with real-life practical counsel. *Departing in Peace* deserves to become the go-to book for those seeking solid guidance on difficult end-of-life decisions."

—**James N. Anderson**, Associate Professor of Theology and Philosophy, Reformed Theological Seminary, Charlotte

"Though we are supposed to glorify God in all that we do, when we are staring death in the face, that calling is usually not at the front of our minds. Having stared death in the face and gotten a reprieve, I had a change in my sense of priorities. I am glad Bill Davis has taken the time to write this book because it is not an easy topic, nor is it a topic that one considers at the moment that it most needs to be considered. I know this firsthand. But the advice in this work is sound, and the wisdom is timeless. We will all one day wonder whether we are making the right end-of-life decisions for our loved ones. This book fills a void in preparing us for that time."

—**Erick Woods Erickson**, author, *Before You Wake*; editor, *The Resurgent*

"This book is a fine reflection on crucial issues of life and death. As we would expect from Bill Davis, it is careful, thoughtful, and biblical, and it will be genuinely helpful to families and pastors."

—**W. Robert (Bob) Godfrey**, President and Professor of Church History, Westminster Seminary California

"This book is a gift for anyone—adult child, parent, pastor—having to wrestle with, or counsel others through, end-of-life decisions. Davis offers clear, biblically grounded principles for navigating these decisions, and he shares a number of real-life case studies that illustrate poignantly both how complicated these decisions can be and how biblical principles can be applied to them. His approach is both immensely practical—supplying the reader with commentary on his case studies and helpful study questions and definitions throughout—and deeply pastoral. His wise, humble, and compassionate manner make clear that he is no stranger to these difficult matters. I know of no better guide for the Christian who faces the very daunting decisions that surround the end of life."

—**J. Derek Halvorson**, President, Covenant College

"There are good books on dying well in the comfort of Christ. But this book combines mature biblical teaching with the brass-tacks practical questions that we all face with the death of loved ones. These are the things that we don't usually think about until they happen. I highly recommend *Departing in Peace* as essential preparation."

—**Michael Horton**, J. Gresham Machen Professor of Systematic Theology and Apologetics, Westminster Seminary California

"Bill Davis clearly loves three things: critical thinking, biblical authority, and the bride of Christ. In this practical volume, he brings these loves together. As a well-trained philosopher, he helps us carefully navigate through end-of-life issues, even as he draws on Scripture, always seeking the goal of Christian faithfulness. Davis wants God's people to live wisely and well, even when we face some of the most heartrending decisions. Thankfully, with his help we can prepare ourselves, our families, and our churches for the complex theological and practical difficulties that arise in these hard situations. I strongly recommend this book specifically to pastors, who are often placed in the difficult position of giving advice to parishioners who must make end-of-life decisions for loved ones."

—**Kelly M. Kapic**, Professor of Theological Studies, Covenant College; author, *Embodied Hope: A Meditation on Pain and Suffering*

"Bill Davis has provided a remarkable guide to address one of the most sensitive aspects of life. *Departing in Peace: Biblical Decision-Making at the End of Life* clearly imparts needed wisdom so that believers in Christ can complete their lives with the faithfulness that affirms the sanctity of life, yet avoids the perplexity of extending life at any cost."

—**Peter Lillback**, President, Westminster Theological Seminary

"With such rapid advances in medical technology, together with a 'culture of death' that predominates in the West, life-and-death decisions are becoming increasingly complex. Thanks to Bill Davis for bringing both his intellectual acumen and his practical experience to bear on such a timely and crucially important topic. Pastors and elders would be well advised to let this book help guide them in decisions of life and death in their churches. Every Christian will be helped by the clarity and counsel that Davis gives to these discussions."

—**K. Scott Oliphint**, Professor of Apologetics and Systematic Theology, Westminster Theological Seminary

"As a Reformed Christian who has practiced medicine for six decades, read and studied medical ethics for most of that time, and written extensively on such issues, I rejoice in Dr. Bill Davis's book on end-of-life issues. The most distressing dimension of my experience has been the purposeful omission or superficial application of biblical reasoning by evangelical Christians to these ethical problems. Dr. Davis has made a very serious attempt to be fully and accurately biblical, especially concerning the withholding or withdrawal of medical treatments and the responsible application of personal and family economic principles. Considering the complexity of such issues, I cannot agree with all that Dr. Davis has said. Yet his book greatly advances biblical medical ethics, as well as the vital discussion and attention that both Christians and non-Christians need to face these difficult decisions."

—**Franklin E. (Ed) Payne**, MD, Associate Professor of Family Medicine, Augusta Health Sciences University (retired); primary author, 1988 PCA Report on Heroic Measures

"*Departing in Peace* is an excellent road map for preparing to deal with difficult end-of-life issues. Although it is written from a beautifully Christian orientation, the core of the material applies to most people. People of faith will come to treasure its wisdom. People not firmly anchored in faith will find much to hold close. The later chapters on the nuts-and-bolts and money matters are very worthwhile.

"Dr. Davis is an exemplary teacher and guide. His personal experience with end-of-life issues and his experience as a guide to others are invaluable for those who want to be ready.

"As a critical-care physician and colleague of Dr. Davis on a hospital ethics committee, I have come to know and highly regard his opinions. This book is worthwhile for everyone because no one escapes death, and we should be prepared for it."

—**Richard R. Pesce**, MD, MS (ethics), FCCP, FACP, Medical Director of Critical Care, Memorial Hospital, Chattanooga, Tennessee

"Professor Bill Davis has written a book that needs to be part of our seminary curriculums and certainly in the hands of pastors and elders. Just a few months ago, a young man in my congregation called from his father's bedside as he and his family struggled to know whether it was right before God to remove him from life support. By taking the discussion into the realm of faithful stewardship of all that God has given us, and realizing that our ultimate enjoyment in the world comes from our spiritual connection to God and his means of grace, Dr. Davis has moved the discussion of end-of-life decisions on to a firmer biblical foundation than merely being pro-life. After more than twenty years in pastoral ministry, I am grateful to the Lord Jesus that he has equipped Bill to write a book that I have needed and I'm sure many more do as well. Take, read, pray, and apply."

—**Kevin M. Smith**, Senior Pastor, New City Fellowship of Chattanooga (PCA)

"With *Departing in Peace*, Bill Davis has provided a thorough and excellent resource for Christian believers seeking a consistent biblical approach to the bewildering challenge of planning for the end of life. Davis provides thoughtful insights from his own personal experiences with a family member and others who have approached death. With strong opinions (some subject to debate), Davis brings a wealth of knowledge from his work on hospital ethics committees and in teaching at a Christian college. Most useful is his practical, step-by-step guide to completing an advance directive. This book will be helpful both in my medical practice and to individuals and families asking these questions."

    —**R. Henry Williams**, MD, FACP, Board Chair, Tennessee
       Center for Bioethics and Culture

DEPARTING IN
PEACE

DEPARTING IN
PEACE

BIBLICAL DECISION-MAKING
AT THE END OF LIFE

BILL DAVIS

PUBLISHING
P.O. BOX 817 • PHILLIPSBURG • NEW JERSEY 08865-0817

Printed in the United States of America

ISBN: 978-1-62995-259-8 (pbk)
ISBN: 978-1-62995-260-4 (ePub)
ISBN: 978-1-62995-261-1 (Mobi)

Library of Congress Cataloging-in-Publication Data

Names: Davis, Bill (Professor of Philosophy), author.
Title: Departing in peace : biblical decision-making at the end of life / Bill Davis.
Description: Phillipsburg : P&R Publishing, 2017. | Includes bibliographical references and index.
Identifiers: LCCN 2017022784| ISBN 9781629952598 (pbk.) | ISBN 9781629952604 (epub) | ISBN 9781629952611 (mobi)
Subjects: LCSH: Death--Religious aspects--Christianity. | Death--Planning.
Classification: LCC BT825 .D345 2017 | DDC 261.8/32175--dc23
LC record available at https://lccn.loc.gov/2017022784

For Lynda

Download free, complete lesson plans for Sunday school classes and church discussion groups from the *Departing in Peace* page on P&R's website, www.prpbooks.com.

CONTENTS

ANALYTICAL OUTLINE

FOREWORD

I was a young man—still in my mid-30s—when I learned that I had been named executor of the estate of an elderly couple in my church who had just died. Bone cancer had taken Nell about a month earlier. Then, quite unprepared for the shock of living alone, George dressed for church on a Sunday morning, but succumbed to a heart attack before getting out the door.

Nell was pretty much ready for death—George considerably less so. But the fellow they'd asked to look after their affairs? He didn't have a clue.

Death, even for a Christian, tends to be something of a mystery. That's the case on a number of fronts. The departure of our souls from our bodies and all that's associated with breathing our last—well, let's just say that it can be a bit "spooky." The medical decisions that we're called on to make can border on the heartless. And the high cost of dying can leave surviving families surprised, embarrassed, and sometimes broke.

And it all comes at you so fast that you're bound to ask, "Why didn't someone warn me?"

Well, here is that warning. But it comes at you here in gentle, helpful terms. Dr. Bill Davis's bedside manner is one that you will cherish the rest of your life.

This isn't primarily a step-by-step manual to equip you to deal with doctors, lawyers, and undertakers. It comes instead from the very practical mind of a philosophy professor who is gifted in helping his students take basic principles and apply them to the hard issues of life. And always, Professor Davis insists that those basic principles be thoughtfully and helpfully anchored in the great themes of Scripture.

Sooner or later, you're likely to find yourself helping to look after the affairs of a loved one who is close to death or who may even have just died. Or you may be trying to order your own affairs to make things easier for those who must look after you. In either case, you will thank Bill Davis for helping you work so thoughtfully through such important matters.

Joel Belz
Founder, *WORLD* magazine

PREFACE

This book is for people who suspect that they may eventually die. It is also for those who have faced death up close. Anyone who has been close to a loved one making end-of-life medical decisions already knows that principled advice is valuable. All of us can do ourselves and our families a big favor by thinking these things through long before the crisis hits. Only healthy people who die suddenly will avoid making hard decisions about end-of-life medical treatment. The rest of us will have to make these decisions, and waiting to think about it will only make things harder. It is not easy to think clearly when we are sick. Disease and dysfunction may even deprive us of the ability to make decisions about our own care. Our family, our friends, or our doctors will be left to make those decisions. If we leave no instructions about our goals and values, their grief over our illness will be compounded by distress and uncertainty.

Christians will be most comfortable with this book's approach to moral reasoning, but other readers should find the discussion helpful as well. Most people have serious convictions about the value of human life, the close relationship between responsibility and agency, and the inappropriateness of prolonging pointless suffering. These convictions are fundamental to end-of-life ethics. They are taught by the Bible, but also by other religious and ethical systems.

This book appeals explicitly to Scripture because Bible-believing Christians are too often persuaded that the Bible requires us to use medical means to extend physical life as long as possible. I will be arguing against this supposed requirement. My argument is built both on general ethical principles and on what the Bible teaches. The Bible does not require doing *everything* as death approaches; instead, the Bible requires something else. This "something else" locates our obligations about end-of-life decisions inside our more general obligation to serve God's glory and our neighbors' good in all that we do with our resources of time, energy, opportunity, and wealth.

The central ethical argument of this book is given in chapter 2. Working from Jesus' teaching in Matthew 25, I establish that all our decisions are made as servants. Our aim is not merely to do what is *right* rather than what is *wrong*; it is also to be found *faithful* rather than *unfaithful*. The question, "Is it wrong to turn off the ventilator that is keeping Gladys breathing?" is more helpfully stated, "Would Gladys be an unfaithful servant of her Master if she had the machine turned off?" Put this way, the issue is then about a Master-servant relationship: "Does the Master require his servant, Gladys, to keep the ventilator on as part of her service to him?" The decision is not about Gladys's conformity to an abstract rule in isolation from the details of her situation. It is about her relationship with her Master and using all her resources to honor him.

Framing end-of-life decisions in the biblical idiom of faithful service shows the appropriateness of paying close attention to Gladys's specific circumstances. Does faithful service mean using medical treatment that is ineffective? No. Would her Master require her to suffer merely to stay alive a few days longer, dramatically limited in her ability to serve others? Seen this way, it is hard to say yes. What if Gladys's treatment offers only the benefit of a slightly longer life in the hospital and imposes the burdens of physical pain, social isolation, drained finances, and spiritual deprivation? Might faithful service for Gladys allow discontinuing the treatment? I will argue that in some situations Gladys can faithfully discontinue the burdensome treatment even if it means that death will overtake her sooner. It is never faithful for Gladys to use medical or other means to hasten her death, and it is always part of faithful service for Gladys to pray that she be restored to health. But she can faithfully decline ineffective or excessively burdensome medical treatment.

These conclusions about what faithful service means follow the lead of a study committee report adopted by the Presbyterian Church in America in 1988. The report identifies a number of biblical principles and applies them to the medical realities of the late 1980s. This book expands and details the biblical basis for the report's principles and advice, answers common objections to the report's findings, and applies its guidance to the medical practices current in 2017. While consistent with the report's findings, my discussion goes beyond the report by highlighting the spiritual burdens imposed by most life-sustaining treatments. The first half of chapter 2 builds the biblical case for the principle that we may decline ineffective or excessively burdensome treatment. The second half of chapter 2 focuses on answering common objections to this principle. I affirm that suicide of any kind (including physician-assisted) is biblically forbidden, and I insist on the value of prayer even as I argue that it is inappropriate to use medical means to "give God time to work a miracle." God does not need that kind of help.

Chapter 3 continues to develop biblical principles to inform end-of-life treatment decisions, first by considering four medical conditions that call for discussions about limiting treatment and then by discussing four kinds of treatment options that might be limited. The structure of this chapter follows the lead of the many state legislatures that have devised forms to guide people in leaving useful instructions about what they want done if they become unable to direct their own care. "Advance Directive" forms (which used to be called "Living Will" forms) have been available in every state since 2010. They provide an excellent way for people to make their values available to family members and medical professionals. In chapter 5, I use the biblical principles from chapters 2 and 3 to explain how I filled out my own (Tennessee) advance directive.

Most of the advice offered in chapter 3 is uncontroversial. People regardless of religious identity now agree that performing CPR on a person who is permanently unconscious is not morally required and may impose great and needless burdens. CPR is the first of the three kinds of medical treatment options discussed; permanent unconsciousness is the first of the four medical conditions discussed. Other recommendations offered as biblically warranted are more controversial.

I affirm the importance of defending all life because everyone is made in the image of God. Along with that affirmation, however, I argue that I may faithfully decide in advance that I do not want to be force-fed through a tube if I am permanently confused. While it is inappropriate to remove life support from me if I want it and can afford it, Christ does not require me to be force-fed to stay alive if I am no longer able to enjoy spiritual goods and serve others.

Chapter 4 tells six true stories about people making end-of-life decisions. The stories place the reader in the position of a friend who is being asked for advice about what to do. The narration is periodically suspended to ask a specific question, to offer three possible responses from which to choose, and then to explain the merits of each option. Most of these questions were asked of me when I was the friend giving advice in the midst of the actual crisis. In teaching this material to college, seminary, and Sunday school classes, I have used these stories as a way to start our discussions. Students are often surprised that anyone really faces questions like these. Medical professionals know that they are sadly common. Each story concludes with an epilogue that briefly explains how the story continued after the decision crisis passed.

Chapter 6 is about money. The original design of the book did not include this chapter, and I am grateful to John Hughes and the editorial staff at P&R Publishing for insisting that it be added. (This is not my only debt to John and the editorial staff, but it is an important one. Their direction and support have been outstanding. Karen Magnuson's detailed attention to the footnotes and thorough copyediting have been an especially great help.) I wanted to avoid financial matters entirely because I have never been part of an end-of-life decision involving real people in which adding money to the conversation made things better (clearer, more biblically illuminating, more faithful). Writing chapter 6 helped me to see that it is not money itself that corrupts the discussion. What undermines end-of-life discussions is distrust. Money focuses distrust and makes it seem reasonable even when it isn't. Families who distrust medical professionals find it easy to believe that the doctors care *only* about money. Family members who distrust each other find it easy to say that the others are greedy and not loving. Money is purposely left out of discussions about end-of-life care on the ethics committee at the hospital where I volunteer as an ethics consultant, and that has seemed like the best approach.

But placing considerations about finances inside the task of faithful service to Christ makes a big difference. Instead of being a discussion-ender, it puts money alongside time, energy, and opportunity as resources that we might use faithfully or not. Medical care near the end of life is expensive, but money is not the only cost involved. Living longer may cost great pain, spiritual deprivation, and burdens borne by others. Devoting resources to living longer may mean *not* using those resources to realize other great goods. Putting money in its proper place made me realize the biblical necessity of dealing with every decision inside the task of making faithful use of all our resources.

The final two chapters are even more practical. Chapter 7 describes how changes in American hospital practice affect the task of making end-of-life decisions. Twenty years ago, most people were talking to personal physicians whom they had known for years when they made the fateful decisions about care. Today, most decisions are made in consultation with doctors and nurses employed by the hospitals. This change means that the medical care is more specialized and less likely to be delayed by misunderstandings about hospital policy, but it also means that sick people and their families are talking to strangers. The chapter focuses on getting the most out of this system, and especially on the crucial task of getting the overall medical picture. Chapter 8 addresses what we might be doing now *before* we are in the hospital, facing end-of-life choices for ourselves or our loved ones. Some of the things we might be doing now call for difficult family conversations. Others call for church or community educational efforts. All of them will have the payoff of diminishing the awfulness of making choices when the time comes.

The biblical analysis and practical advice offered in this book have been road-tested, both in the hospital and in the classroom. **Sometimes the practical advice makes observations about legal matters, but I am *not* a licensed attorney and these observations should not be construed as legal advice. Concerning legal matters, readers are** encouraged to seek the advice of qualified legal counsel. I am also not trained in medicine. My qualifications are only as a philosopher and teacher with experience and some training as a hospital ethics consultant. With this background, I am grateful to the leadership at Lookout Mountain Presbyterian Church (PCA) for allowing me to lead Wednesday-night discussions and Sunday school classes through this material. The curricula for these educational events are available through the P&R website. The Wednesday-night discussions depend on the availability of doctors and nurses willing to talk through and answer questions about specific cases. The four-week Sunday school curriculum is driven by scripted dialogues acted out by class members. The expertise of medical professionals is not required for the Sunday school curriculum, but when they are present, it helps a lot. I am also thankful to the leadership of Chattanooga Valley Presbyterian Church for inviting me to teach the Sunday school material to their adult class.

My students at Covenant College and Reformed Theological Seminary Atlanta also contributed to refining the argument of this book. My Bioethics class at Covenant helped focus the stories and questions in chapter 4. My Christian Mind students at Covenant proofed and commented on the first complete draft. The Pastoral & Social Ethics class at RTS Atlanta reviewed and corrected the thirty-three biblical principles that are developed in the book and summarized in Appendix A. The thirty teaching and ruling elders on the session at Lookout Mountain Presbyterian Church also vetted these principles.

The administration and my faculty colleagues at Covenant College also played an important role in making this book possible and shaping its contents. I enjoyed a semester-long sabbatical from teaching in 2014 to do research, and the administration funded my trips to the PCA General Assembly to lead seminars on aspects of the book in 2013 and 2016. John Wingard (philosophy), Bill Tate (English), Hans Madueme (theology), and Brian Crossman (physical education) all pestered me about progress and pushed back when my ideas were foggy (or worse). I am grateful to all of them for their thoughtful help and encouragement. Also at Covenant, the Philosophy Department work-study aide, Caroline McLeod, did excellent work in compiling the glossary of terms.

I am indebted to many other people for their help with this book. They answered questions, read drafts, and gave thoughtful responses to the principles I recommend. Some are physicians: Robert Goldman, MD (palliative-care specialist, Memorial Hospital, Chattanooga, Tennessee), and John Risley, MD (urgent care medicine, Chattanooga). Others are nurses: Christine Dominguez, Karen Frank, and Jerry McCrary. Some are hospital chaplains (Betsy Kammerdeiner and Father Fausto Kevarengai), teaching elders in the PCA (Paul Bankson, Dan Gilchrist, Frank Hitchings, Joseph Novenson, Brian Salter, and Len Teague), or ruling elders at Lookout Mountain Presbyterian Church, PCA (Frank Brock, Tommy Gifford, Robert Huffaker, and Donald B. Kent).

Friends and colleagues have been especially helpful with comments on drafts and by praying: Barby Gifford and Hollie Kent. I am also indebted to Carl Middleton at Catholic Health Initiatives (Denver, Colorado) and Sister Eileen Wrobleski, the former vice president for mission integration at Memorial Hospital, as well as the other members of the ethics committees at Memorial Hospital, and the Alexian Brothers PACE program in Chattanooga. The board, administration, and faculty of Covenant College granted me a sabbatical in the spring of 2014 to do research on this project.

Many of my Covenant College and Reformed Theological Seminary students have been involved: Joshua Alford, Ben Benson, Chris Blackman, Grace Brown, Jason Cunningham, Terry Dykstra, Meagan Fernsler, Daniel Freman, Isaiah Gordon, Emma Grimes, Alex Kim, Michael Kirkland, Joanna Kolkman, Michael Lancour, Jimmy Latham, Lorette Mathe, Caroline McKissick, Mark Miller, Michael Morris, David Newberry, Morgan Nix, Matthew O'Sullivan, Noah Rallo, Sally Anne Russell, Luis Sanchez, Libby Scott, Anna Stogner, John Tremann, Hannah Umhau, Roy Uptain, Sophie Westbrook, Annalisa Yew, Joshua Youssef, and Kristie Zeigler.

Finally, I must thank friends and family for their input and support. Dr. R. Henry Williams, internal medicine, and ruling elder at Lookout

Mountain Presbyterian Church, provided uncommonly detailed and insightful questions about many aspects of an early draft of this book. Dr. Rich Pesce, the chief intensivist at Memorial Hospital, Chattanooga, has been my best-informed resource about the many medical matters discussed in the book. His command of the medical and ethical literature is encyclopedic, and he has endured my numerous ignorant questions with patience and provided consistently helpful answers. Karen Frank, DNP and head of safety and security at Memorial Hospital, has walked me through best practices for getting the big picture. If I'm ever in the hospital, I want Dr. Pesce overseeing my medical care and Karen as my case manager. And if I can't make decisions for myself, I want my wife, Lynda, making them. We have discussed all manner of distressing end-of-life cases. Her sense of what faithfulness calls for in these cases has been clear when mine was cloudy. I have complete confidence in her judgment, but I hope she never has to use it to make decisions about my care. I would prefer that Jesus return before those decisions are necessary. Because this book will be useful only if Christ tarries, I hope it is never used by anyone.

1

INTRODUCTION

MY FATHER'S DEATH

During the first week of June 2014, my earthly father died in a hospital bed in Wenatchee, Washington. My twin brother and I were in the room when he died, and we had participated in his decision to stop using the mask that was forcing air in and out of his lungs. Rather than staying on the mask and struggling to breathe, he decided to focus instead on being comfortable. He knew that it would mean that he would die before long, but he had been fighting a gang of physical challenges for a week. Together we agreed that his fight to get better had been faithful, and that he was never going to leave the hospital. While it was very sad to lose him and difficult to accept that his time had come, it was not difficult to decide to stop doing everything that medicine could do to extend his life. The decision was not difficult in part because my father had decided long before his final illness that he did not want to be kept alive on a ventilator and did not want to be resuscitated if his heart stopped. He had put these wishes in a legally sound form and explained them to me. I did not have to wonder whether he would want to have either of these means used to keep him alive.

A summary of my dad's final hours that I wrote for my family shows another reason that the decisions involved were not difficult:

Friends,

Last night at 9:45 my dad went home to be with the Lord. The end came much more quickly than I thought possible, but it was peaceful and may have happened exactly as he would have scripted it.

At 11:00 A.M. yesterday, my dad spoke his last clear word. He had fallen asleep earlier in the morning during the family conference with the doctors, his wife, Carolyn, two of my siblings, and me. At that conference we came to the conclusion that (a) he would never be strong enough to leave the hospital and (b) all of the ways forward involved fatal risks. Even the BiPap mask pushing his oxygen involved the risk of making him nauseated to the point of vomiting. And vomiting into the oxygen mask would bring a rapid and painful death by aspiration. Discontinuing the mask would be much more comfortable, but without it his carbon dioxide level would rise, eventually to a fatal degree. But the slow buildup of CO_2 would not be uncomfortable provided he had morphine to manage the air hunger drive. In light of all this, the family decided that he would want to have the mask removed and to be made comfortable.

Before changing his treatment level, we asked the doctors to let us discuss it, this time including Dad in the conversation. (The only unsatisfying part of the medical care Dad received was the last hospitalist's unwillingness to take the time to try to explain Dad's situation *to Dad*. The hospitalist had decided that Dad was too out of it to direct his own care. Neither Carolyn, nor Russ, nor I agreed with the hospitalist's judgment about Dad's ability to follow and participate. The hospitalist had been on the case only a couple of hours, and he did not make a serious attempt to wake Dad up to talk to him.) So with the doctors out of the room, we slowly explained to Dad what we had learned about his condition (that the attempts to restore his breathing capacity were not working), his prognosis (that he would never be strong enough to leave the hospital and that continuing to use the mask involved risks), and his options (to stay on the mask and accept the discomfort and the risks involved or to change the goal of his care from curing his many illnesses to maximizing his comfort). When we were convinced that he understood enough of this, we said we thought he would want to focus on being comfortable and to take off the mask. He visibly summoned his strength, looked each of us (Carolyn, Russ, and me) in the eye, and said "Okay" through the mask. It was a great blessing to have him confirm the decision.

At 1:30 P.M. the equipment and specialists were assembled. They turned off the monitors. They started an IV morphine drip to make sure he would not have unmanageable pain. After 10 minutes on the morphine, they took out all the other IVs, took off the oxygen mask, and put on the nasal cannula (high-flow oxygen). He did not struggle to breathe, but it did take 15 minutes to find a comfortable position in the bed.

When my dad was settled on the initial dose of morphine, the palliative-care specialist, Dr. W, started to leave the room, insisting that the nurse, Greg, was fully able to supervise the process of finding the appropriate level of morphine. I did not doubt Greg's competence at all, but I did not want Dr. W to leave the room. So I stood in the doorway and asked if he could stay. As he had been throughout his time caring for my dad, he was willing to meet my needs as well as my dad's: he stayed to oversee the process. Morphine is a powerful pain suppressor, and it is wonderful for controlling the air hunger drive. The morphine would enable my dad to sleep easily for the first time in days. But morphine also suppresses breathing, and I did not want the morphine to be the cause of my dad's death. I wanted him to be comfortable, but not to be terminally sedated. With patience and careful monitoring, the specialist would be able to find a dosage high enough to end the pain and anxious struggling but low enough for him to continue to breathe.

Over the next 45 minutes the morphine drip rate was slowly increased under the supervision of the palliative-care specialist. We watched for signs of struggle or restlessness, confident that if he could go 15 minutes without jerking, grimacing, or crying, his pain and anxiety were under control. Three times the specialist directed Greg to give Dad a shot of morphine and to increase the drip rate on the IV slightly. After each increase, we watched for signs of discomfort. After the third increase, he went 15 minutes breathing steadily and showing no signs of distress.

After switching from curative care to comfort care, my dad rested as Russ, Sarah, and I talked about our children. He would open his eyes from time to time and smile. It is likely that he was listening almost all the time. His breathing was not regular like he was asleep, and sometimes he would shake his head and smile at a funny turn in a story. He never opened his eyes, but we could tell he was with us.

Between 3:30 and 8:00 P.M. I went to the hotel and slept. Russ and Sarah stayed with Dad and continued to talk. His breathing was consistent and on the few occasions when he furrowed his brow or squirmed, the nurse would give him a 1 mg shot of morphine on top of the drip.

At 9:00 P.M. they moved him out of the ICU to a comfort-only room on another floor. He did not open his eyes during the rather complicated move, but his breathing remained steady and strong at 16 respirations per minute. Russ was about to go back to the hotel and get some sleep. I was settling in for a night of watching and read-ing the Psalms to Dad. But with Dad breathing steadily, Russ and I started talking about Richard Feynman's lectures on quantum phys-ics. We lost track of time. At 9:43 Russ noticed that Dad's breathing pattern had changed. We went to the bedside (all of four feet away) for a closer look. His breathing was very shallow, and now about 2 breaths per minute. I went to find a nurse to see if something needed to be done, although Dad was not struggling and looked like he was sleeping peacefully.

The nurse came a couple of minutes later. She examined him and said, "He has passed. I'll get another nurse to confirm it." We were shocked at how quickly it had happened, and a little unhappy that we hadn't noticed that his breathing was decreasing as we talked. But on reflection I believe that Dad would have wanted to drift out of this life listening to his children enjoying each other's company. When Russ and I were seven years old, Dad would help us get to sleep by playing recordings of Dr. Edward Teller explaining Einstein's theory of relativity. I'm sure Dad did not mind being helped in his final sleep by our talking about physics. He was a nuclear engineer most of his life. He may have thought that the loop was closing in an appropriate way.

My dad made arrangements to be buried at sea. We found a card in his wallet with a number to call, and they (the Neptune Society) took care of everything concerning the disposition of his body. I'll see him again when the sea gives up its dead.[1]

Thanks for all your prayers and friendship.

In many ways, it is clear to me that God was merciful to my dad, my brother, and me. My dad may have continued breathing for days, or even weeks, probably never waking up and possibly in some pain. If he had continued to breathe, we would have had to figure out whether to set up a schedule to keep watch over him. It may have been necessary to find a facility that could care for him in a minimally conscious state. Every day would have given us the opportunity to second-guess our decision. As it happened, we could see that he was comfortable, and we were there when he breathed his last. We have not had to wonder whether he died for lack of close attention or someone's mistake. It was a more peaceful passing than I could have invented with a blank sheet of paper.

The final decision was not difficult because Dad had left crucial instructions. Its difficulty was also diminished by my own preparation for making biblically appropriate end-of-life decisions. I am a philosophy professor with no formal medical training. While I teach bioethics at Covenant College and Reformed Theological Seminary, what I know about morphine, palliative care, oxygen-delivery options, and the difference between hospitalists and nurses comes from serving for seventeen years as a volunteer community member on the ethics committee at Memorial Hospital and with the PACE program in Chattanooga, Tennessee. I have an MA from Westminster Seminary

---

1. Rev. 20:13. The Neptune Society is a cremation service; see https://www .neptunesociety.com/. I believe that cremation is biblically permissible, and I am sure that those cremated will be bodily raised without difficulty. When financially feasible, however, burial provides a way of visibly proclaiming our confident hope in the resurrection.

California and a PhD in philosophy from the University of Notre Dame.[2] That training prepared me to think through the biblical principles that informed the final decision for my dad. Without the years of experience on the ethics committee, including serving as an ethics consultant on cases at the hospital (always with at least one doctor and one nurse), I would not have known how to connect the biblical principles to the practical demands of decision-making in a hospital context.

Since 2013, I have served as a ruling elder at Lookout Mountain Presbyterian Church (PCA), pastored by Joe Novenson. In that role, I have had the difficult privilege of advising families faced with end-of-life decisions about their parents and their children. One of the more recent cases involved the decision not to resuscitate a 2-year-old who had suffered a global brain injury but still had a functioning brain stem. Between the ethics committee work and cases referred to me by PCA churches, I have talked, walked, and prayed with people through more than thirty end-of-life situations. Every one of these cases has been emotionally taxing, but it has been an honor to be a part of each one.

This book is driven by the most common source of anxiety expressed by Christians as they have faced end-of-life decisions. Desiring to honor God's Word and obey his commandments, they have often thought that they were obligated to do everything medically possible to extend earthly life as long as possible. It is common for sincere believers to say something like this: "Because life is precious to God, I must be called to do everything possible to keep my loved one (or myself) alive." Medical technology is now able to extend earthly life in ways that would have seemed miraculous even fifty years ago. Very often it is *possible* to extend life for a long time even though there is no human reason to think that the person will ever regain consciousness. Sometimes the medical means are available but come only with great

2. John Frame's course The Doctrine of the Christian Life was especially important in shaping my thinking. This course was the basis for Frame's *The Doctrine of the Christian Life*, A Theology of Lordship (Phillipsburg, NJ: P&R Publishing, 2008).

pain, confusion, isolation, and radically diminished spiritual opportunities. Even when the gains from medicine are meager, sincere believers find it hard to resist the conclusion that they must seize every medical treatment because God requires it.

GOD'S LAW: A GIFT TO GOD'S PEOPLE

If I believed that God's Word required us to use every means available to extend life as long as possible, I would not have agreed to removing the BiPap mask from my dad. And I would have urged him not to accept a do-not-resuscitate order when asked by his doctors. It would be foolish to trust my own understanding more than God's law. God's law is perfect and the only inerrant source of guidance. God's revealed will is for our good at the beginning of life, at the end of life, and at every moment in between. God's Word speaks to every area of life as well. While we can ask questions that God's Word does not answer in detail—such as "Should I ask my boss for a raise?"—it shines light on the path ahead of us with warnings, principles, and direction. Even when I do not understand how God's law is for my good, I know that it is. As the world around us grows less and less curious about God's design for our good, followers of Christ should continue to look to God's Word as our rule of faith and life.

Because the culture around us is increasingly comfortable treating life as cheap, Christians are right to be suspicious about trends away from fighting for every life. In 1985 I moderated a panel discussion on end-of-life care at Mercy Hospital in San Diego. I was a seminary student at the time, and I was eager to speak boldly for the protection of life. One of the physicians on the panel was not a believer, and he was openly frustrated by my resistance to discontinuing treatment that was not showing any benefit. When I asked him whether he was "playing God" when he turned the machines off, he said, "Of course I'm playing God. That is what doctors are paid to do." It was not a helpful response. I assumed (wrongly) that he was saying what any doctor would say, and it led me to think that Christians must double their resolve to extend life regardless of the obstacles. Without studying what the Scriptures have to say about life and death, I set out to defend what I thought the Bible must be saying.

My confident presumption that I knew best led me next to dis-agree forcefully with a Christian doctor in my home church. In casual conversation about a friend who was in the hospital but in decline, he said that the decision to turn a life-support machine off is ethically the same as the decision not to turn it on in the first place. This seemed dangerously incorrect to me. Turning a machine off would mean *killing* someone. Not turning it on would be merely *letting the person die*. I argued (proud of my insight and holiness) that turning on a machine to keep someone alive implied a promise to keep it on as long as it was doing its job. His response was simple, and I now know that it is decisive: if turning a machine on brings with it a promise to keep it on, then first responders (paramedics, ER personnel, etc.) will be forced to make long-term promises without vital information. Often, no one knows what effect a course of treatment will have. It might be just what the person needs, but it might also do very little good and even cause great pain, isolation, and spiritual deprivation. If ineffective or greatly burdensome care cannot be withdrawn when the true impact of the treatment is finally known, then emergency workers will have to see the future or make promises that everyone will regret. As I will show in chapters 2 and 3, I am now sure that this Christian doctor's reasoning was both biblical and sound. At the time, however, I insisted that he was rebelling against God's Word, duped by the world's indifference to the sanctity of life.

In the thirty years since loudly taking these positions, I have served on three different ethics committees. Most hospitals now have eth-ics committees because it is expected by the Joint Commission that accredits hospitals to receive government funds. Some hospitals don't make much use of these committees, but I have had the pleasure of volunteering for three that were active. All three did "consults," work-ing with caregivers to sort through contentious decisions. Two of them made and reviewed hospital policies about informed consent, privacy, and how to limit medical treatment that was excessively burdensome. The one on which I currently serve does all that and also works hard at educating everyone about ethical challenges—sick people and their families, doctors, hospital staff, and the local community. Each of these committees on which I have served spent well over 75 percent of its time on end-of-life decisions. The decisions involved are momentous, urgent, medically complex, and typically plagued by communication breakdowns. As a philosophy professor, I find the committees' deliberations fascinating. As a follower of Christ, I find that they make my heart sick. The ravaging effects of the fall cluster together as death, fear, greed, and broken relationships combine to make an awful stew.

In part from serving on these committees, I became friends with many excellent physicians and nurses, both Christians and non-Christians. To my surprise, most of the non-Christian doctors and nurses have been zealous for the defense of human life. While the business and legal folks on the committees were sometimes willing to give up on sick people near the end, the physicians and nurses rarely did. They are trained to heal, and not to give up. The Christians have been even more solidly and actively pro-life. Some are leaders in the antiabortion effort; others are career medical missionaries; and all are respected by their medical colleagues. To my surprise (and chagrin), I also discovered that every last one of these people—including the Christians—disagreed with both of the principles that I had insisted were biblical. The Christian medical professionals have all believed that God's Word allows us to stop using treatment that is greatly burdensome, even if it is extending physical life. And they have been even more sure that God's Word does not obligate us to continue treatment once it is started.

Finding so many sincere, Bible-believing Christians who disagreed with my opinions about what the Bible teaches should have been enough to drive me back to Scripture. Sadly, it wasn't. It was working on the ethics committees that forced me to look carefully at what God's Word says about life and death. Reading the details of what it takes to extend sick people's lives medically was disquieting. Seeing and smelling the realities of what it meant for people to have the medical means used on them was even more moving. Resuscitating someone whose heart has stopped looks like a violent assault. Maintaining someone's breathing on a ventilator looks like a miracle when it makes recovery possible. But for a person with no medical prospect of ever leaving the ICU, it looks much more like a prison sentence. Cancer treatments often involve drugs or methods just short of fatal: killing the cancer means nearly killing the person. For people already weak for other reasons, the physical, psychological, and spiritual toll can be devastating without being likely to succeed. If God's Word taught that we must do everything medically possible to extend life, then I would have to learn how to deliver that hard word in a gentle but firm way. First, though, I needed to be sure that God's Word demanded it.

Chapters 2 and 3 of this book summarize what I learned when I returned to the Scriptures, applying the tools I had gained at Westminster Seminary years earlier. (I realize that I should have been searching the Scriptures from the outset. I regret the years of being a pain or a bore to my Christian medical friends, thankful only that I did not do too much damage on the ethics committees before admitting that I had not carefully studied what the Bible says.) The order of the topics in chapters 2 and 3 follows the pattern I use when I teach the principles to adult Sunday school classes and to students at Covenant College and Reformed Theological Seminary. Teaching end-of-life decision-making to biblically serious Christian adults has shown me two crucial things about this difficult material. First, the discussion must stay connected to what the Bible says about life, death, stewardship, and the significance of spiritual benefits and burdens. Discussions that wander away from the Bible's teaching on these things will generate anxiety rather than confidence. Second, everyone has a personal connection to the practical challenges involved. These people need to be encouraged to tell their stories. Often, the stories are full of sorrow, confusion, and even regret. People who are living to serve Jesus and obey God's Word are often hurting because they think they gave up on a loved one too soon. They also think they displeased Christ by giving up. The principles presented in chapter 2 can help them deal with their complicated grieving, but they can also benefit from drawing the rest of the class into their story. Their grief has often been lonely precisely because they thought they had failed God's law.

THE PCA REPORT ON HEROIC MEASURES

The testimony of Christian medical professionals, together with what I saw while volunteering on the ethics committees, and my own study of God's Word, led me to believe that the Bible does not require us to do everything medicine offers when the medical treatment either is ineffective or imposes an excessive burden on the person who is nearing death. Only after reaching that conviction did I learn that my own denomination—the Presbyterian Church in America (PCA)—had appointed a committee in the late 1980s to study what God's Word says about end-of-life care. The PCA had adopted the committee's findings in 1988, but I did not learn of its existence until 2013. I read the report eagerly (and with a little apprehension). The report's central finding is that God's Word does not require us to use ineffective or burdensome treatment to extend our physical lives. This can be stated as a biblical principle, and it is the most important principle in this book:

Permission to Decline Treatment: God's Word permits us to decline life-sustaining medical treatment that is ineffective or that we, as servants of Christ, judge to be excessively burdensome.[3]

The 1988 PCA Report on Heroic Measures reaches its conclusions by using the Word of God as its standard. God's Word does not change, and the principles recommended by the report are still valid and helpful. American society and medical practice, however,

---

3. The exact wording of this principle in the PCA Study Committee Report on Heroic Measures at the End of Life is as follows: "treatments that are ineffective, minimally effective or have frequent and serious side effects are not obligatory" (§ III.6). I have replaced "serious side effects" with "excessively burdensome" to reflect the terminology commonly used in hospital practice and to emphasize (as the report intends) that side effects are "serious" when they are greatly burdensome to the person who must endure them. The authors of the report were William Hall, James Hurley, Reginald F. McLelland, PhD, F. Edward Payne, MD, and John Van Voorhis. The full text of the report can be accessed at http://pcahistory.org/pca/2-378.html. From here on, this report will be called the "1988 PCA Report on Heroic Measures."

have considerably changed since 1988. Those changes make the report practically difficult to use today. The language used in the report is not just outdated. Some of its key phrases now mean something very different. The report makes assumptions about a doctor's role that would seem quaint or even dangerous today. Most importantly, the report discourages believers from using "Living Will" forms for reasons that no longer apply to today's legal environment and hospital practice. (Living wills—now called *advance directives*—are today more standardized, better understood, and more likely to be welcomed by physicians as a source of guidance.) This book aims to make a more detailed biblical case for the principles found in the 1988 PCA Report on Heroic Measures, and to give more practical guidance about how to apply those principles, especially in the hospital setting of today.

The final recommendation of the 1988 PCA Report on Heroic Measures drives the writing of this book:

> A person or committee in each church should be designated for special study concerning the terminally ill. The seriousness of the issues and their complexity require more than a casual or wait-until-something-happens approach. Further, virtually everyone will face some facet of these problems with some family members. A resource is needed locally to offer Biblical advice and options to those involved. It is doubtful that every pastor will have the time necessary to devote to this particular area. Formal teaching sessions and distribution of literature for the congregation should also be arranged. Physicians in the congregation should be involved as well.[4]

The recommendations about end-of-life medical decisions given in the 1988 PCA Report on Heroic Measures are sound, but the biblical support for its principles is not developed in detail. My goal is to provide a "resource" that can be used by believers to "offer Biblical advice and options," and to give pastors and other leaders the biblical basis for the principles they will need to assist believers and their families

4. Ibid., § IV.5.

when medical decisions must be made. My experience in teaching these principles to adults in PCA churches has helped me to see where the reasoning needs to be especially attentive to the text of Scripture. Those teaching opportunities also helped me to see the importance of illustrations that match what people are facing in the hospital context today. I would be very pleased to learn that this book helped to fulfill the recommendation that "literature for the congregation should . . . be arranged."

In addition to recommending biblical principles and preparing people for practical hospital realities, this book follows the 1988 PCA Report on Heroic Measures' emphasis on the role that *spiritual implications* should play in end-of-life decisions by and for believers. Christian reflections about our approach to death often highlight the spiritual delights that await believers in an endless life in Christ's presence. I will do nothing to diminish that grateful anticipation or dim that glorious truth. Instead, I hope to focus on the spiritual burdens that are endured by many who are kept physically alive by medical treatments that offer no natural prospect of recovery. We too easily forget that the greatest joys that this life affords are spiritual. To the world, spiritual joys look paltry. We should know better. The delight of reading God's Word and hearing it preached, the unity found in taking the sacraments with other believers, the peace and involvement known in corporate prayer, and the thrill of singing God's praises together with God's people are more fulfilling to our whole selves than anything else on earth.

Today's medical treatments can extend earthly life, but often only by cutting people off from all these spiritual joys. In chapter 5, I use my own advance directive to illustrate a step-by-step approach to completing a legally effective document to make sure that your wishes are known if you become too sick or injured to speak for yourself. At the heart of the instructions I have left with my doctor is the desire not to have medical means used to keep me alive *unless* the means are humanly likely to restore to me the ability to enjoy "the ordinary means of grace." These ordinary means are the spiritual goods just mentioned above: access to God's Word, the sacraments, corporate prayer, and worship. Living cut off from those things is a great spiritual burden. It would be a burden much greater than the benefit of being alive in a hospital bed or permanently confused. I would rather be at home with the Lord.

TERMS AND METHODOLOGY

Why There Are No "Patients" in This Book

The words we use to describe things affect the way we feel about them. Talking about medical choices can be distressing even when all the words are carefully chosen and we know what they mean. For most of us, the language of medicine is a foreign tongue. Medical training and constant use give hospital workers a large vocabulary for describing body parts, bodily functions, and rapidly changing range-of-treatment possibilities. Even with more than twenty years of experience on hospital ethics committees, I regularly have to ask for explanations of words that everyone else at the table clearly understands. Throughout this book, I intend to use medical jargon only when it is necessary, and to explain the technical terms when they can't be avoided.

Technical terminology can be unnerving for anyone visiting a hospital. It has to be even more distressing for the person who is seeking medical attention. Inside the hospital, anyone seeking medical attention is called a *patient*. It is a compact and clear way of referring to a person under the medical staff's care, but using the term *patient* involves some risks. Recent critics of hospital practices have warned that Western medicine has grown too comfortable in treating sick people as mere objects for medical science.[5] Merely using the word *patient* does not dehumanize sick people, but continuing to use it runs the

5. The most compelling of these critics is Michel Foucault, especially in *The Birth of the Clinic* (London: Routledge, 1963; repr., New York: Vintage Books, 1994). Paul Ramsey's *The Patient as Person* (New Haven, CT: Yale University Press, 1970) was an early voice inside the world of medicine warning against seeing sick people as mere puzzles or problems and instead remembering that each one is a person. The move away from a paternalistic model (doctor = father, nurse = mother, patient = child) toward the autonomy of sick people to direct their own care is one of the fruits of these warnings.

risk of thinking of sick people as "them" rather than "us." Calling a sick person a *patient* (one who suffers or waits) makes it easier to put that person at an emotional distance. A *patient* can be a featureless stick figure in a bed or attached to an IV stand. But this is not why hospital workers use the term. *Patient* for them is the universally approved term for someone under medical care. They are aware of the threat of reducing people to nothing more than a set of symptoms and behavioral challenges. Most hospital workers take steps to maintain an appreciation for the humanity of those needing their attention. Yet the danger remains.

This book discusses the choices that people face in the hospital. Using the word *patient* in this book the way hospital workers do would be efficient and make sense. The 1988 PCA Report on Heroic Measures uses the word *patient* fifty times in the space of eleven pages. With the efficiency, however, would come the continued risk of obscuring the humanity of those in the midst of their own personal health crises. Instead of *patient*, I will use *sick person, person in the bed*, and similar phrases. Often, this will make the descriptions feel clunky. Yet the advantage of using the other terms is evident even in their clunkiness. Reading *sick person* instead of *patient* encourages us to picture a real person. A *sick person* was once healthy, and probably wants to be healthy again. A *sick person* has loved ones who are often anxious and sometimes hurting.

Using someone's name is much better than using either *patient* or *sick person*. Whenever possible, including in fictional illustrations, I will use the name of the person involved to reinforce the habit of focusing on an individual human being rather than a set of symptoms or a kind of problem. The differences between *patient, sick person*, and *Mindy* are large enough to aim for consistency in avoiding the use of *patient* in this book.

The Power of Stories

Making ethical decisions can be agonizing. As the true stories in this book will illustrate, the decisions that we are asked to make about medical care can be daunting, overflowing with complexity and values that cannot all be honored. Over the last two hundred years, the approach to ethical decision-making taught in Western schools has emphasized formulas and rules. This "modern" approach holds that the right formulas and rules will make the one right answer obvious to *anyone*. Godliness and the wisdom that comes from experience might be nice to have, but they are now thought to be unnecessary, even when the decisions are difficult. God's Word treats decision-making very differently. Although no one can say that lack of godliness and wisdom is an excuse for not obeying God's law, the Bible says that "the fear of the LORD is the *beginning* of wisdom" (Prov. 9:10). We are encouraged to heed the instructions of our parents and older people (the "hoary head" of Leviticus 19:32). The law of God is certain, pure, and a light to our path; but we are not told that it is simple to apply in every situation.

The recent focus on formulas and rules replaced thousands of years of emphasis on wisdom and the role of godliness in making good choices. The law of God is not just a set of rules. It is the way of blessing, life, and fellowship with God and peace with our neighbor. Decision-making in the Bible is most often a matter of recognizing a similarity of the current challenge to a challenge described in Scripture. Consider just three examples:

Proverbs 6:6–11: "Go to the ant . . . ." To recommend hard work over laziness, the teacher says, "Be like the ant." Godly industriousness is not easily expressed as a rule, such as "Work until you are sweating for at least eight hours a day." It is instead shown by an example or an analogy. Lazy people who don't see how the example of the ant helps will not be helped by a precise rule to follow.

Matthew 6:25–34: "Consider the lilies . . . ." Rather than only giving the rule "Do not worry," Jesus directs our attention to birds and lilies. They do not fret, and God provides for them abundantly. Before and after pointing to the birds and lilies, Jesus says, "Do not be anxious." Jesus uses the analogies to show us what to do instead of worrying.

First Timothy 5:17–18: "You shall not muzzle an ox . . . ." To teach Timothy about the honor (and pay) due to pastors, Paul refers to what Deuteronomy 25:4 says about feeding beasts of burden. Paul is not saying that pastors are little more than dumb oxen. He is using an analogy between pastors and oxen to show that since even oxen deserve support, so do pastors.

Before the rise of the modern fascination with formulas and rules, reasoning by analogy was the most common way of helping Christians make difficult decisions. Should I forgive my brother? Jesus answers with a story about a servant forgiven of a great debt who refuses to forgive a small debt. Should David repent of murder and adultery? Nathan tells a story of a wealthy man and a poor man. These stories do not replace the prohibitions and obligations given in God's law. They show how the commandments apply in difficult situations by highlighting the similarity to situations in which the choice is more obvious. Applying God's Word by using analogies helps everyone see the factors that should matter most, often drawing attention to things that might otherwise be overlooked. Another benefit of giving advice by way of analogy is the help it gives in making sense of the decision long after it has been made. "We chose this path because we were facing a situation like this other situation (in which the choice would have been easy)." One of the most important parts of giving godly advice is showing people how to weave what they are facing into the larger story of their walk with Christ. Advising by analogy not only helps people make more confident decisions, but also helps them make sense of the difficult time when they reflect on it later.

As with the sterile application of formulas and rules, advising by analogy can be abused. An illustration should help to show both the value and the potential risks involved in advising by analogy. Starting in the Netherlands in 1994 and now including U.S. states such as Oregon and Washington, laws have been changed to allow physicians to prescribe lethal doses of sedatives to people who want to die "in a humane and dignified manner."[6] These laws aim to give a medically managed way of escape for people who are terminally ill and likely

6. This is the phrase used in the Oregon Revised Statutes (ORS) (https://www.oregonlegislature.gov/bills_laws/ors/ors127.html). Oregon law in 2015 includes a

to spend their last days of life in great pain. By allowing doctors to assist people with such grim prospects, the laws intend to help people who are eager to die to do it efficiently and painlessly rather than in a messy, possibly unsuccessful way. Some people have supported these changes in the law out of compassion for people who are facing a horrific end. It is appropriate to have our hearts break for people in pain. They bear the affliction of the fall in ways that many of us do not. And if we see physician-assisted suicide only as a way to diminish someone's pain, it is hard to see how it could be wrong. Comparing physician-assisted suicide to relieving someone in pain is moral advice by analogy. If relieving pain is the only consideration, then we should be in favor of physician-assisted suicide. But of course, it is not the only consideration. The fastest way to see that more is involved is to tell another story.

Imagine that dangerous levels of toxic mold and asbestos have been discovered in the basement of your house. The upper floors and attic are not affected, but the basement is irreparable. The insurance company will pay to have the house completely demolished and a new house built on a different site, so you hire a demolition crew and tell them to destroy the house. As the crew is looking around the attic to see where to begin, they find two paintings. An amateur historian working on the crew recognizes them as Rembrandts. Pinned to the frame of each is a note: "On loan from the Louvre." The leader of the demolition crew says, "Because these are in a toxic-hazard site, it will be hideously expensive to save these paintings. It will set the work back for months." In light of the great hassle involved, would it be okay for the crew to destroy the paintings along with the house?

The obvious answer is "No!" The paintings are masterpieces. They do not belong either to the demolition crew or to you, the owner of the house. Even though it will be a massive headache for you to rescue and return the paintings, it would be wrong for you to destroy them,

---

clause that insists that dying from a physician-prescribed overdose is *not* suicide (ORS 127.805 § 2.01; ORS 127.880 § 3.14). Officially, then, it is not "physician-assisted suicide," because according to the law it is not suicide at all.

and it would be wrong for you to ask the demolition crew to use their expertise to destroy them. The paintings are not yours, and they are not trash.

Physician-assisted suicide is even more like crew-assisted painting destruction than it is like helping to relieve someone's pain. We know this because God's Word tells us that human life is precious in his sight, and that it belongs to him and not to us. Even if you see the paintings (or your life) as a huge obstacle to getting what you want (a new house, or relief from pain), the paintings (and your life) are still valuable. Wise friends would encourage you to learn about the value of the paintings and to think harder about what it means to be a borrower rather than an owner. People facing a painful last illness need people to draw close to them to cherish the value of what they have. They do not need people confirming their sense that their life is pointless and that the pain is the only reality.

For someone seriously seeking to commit suicide, a fictional story about paintings in an attic is not likely to be persuasive. But it ought to be helpful to someone trying to decide whether to help someone else end his or her life. Believers who are eager to see what God's law says about our good should find it even more persuasive. It should help us remember what God has revealed about his glory and our good.

These competing analogies about physician-assisted suicide high-light both the power of advice by analogy and the importance of taking steps to limit the risks involved. In the hands of unscrupu-lous or wicked people, *every* approach to moral advice can be used to justify wickedness. Cost-benefit (utilitarian) reasoning can ignore the costs imposed on the weak or the poor. Duty or rights-focused (deontological) reasoning can treat the rights to sexual expression as more important than all other rights. Advice by analogy can offer analogies that ignore crucial ways that the situations are *not* alike, sowing confusion rather than clarity.

A memorable story can make bad moral advice seem better than it should. When we find a moral analogy compelling, it is wise to take steps to limit the risk that the story is making a biblically inappropriate choice attractive. The most important of these steps is to seek godly counsel. Spiritually mature believers are likely to see that the story is leading us astray. People older in the Lord may see that we are overlooking clear biblical teaching. We should trust them to open our eyes to passages of Scripture that we need to take into account. Spiritually mature brothers and sisters can often give advice from their own experience. Sometimes they will tell us about a choice they faced that is more similar to our situation than the choice faced by the fictional hero of the analogy that we are considering. At other times they will propose a different analogy from the one that seems so helpful to us. This new analogy may reinforce the recommendation of the original analogy, but it may also encourage a different choice. Either way, the road ahead will be easier to see. Finally, godly fellow believers can help us see where our own immaturity may be getting in the way. If someone else used the analogy to support bad advice, they will be able to help us see who ought to be trusted. If, instead, we are embracing the story because we are ignorant, confused, or in love with the wrong things, they can alert us to the danger we are in.

Stories about choices in analogous situations can give clarity and comfort. This book uses both true and fictional stories to reinforce recommendations. Applying these stories to other situations should be done prayerfully and with the advice of wise friends.

A PRESSING NEED

Two recent occurrences made it clear to me that this book could be helpful. The mother of a good friend passed away after a full life. The final days of her life involved many questions about starting or stopping medical treatments. When I met my friend in the receiving line at the memorial service, my friend said, "Thank you [for what you taught in Sunday school]. Mom had lost the ability to enjoy the means of grace. Medicine could not do anything to restore it. I could say no [to some options without worry]."

Finally, as I was trying to decide whether to pursue publishing this book, a woman told me that she wanted a Christian philosopher's help with a problem. She had been recently diagnosed with an aggressive form of breast cancer for which there is no known treatment. Her oncologist told her that she was likely to live only five more months. The oncologist also told her about an experimental drug trial that she might enroll in. If all went well, she would live seven more months rather than five. The experimental drug came with serious side effects, however. She would be sick to her stomach, bloated, confused, and lethargic as long as she was on the drug, and that could be for four months. She knew what she *wanted* to do: she wanted to decline the drug and focus on making the most of her five months of mostly gradual decline. But she also wanted to obey God's Word. If God was calling her to endure discomfort and confusion in order to stay alive as long as possible, she was willing to trust him through it.

The choice that this dear woman was facing was hard. It was made even harder when she started looking for biblical advice about how to make it. She described to me the approach she had taken to finding sound biblical counsel. She had regularly prayed for guidance. She had talked to pastors. She described sophisticated approaches to library and Internet resources she had used. What she had found was discouraging. Sources serious about the authority of God's Word either said nothing about her situation or said that she was obligated to do everything possible to live as long as possible. Life is precious to God, so any cost is worth it. The sources not serious about the authority of God's Word generally recommended that she minimize her pain by whatever means possible. A distressing number of those sources described in detail how she could end her life painlessly before the symptoms became unpleasant. She did not find any sources with a high view of Scripture that addressed her situation and said that God's Word allowed her to decline participation in the experimental trial.

As she was telling me about her situation, I assumed that she had heard that I was working on this book. She might have heard that I taught bioethics at Covenant and expected me to know what she had not read. Or maybe she had heard that I served on the ethics committee downtown. When she finished her story, however, I learned that she did not know anything about me, my research interests, or my activities. She only knew that I was a Christian who taught philosophy.

I was able to suggest some books that might help her,[7] but what she had found in her highly motivated research is accurate: very few books or websites are helpful for people serious about the authority of God's Word and facing hard decisions about burdensome medical treatment. This book aims to provide the biblical principles needed to answer this woman's question.

KEY TERMS

> advance directive
> casuistry
> do-not-resuscitate (DNR) order
> heroic measures
> 1988 PCA Report on Heroic Measures

STUDY AND *DISCUSSION QUESTIONS

1. What decisions had the author's father made before his final health crisis that decreased the author's distress in making his own crucial decisions?
2. What difference did the palliative-care specialist make in the sequence of choices?
3. How long did the author's father live after the *decision* to move to comfort care only?
4. *Did the author make the right decision about discontinuing the use of the BiPap support for respiration? Why or why not?
5. How is God's law a gift to God's people?
6. What reasons are given for thinking that withholding and withdrawing medical treatment are morally equivalent?

---

7. David VanDrunen, *Bioethics and the Christian Life: A Guide to Making Difficult Decisions* (Wheaton, IL: Crossway, 2009); Gilbert Meilaender, *Bioethics: A Primer for Christians*, 2nd ed. (Grand Rapids: Eerdmans, 2005); Kenneth P. Mottram, *Caring for Those in Crisis: Facing Ethical Dilemmas with Patients and Families* (Grand Rapids: Brazos, 2007).

7. What pattern did the author discover about end-of-life challenges through his work on hospital ethics committees?

8. *Was the author too quick to agree with the physicians who urged him to see withdrawing and withholding as equivalent?

9. What are the principal findings of the 1988 PCA Report on Heroic Measures?

10. Why is the 1988 PCA Report on Heroic Measures difficult to use today (in 2017)?

11. *What role should the findings of the 1988 PCA Report on Heroic Measures play in the decision-making process of a PCA church officer? Of a PCA church member? Of a Christian who is not a member of a PCA church?

12. Why does the author not use the term *patient* to refer to people who are sick?

13. What reasons are given for the extensive use of stories in advancing the argument of this book?

14. *Why does dictionary.com define *casuistry* (which technically only means "the application of general ethical principles to particular cases," usually by appeal to analogous cases) as "specious, deceptive, or oversubtle reasoning, especially in questions of morality"?

15. *Should true stories matter more than fictional stories in forming biblical moral principles?

16. *What advice should be given to the woman with breast cancer about pursuing treatment?

FOR FURTHER READING

Bane, J. Donald, Austin H. Kutscher, Robert E. Neale, and Robert B. Reeves Jr., eds. *Death and Ministry*. New York: Seabury Press, 1975.

Beauchamp, Tom, and James Childress. *Principles of Biomedical Ethics*. New York: Oxford University Press, 1979.

Downie, Robin. "Guest Editorial: A Personal View: Health Care Ethics and Casuistry." *Journal of Medical Ethics* 18, 2 (1992): 61–66.

Ethical and Religious Directives for Catholic Health Care Services. Washington, DC: United States Conference of Catholic Bishops, 2009.

Foucault, Michel. *The Birth of the Clinic.* London: Routledge, 1963. Reprint, New York: Vintage Books, 1994.

Hall, William, James Hurley, Reginald F. McLelland, F. Edward Payne, and John Van Voorhis. *Study Committee Report on Heroic Measures,* adopted by the 1988 General Assembly of the Presbyterian Church in America. http://pcahistory.org/pca/2-378.html.

Higgins, James. "Casuistry Revisited." *Heythrop Journal* (2012): 806–36.

Jonsen, Al. *The Abuse of Casuistry: A History of Moral Reasoning.* Berkeley, CA: University of California Press, 1988.

Ramsey, Paul. *The Patient as Person.* New Haven, CT: Yale University Press, 1970.

2

FOUNDATIONAL
CONSIDERATIONS

TWO FUNDAMENTAL BIBLICAL OBLIGATIONS

Matthew 25:14–46 records the last two stories that Jesus told before he was arrested and led to the cross. The parable of the talents (vv. 14–30) highlights the joy of hearing the master say, "Well done, good and faithful servant." The account of the sheep and the goats at the last judgment (vv. 31–46) underscores the horror of hearing "Depart from me, you cursed," and the surprise of the faithful who cared for "the least of these my brothers." In these vivid stories, Jesus shows the ultimate importance of living to fulfill the tasks that God has given us, seeking to please our heavenly Master rather than earthly fads and fashions. Jesus' words in Matthew 25 give us crucial principles that should inform the decisions we make about life-sustaining medical treatment. After explaining the principles in this passage, the remainder of the chapter will show the biblical case for principles about our authority to make decisions, our permission in some cases to do less than everything medically possible, the difference between killing and allowing death to occur, and the role of prayer when facing end-of-life decisions.

Faithful Stewardship

Matthew 24–25 emphasizes the importance of always being ready for Christ's return. We do not know when the Son of Man, the Master, the Bridegroom, or the Judge will appear. These figures refer to Jesus himself. He is coming to hold us accountable for doing what he expects us to do with the time, talents, and opportunities that we have. In light of this multipart warning, we should be eager to know what the Lord expects from us. For that, we need to go to Genesis 1 and the tasks that God gave to Adam and Eve. They were given the tasks (and the delights, before the fall) of multiplying, stewarding, and honoring.

The first task of multiplying is obvious: part of our faithful (corporate) service to the Master is to procreate. The second task of stewarding creation is less obvious. It includes nearly everything we do with our talents. All our gifts of skill, power, and understanding are to be used to encourage the flourishing of God's creation within the design limits set by God's revealed will.[1] Creation belongs to the Lord and not to us. We are stewards, entrusted like gardeners with the task of glorifying the owner by tending the garden according to the owner's design. The biblical principle here might be expressed this way:

The Duty to Steward Our Resources: God's Word requires us to make faithful use of all our talents, opportunities, and resources: time, energy, attention, and money.

Showing Honor and the Image of God

The third task of showing honor is the obligation to treat all that the Master values with respect and reverence. The task of honoring deserves close attention because it bears directly on end-of-life decision-making. Genesis 1:26 gives us a glimpse into the intra-Trinitarian conversation before the creation of Adam and Eve: "Let us make man in our image, after our likeness." This divine decision leads to Genesis 1:28: "And God said to them, 'Be fruitful and multiply . . . , and have dominion.'" With these words, God commissions Adam and Eve to be divine representatives, ambassadors sent from the divine throne room to speak and act for God in the midst of God's created realm.

---

1. Andy Crouch's *Playing God: Redeeming the Gift of Power* (Downers Grove, IL: InterVarsity Press, 2013) is quite helpful on this point.

It is significant that Moses is the author of Genesis 1. Raised in the court of Egypt, Moses would have known something of the way that Pharaoh commissioned his provincial governors. So when Moses wrote Genesis 1:26–30, he likely had such a ceremony in mind. Like many other rulers of the ancient world, Pharaoh had extended his domain by conquest. Conquered people could avoid being annihilated by accepting a treaty—a covenant—that would make them vassals under Pharaoh, submitting to him as their suzerain king. These subjugated vassal people would agree to pay tribute, to provide soldiers, and to obey the rule of a governor. The Hebrew word for "image" in Genesis 1:26 is the title given to a governor commissioned to exercise dominion over vassal subjects. Adam and Eve are the *image* of God because together, male and female (Gen. 1:27), they have been given the task of exercising dominion in God's name.[2]

Often, we think of the image of God as referring first of all to humans' being *like* God. It is true that humans are made in the likeness of God, but "image" and "likeness" are not the same thing in Genesis 1. The word for "likeness" in Genesis 1 is used elsewhere in Scripture, referring to external similarity or looking like.[3] Humanity exhibits the true God's attributes (such as rationality, volition, and creativity).[4] Those attributes are part of our being the image of God because they equip us to fulfill the tasks assigned by the Suzerain King of all creation, our Master and Lord. Killing a human is an act of treason against this Master because it deprives the Master of a member of his ambassadorial team. The parable of the talents reminds us of this

---

2. For another expression of this understanding of the "image of God" as task or function, see Richard Middleton, *The Liberating Image: The Imago Dei in Genesis 1* (Grand Rapids: Brazos, 2005).

3. Over half the twenty-five Old Testament uses of the Hebrew word for "likeness" (as in Genesis 1) occur in Ezekiel, referring to what his visions looked like (wheels, living creatures, etc.). For a detailed discussion of recent scholarship on "likeness" in the Old Testament, see W. Randall Garr, *In His Own Image and Likeness: Humanity, Divinity, and Monotheism* (Leiden: Brill, 2003), 118–32.

4. A clear statement of the view that the image of God is in humanity's intellectual powers is found in Thomas Aquinas, *Summa Theologica* 1.93, especially article 6, and articles 7 and 8 in which Thomas cites Augustine's *De Trinitate* XIV as his authority.

commissioning and ultimate calling to account. The tasks of multiplying and stewarding are assigned by the Master, and only the Master has the authority to recall a member of the ambassadorial team.

The picture that Jesus paints of the judgment of the sheep and the goats highlights another aspect of the commissioning of Adam and Eve (and thus all humanity). Some kings of the ancient world, including Pharaoh, would sometimes appoint a visibly deformed person as their image-bearer/ambassador. Pharaoh and others would send governors with a club foot or a speech impediment to exercise dominion. (Moses himself had difficulty speaking when he was commissioned by God to go to Pharaoh and demand that the Israelites be allowed to leave Egypt [Ex. 3–4]. Pharaoh would have understood the irony, and Moses' reluctance to go may have been related to the clear rebuke in that irony.) The kings would appoint deformed image-bearers in order to test their vassal subjects. An image-bearer was sent to speak for a great king. The subjects were obligated to receive the image-bearer with all the honor and dignity that they would show to the great king himself if he were to visit them in all his splendor. If the subjects mocked or snickered at the ambassador's infirmity, the great king would punish the subjects for failing to honor *him*. Jesus specifies "the least of these my brothers" as those who are hungry, thirsty, strangers, naked, sick, and in prison (Matt. 25:35–40). The sheep on Jesus' right had treated these people with the honor that they would have shown to Jesus himself. The goats had not.

At the end of Matthew 25 (vv. 34–40), Jesus commends the sheep who gave "the least of these" food when they were hungry, drink when they were thirsty, welcome when they were strangers, clothes when they were naked, and visitation when they were sick or in prison. He says that these sheep are "blessed by my Father," both because they will inherit the kingdom and because they have been doing what the Father is said to do throughout the Old Testament. Psalms 146:7–9 and 147:3 describe the Lord as lifting up those who are bowed down and binding up the wounds of the brokenhearted. When Jesus inaugurates his ministry (Luke 4:16–21), he quotes Isaiah 61's promise that the Lord will heal and set the oppressed free. When John's disciples ask whether Jesus is the Messiah, Jesus answers by healing people (Luke 7:21–23), and he offers his ministry to the sick and needy as proof of who he is.

The task of defending and protecting those without a champion is explicitly given to God's people. The Israelites' failure to imitate God in this way is a common part of the prophetic word of judgment against them. Isaiah 58:6–10 calls Israel to make the acceptable sacrifice of setting the oppressed free, giving food to the hungry, and clothing the naked. Jeremiah 5:27–28 warns that Israel is evil for failing to defend the rights of the needy. And Ezekiel 34:1–10 condemns the shepherds of Israel for not strengthening the weak, not binding up the injured, and not bringing back those who wander. Jesus' commendation of the sheep in Matthew 25 is for doing what he has been doing in his earthly ministry. When we, Christ's followers, are entrusted with the task of making decisions for those whom we do not know well enough to speak for, we should aim to choose as Christ would have us choose for them. Even when we lack the biblical authority to choose what they would choose, we still have the biblical authority to defend and protect them:

Protection for the Least of These: God's Word calls us to seek to defend and protect those who are voiceless and suffering.

The obligation to defend the voiceless is typically joined to the obligation not to make false promises and to steward others' resources carefully. But in the absence of information about what someone would choose for himself or herself, we should focus on defending that person. Rather than choosing what we would want for ourselves or trying to guess what the person would choose if he or she could speak, we should aim to protect the person from being neglected.

From Matthew 25 we learn that physical death is not the most awful fate. We should be more afraid of being found unfaithful by our Lord than of the death of our bodies. The faithless servant in the parable of the talents is "cast . . . into the outer darkness [where] there will be weeping and gnashing of teeth" (v. 30). The goats are told, "Depart from me, you cursed, into the eternal fire prepared for the devil and his angels" (v. 41). The lot of the faithless is *spiritual* death. They are unfaithful because they rebel against fulfilling the tasks that humanity was given in Genesis 1: to multiply, to steward creation, and to treat God's rule with honor, including all those whom he has entrusted with his image. In every decision near the end of life—as with every other decision of any kind—we must make faithfulness to our Master our first concern.

THE AUTHORITY TO MAKE CHOICES

Authority to Direct Our Own Lives

As image-bearers, we each have the authority to make the choices necessary to steward our own talents and opportunities. These choices are not made in isolation from our family and others, but we will be held ultimately responsible for serving Christ well. Our health affects our ability to use our time and talents, so the many choices we make about diet, sleep, exercise, and medical attention are a vital part of our stewardship task. Luke 12:35–48 recounts Jesus' words about our obligations as servants awaiting his return. All our choices are included. The following biblical principle is foundational to end-of-life decision-making:

> **Servant Authority to Make Medical Choices:** God's Word teaches that every adult has the authority to accept or decline medical attention as part of his or her responsibility as an image-bearer of God. (The authority does not reside in each of us absolutely. The authority is delegated to us by God as his servants.)

This principle is foundational because it sets limits on the choices that we are authorized to make. We are not authorized to make choices that are contrary to God's revealed will. Our choices are to serve God's purposes in the world. Most of the time, our own health needs and God's purposes overlap: we serve God faithfully by making choices that serve our own needs as well. Living according to God's law is always what is best for us.[5] At times, though, we can ask questions that God's Word does not answer with a simple yes or no. When that happens, we are still guided by what the Scriptures teach about God's priorities for us. Living as faithful servants means eagerly seeking to understand what the Master loves and living to realize his purposes rather than living to please only ourselves.

Even when deciding about medical treatment for ourselves, our authority is not absolute. We have the authority to choose according to God's values. We are stewards of the lives that he has given us. An important implication of seeing our authority this way is the limit that it places on those who make choices for us when we cannot. At some point in our lives, many of us will be too sick or confused to make choices about our own care. When that happens, someone else will have to step in and make choices for us. That person's authority to make those choices comes from us, and our authority comes from God as his image-bearers. Using myself as an example, someone who speaks for me in making a medical decision is responsible for saying what I would say if I could understand the question and express an answer. This is what both God's law and the states' laws expect if someone is going to speak as a surrogate decision-maker or agent.

Extensive knowledge of what I value and what I hope to gain from medical attention will equip my surrogate decision-makers to choose for me. Years of conversations with me about my health challenges and the choices I have already made will also be helpful. Written instructions that anticipate decisions that are likely to arise will be golden. In order to prepare others to make decisions that carry on my effort to be a faithful steward of all I have, I have been thinking through the decisions that may be coming and have left instructions to inform my surrogates. The Bible teaches that we all have the authority to look ahead and anticipate choices in this way. This is implied in Paul's

---

5. David Clyde Jones, *Biblical Christian Ethics* (Grand Rapids: Baker, 1994); Cornelius Plantinga, *Not the Way It's Supposed to Be: A Breviary of Sin* (Grand Rapids: Eerdmans, 1995).

instructions in his letters (see, e.g., Col. 4:10). Applied to medical treatment, this is the biblical principle:

Authority to Make Choices in Advance: God's Word permits us to accept or decline medical treatment in advance, including leaving an advance directive or other instructions. These instructions are binding if they conform to God's law.

As obvious as this authority may be, it is important to spell it out. Just as the authority to accept or decline treatment is only that of a servant's authority to pursue his Master's purposes, our surrogate's authority is only that of a spokesperson seeking to pursue our purposes. If our values and desires are not known, our surrogates will find it difficult to make choices with confidence. They will have to guess what we would want, sometimes in the midst of a medical crisis when a quick decision is needed. No matter how much time they have, they will also have to wonder whether their own selfish desires and fears are the source of their guesses about what we would say. Genesis 50:25 reports that Joseph gave instructions about taking his bones back to the land of his fathers, and Exodus 13:19 tells us that his instructions were remembered. The value of decisions made in advance is another biblical principle:

Advance Directives Can Be a Blessing: God's Word encourages us to take steps to remove unnecessary distress from those we love and ought to honor. Legally executed advance directives diminish the burdens of fear and indecision from all those who will have to make medical decisions for us if we cannot make them for ourselves. Advance directives clarify who is to decide if we cannot, and they reduce the need for anyone to guess about our wishes.

Just how great this blessing can be for our loved ones will be illustrated by the situations that are described in the next two chapters. Detailed instructions about completing an advance directive will be given in chapter 5.

As long as we are able to make decisions for ourselves, instructions for our loved ones and agents are not crucial. In the hospital, these instructions start to matter when a doctor or a nurse determines that we lack decisional capacity.

Decisional Capacity

Decisional capacity is the term that hospital personnel are likely to use when determining who should be making treatment decisions. Some may talk about whether we are *competent* or not, but doctors no longer have the power to declare someone *incompetent*. Adults are now presumed to be competent unless they have been declared incompetent by a judge in a court proceeding. People deemed incompetent are no longer legal agents.[6] They cannot write or change their wills; they cannot write checks or enter into contracts. People who are declared incompetent can have their legal powers restored only by a court order declaring them competent again.

The process of getting someone declared incompetent can be long and expensive. If someone needed to be declared incompetent before his or her advance directive took effect, then advance directives would rarely matter. Desiring to have people's wishes honored in treatment decisions, state legislatures in the early 2000s passed into law legal forms that take effect when their authors are *decisionally incapable.*[7] People who retain their legal competence may be deemed by a doctor or nurse to be incapable of making the decisions necessary to direct their own care. Determinations about decisional capacity are not about whether someone is able to make contracts or change a will. Being *decisionally capable* means being able to understand the question that is being asked, having a system of values and the ability to connect

6. For a discussion of competence and capacity, see Jalayne J. Arias, "A Time to Step In: Legal Mechanisms for Protecting Those with Declining Capacity," *American Journal of Law and Medicine* 39, 1 (2013): 134–59.

7. A typical definition of decision-making *capacity* is included in the Tennessee Health Care Decisions Act, Tennessee Code Annotated § 68-11-1802(a)(3): "'Capacity' means an individual's ability to understand the significant benefits, risks, and alternatives to proposed health care and to make and communicate a health care decision."

those values to the choice involved, and being able to communicate an answer to the question.

When doctors or nurses judge that someone under their care cannot do these things, they are eager to have the decision made by someone who can speak for the person. The medical team's first choice is to have an advance directive that makes it clear who the agent is. If no advance directive is on file, then the doctors and nurses are forced to look for guidance to the person that the law says has the highest claim to speak as the surrogate decision-maker. The legal hierarchy is clear—spouse, children, parents, siblings, etc.—but unless the party with the legal claim is present, the process of finding the legal surrogate can delay important decisions. Sometimes decisions are delayed because the law requires that a group of people agree about what is to be done. Most hospitals require that children (or parents, or siblings) be unanimous in order for their decisions to be recognized as speaking for the person under the doctors' care. Often, the task of achieving unanimity delays treatment decisions significantly. Having an advance directive that names an agent means that the doctors and nurses will need only one person (the agent) to decide what should be done.

Our legally designated agents have the biblical authority to make nonsinful choices for us because we have the authority to empower them to speak for us. Advance directives identify our agents as the people best equipped to say what we would choose if we could choose for ourselves. If no agent has been specified by an advance directive, our spouses have the biblical authority to say what we would choose:

Covenant Decision-Making Authority: God's Word authorizes spouses to speak (give a substituted judgment) for each other.

This principle is implied by the use that both Jesus and Paul make of Genesis 2:24. Jesus says that in biblical marriages, the husband and wife become "one flesh" (Matt. 19:4–6). Paul emphasizes that this oneness is a mystery that includes responsibilities (Eph. 5:25–33).

When no spouse is available to speak for us, our families have the biblical authority to say what we would choose:

Family Decision-Making Authority: God's Word permits our children and parents to make choices for us when we are unable to make them for ourselves as part of the authority structure implicit in the fifth commandment.

The fifth commandment as it is given in Exodus 20:12 connects honoring our parents to long life in God's promised land. While this commandment joins family members in receiving a promised gift, the second commandment (Ex. 20:4–6) connects generations of families in the consequences of rebellion. In a vivid and terrible display of this connection, Joshua 7 recounts the stoning of Achan and his whole family for Achan's sin. Israel and Judah are exiled as a people, with children sharing in the travails earned by their parents. Ephesians 6:1–4 invokes the promise of the fifth commandment and reaffirms the tight connection of responsibility and honor that exists between parents and children. The authority that parents have to choose for their minor children flows from their covenant obligation to nurture and discipline them, speaking for them and teaching them to speak for themselves as faithful servants of Christ. The authority that children have to speak for their decisionally incapable parents flows from their covenant obligation to honor and obey them. Parents are not to choose according to what their minor children would choose, since the minor children are ignorant and immature. Children are not to choose for their parents what they would want for themselves because they are to honor their parents' values. Children are to choose for their parents what their parents would choose for themselves.[8]

Being decisionally incapable may last for only a short time. Medications to manage pain, lack of sleep, and recovery from surgery are just a few of the conditions that can limit decision-making ability. Until decisional capacity is permanently lost from an injury or cognitive

8. A short, helpful exposition of what the fifth commandment means by "honor your father and your mother" can be found in Jochem Douma's *The Ten Commandments: Manual for the Christian Life*, trans. Nelson Kloosterman (Phillipsburg, NJ: P&R Publishing, 1996), 171–74.

dysfunction, doctors and nurses typically reassess a person's ability to make his or her own decisions every time a new decision is needed. If it is likely that decisional capacity will return before the decision must be made, doctors will usually wait to see whether that happens before asking the agent to make the decision. This practice conforms to God's Word. Because our authority to make medical decisions is based on our responsibility as stewards of all that Christ has given us, we should be making decisions about our own care whenever we can. We may need to ask to have the situation explained slowly, in small words, or more than once, but we should be choosing whenever possible.

BIBLICAL PERMISSION TO DO LESS THAN EVERYTHING MEDICALLY POSSIBLE

CPR and breathing machines changed death and dying. Before these life-sustaining measures became common in the 1960s, doing everything medically possible did not result in long periods of unconsciousness before death. If someone's heart stopped beating, there was nothing to be done. If someone's breathing stopped, there was no way to breathe for that person. Someone who was unconscious might wake up, but if his or her heart or lungs stopped working, the person was dead.

Now, fifty years into the age of life-sustaining medical treatment, "do everything" covers a much wider range of medical possibilities. It is now possible to keep someone's heart and lungs working for months even when the person is unconscious and his or her organs are too weak to function without help. When life-sustaining treatments are used to help in curing an infection or an injury, the treatments are a great blessing even when they are quite expensive. Often, however, life-sustaining treatments do not contribute to a cure, at least not humanly speaking. Ventilator support for someone who is unconscious from a massive head injury is not part of a medical plan to cure the injury. God can always intervene supernaturally, but life-sustaining treatments may be extending physical life only by imposing serious burdens on the person who is sick. In this section, I will explain the principles taught by God's Word that make it permissible in some cases to decline or discontinue life-sustaining treatment.

Most of the reasoning in this book depends on the claim that I am making here: God's Word permits us in some cases to say no to life-sustaining medical treatment. If I had written on this subject one hundred years ago, I would have rejected this key principle. Yet the Word of God has not changed. What has changed is the range of medical options. I was born in 1960, four years before CPR became a standard part of a medical-school education. Kidney dialysis, defibrillators, and ventilators (machines to support breathing) were developed even later than CPR. In 1960, people who are today kept alive "by machines" would all have died from their diseases. The medical advances of the last sixty years have been exciting, but they have also made it harder to think through our obligations about medical care.

The Bible teaches that we must accept medical attention that is likely to cure us of our diseases. As Christ's servants, we are called to maintain our health so that we can serve him well.

Obligation to Accept Care: God's Word obligates us to accept loving care that is likely to maintain or restore our health.[9]

Before the development of life-sustaining medical treatments, this obligation to use medical means to maintain our health would have meant that we were obligated to use all available medical means to stay alive. In John 5:2–9, we are told of a man who sought the only healing help available at the pool of Bethesda. Until medical skill was able to keep people alive in an unconscious or permanently confused state, it was correct to say that we are obligated to use all medical means possible

---

9. According to the 1988 PCA Report on Heroic Measures, it is wrong to refuse treatment that is clearly able to heal, restore, or maintain the life of a sick person using only ordinary means (such as food or water by mouth) (§ III.2–5).

to stay alive. God's Word commands us to defend life, but it does not command us in every circumstance to use medical techniques to extend it as long as possible. In order to see this, we must look at what the Scriptures say about life, death, benefits, burdens, and the limits of what medicine can do.

Life and Death in the Bible

From the very beginning, God's Word insists that human life is precious. When God breathed life into Adam and fashioned Eve from Adam's rib, he gave them the task of bearing his image and exercising dominion over all creation (Gen. 1:27–28; 2:7–15; 9:1–7). The application of the Ten Commandments to the life of Israel (in Num. 35) makes it clear that those who intentionally take a person's life deserve to die. More positively, Psalm 91 says that long life is a blessing for the righteous.

Human Life Is Precious: God's Word obligates us to protect and nurture human life.

Life is one of the dominant themes in Scripture. Long life is clearly a great good, and being embodied is essential to who we are. Along with emphasizing the goodness of physical life, the Bible also teaches that long *physical* life is not the *ultimate* good. This is evident in the account of the death of Moses in Deuteronomy 34. We are told there that when Moses died on Mount Nebo, looking into the promised land, he "was 120 years old . . . [and that] his eye was undimmed, and his vigor unabated" (v. 7). His body was strong, and yet God took him home. This suggests that long earthly life isn't the top priority for God, and in 1 Kings 3 God says it directly. When God promised to give the young King Solomon whatever he requested, Solomon asked for wisdom. In praising this choice, the Lord mentioned long life: "It pleased the LORD that Solomon had asked this. And God said to him, 'Because you have asked this, and have not asked for yourself long life or riches or the life of your enemies, . . . I give you a wise and discerning mind. . . . And if you will walk in my ways, . . . I will lengthen your days'" (vv. 10–14).

Earthly Life Is Not the Highest Good: God's Word teaches that long physical life is a great good, but it is not the highest biblical good.[10]

The Lord gives Solomon long life as well as wisdom, but he tells Solomon that wisdom is more important.

The Bible also teaches that spiritual life is more valuable than long physical life. "Life" occurs over four hundred times in Scripture, and of these instances, the vast majority refer to spiritual life, not physical life. The Tree of Life in both the garden of Eden (Gen. 2–3) and the heavenly Jerusalem (Rev. 20–22) is a symbol of the fulfillment of every kind of life: physical and spiritual, individual and communal. For most of us, long physical life and spiritual life do not come into conflict. We can extend our physical life without taking away from our spiritual life. But if we are forced to choose between our spiritual life and our physical life, the Bible calls us to value spiritual life more highly.

Christ's work for us has earned our salvation, so we will never have to choose between living a longer earthly life and living spiritual life in fellowship with God. It may happen, however, that other great spiritual goods can be pursued only by laying aside our physical life. The most obvious example of this is Christ's earthly, physical life. He says about himself that he lays down his life for his friends (John 15:13), and that by it he demonstrates his love for us. Jesus also says that he has the authority to lay his physical life down (10:17–18). If God's Word required us *always* to extend our physical life as long as possible, then Jesus would have violated that obligation when he gave up his life to secure our redemption.

Jesus' atoning death for us is certainly a special case in many ways. Yet martyrs such as Stephen in Acts 6:8–7:60 are also praised for choosing a shorter physical life in order to pursue the spiritual good of proclaiming the gospel. Stephen could have lived a much longer life

---

10. Compare the wording in the 1988 PCA Report on Heroic Measures, where the first principle is: "God's glory is our ultimate aim. So extending our physical life is not an ultimate good."

if he had simply kept his mouth shut. The high priest and the coun-
cil stoned him in a rage because he accused them of murdering "the
Righteous One" (Jesus) (7:52). If he had simply answered the charge
against him (6:13–14), he might have remained alive. He chose instead
to exalt Christ rather than live longer. The vision that he was granted
of Jesus standing at the right hand of God (7:55) shows that God
approved of his choice. The Bible teaches that some things are more
important than living as long as possible.

Physical life is not the ultimate good, and physical death is not the
ultimate evil. Jesus teaches that it would be better to be dead than to
lead God's children astray (Matt. 18:1–6). We are called to fear the
one who can kill our souls in hell more than we fear those who can
kill only our bodies (Matt. 10:28). While death is a consequence of
the curse, Ecclesiastes 3:1–8 says that there is a time for everything,
including a time to die. Abraham dies "full of years," at a "good old
age" (Gen. 25:7–8).

A Time to Die: God's Word permits us to accept death in the
Lord as a blessing when our service to Christ is full.[11]

Paul says that to live is Christ, but to die is gain (Phil. 1:18b–23).
While the last days of physical life may be uncomfortable, for the
believer death is not something to fear. Death has been defeated at the
cross (1 Cor. 15:50–57, echoing Isa. 25:6–8).

Death Is Defeated: God's Word assures us that death is
a great evil, but it is not the ultimate evil, and it has been
defeated by Christ.

11. Section II of the 1988 PCA Report on Heroic Measures, which explains "Biblical Principles," contains this statement: "*Spiritual* death is an absolute evil for human
beings, to be avoided by them at all costs (Cf. Ezek. 18:23, 2 Pet. 3:9). *Physical*
death, on the other hand, is a relative evil in a fallen world. For the Christian it is not
an enemy always to be fought at all costs. 'There is a time for everything,' says the
Preacher, 'A time to be born and a time to die' (Eccl. 3:1–2). And, we might add, a
time to resist death and a time to cease resisting."

We are not to hasten our own death or the death of others (apart from just warfare or capital punishment), but avoiding death should not be our primary goal. We are made to glorify God and enjoy him forever, and the end of physical life will be only one moment in that greater objective.[12]

Benefits and Burdens

Most medical treatment aims at the restoration of health and not merely the avoiding of death. In the case of serious illness, medical treatment typically offers both benefits and burdens. The most obvious of these benefits and burdens are physical. Medical procedures offer the physical benefits of longer life, clearer thinking, better sleep, increased stamina, improved bodily functions, and decreased levels of pain. Even simple procedures can involve some inconvenience, some loss of function, and some pain. Life-sustaining medical treatment typically involves more than a little inconvenience, limitation, and pain. For all sorts of health difficulties, the physical benefits offered by treatment easily outweigh the physical burdens imposed by them. Sometimes the trade-off between benefits and burdens seems about even. When the likely burdens outweigh likely benefits, we are usually comfortable declining the treatment. A few years ago, my doctors prescribed a statin to reduce my total cholesterol. The day after I took the very first pill, I felt awful. I felt as though I had a fever of 103 degrees (F)—muscle ache, fidgetiness, fatigue—but my temperature was normal. When I called my doctor's office, I was told not to take any more. I was in the small percentage of people who react badly to statins. If I had kept taking the pills, they could have killed me. The physical burden (muscle failure and possibly death) greatly outweighed the physical benefit (lower total cholesterol). Saying no to statins was an easy call, and I can't imagine anyone suggesting that I have an obligation to accept that burden in order to achieve the benefit.

12. Westminster Shorter Catechism 1, *The Westminster Confession of Faith and Catechisms as Adopted by the Presbyterian Church in America with Proof Texts* (Lawrenceville, GA: Committee on Education & Publication of the PCA, 2007).

Choices about the benefits and burdens of life-sustaining medical options are more difficult than my choice about taking a statin. The most common end-of-life question that people face in American hospitals is "Do you want to be resuscitated if your heart stops?" If someone does not want to be resuscitated, the doctor writes a DNR order (do-not-resuscitate order) that tells the medical team to allow natural death to occur if the heart stops. Because a resuscitation attempt is an extreme measure with a low probability of success, the burdens involved are high and the likely benefits typically fairly low. Most doctors ask about a DNR order only when they believe the benefit-burden trade-off would be unattractive. More will be said about resuscitation attempts in the "CPR" section of chapter 3.

Decisions about resuscitation are not the only common challenge in the hospital setting today. Mechanical ventilation to support breathing, kidney dialysis, and the mechanical delivery of food and water are widely available. Making choices about whether to use these forms of treatment also calls for thoughtful attention to the likely benefits and burdens. Doctors and nurses can give excellent insight into the physical benefits and burdens involved. They can also help with the psychosocial benefits and burdens that ought to be taken into account. Psychosocial benefits include being able to think clearly, to remember important details, to make plans confidently, and to enjoy the company of other people. Psychosocial burdens, on the other hand, include being confused, forgetful, uninterested in the future, and unable to give or receive pleasure from others' company. These benefits and burdens are often connected to someone's physical condition. Pain can make people confused, listless, or argumentative—but not in every case. Careful consideration of whether the benefits are worth enduring the likely burdens has to be specific to the person receiving the care. This is why doctors and nurses are eager to hear what the sick person thinks about the balance between likely benefits and likely burdens. When the sick person is unable to express an opinion, the doctors and nurses want the sick person's agent to say what the agent believes the sick person would say. Ultimately, the best judge of whether the benefits will outweigh the burdens is the person who will live with the choices being made.

The world around us overestimates the significance of financial benefits and burdens, and it certainly *underestimates* the significance of spiritual benefits and burdens. Doctors and nurses today will tolerate including spiritual implications in discussions about medical treatment, but most doctors and nurses will be uncomfortable about allowing spiritual considerations to be decisive. If spiritual concerns lead away from following doctors' recommendations, the doctors are likely to be frustrated, eager to find a way to get "past" religious ideas that are in the way of what they believe is sound medicine. Christian doctors and nurses may also be frustrated. Experience has taught most doctors that religious language is too often used to avoid dealing with the approach of death. They know that it is hard to accept that medical treatment can do little more than keep a loved one alive in the hospital. They want a discussion that faces what is happening, and when religion seems to be getting in the way of that, it can seem that they want all talk of religion to end. In part, their frustration about religious talk rests on the emptiness and even self-destructive power of *false* spiritual beliefs. Christian doctors and nurses are grieved when false religious convictions lead a person to decline a lifesaving blood transfusion or course of chemotherapy.[13]

What we know from Scripture is not false or self-destructive. It is instead true and life-giving in ways that exceed the many physical and psychosocial benefits. True spiritual benefits are more delightful and ultimately more significant than physical, psychosocial, or financial benefits. The reverse is true for spiritual burdens. Just as spiritual delights are more satisfying than the other benefits, spiritual deprivations are more serious than the other burdens. Moreover, these different kinds of benefits and burdens are usually connected. Medical treatment can greatly affect our spiritual state. Illness and injury can be used by the Holy Spirit to draw us closer to Christ, but they can also

---

13. Jehovah's Witnesses reject all blood products on the basis of a mistaken reading of Deuteronomy 12:23, "the blood is the life." Christian Scientists believe that all physical afflictions are ultimately spiritual problems to be addressed by prayer and *not* medical treatment; see Mary Baker Eddy, *Science and Health* (Boston: First Church of Christ, Scientist, 1994).

lead to spiritual loneliness and despair. All these consequences need to be taken into account.

In the absence of persecution, it is easy to take our spiritual goods for granted. We are prone to forget the many ordinary ways in which God nurtures our faith through activities that are pleasant in themselves. Meditating on God's Word, for example, is delightful in itself. Psalm 19:10 says that the rules of the Lord are more desirable than gold and sweeter than fresh honey. When Jesus by the Holy Spirit opens the Scriptures to us in the faithful preaching of the Word, we are like the disciples on the road to Emmaus in Luke 24. Our "hearts burn within us" (Luke 24:32), our love for Christ deepens, and the eyes of our hearts are opened more fully to the spiritual reality of our glorious inheritance and the greatness of God's immeasurable power (Eph. 1:18–19). Other ordinary sources of joy are worship, prayer, and the sacraments. Worship in God's house for even one day is better than a thousand days doing anything else (Ps. 84:10). When we pray together, Jesus is present with us (Matt. 18:20). In celebrating the Lord's Supper, our souls are fed and we proclaim the Lord's death until he comes (1 Cor. 11:23–26).

> **The Ordinary Means of Grace:** God's Word teaches that the spiritual goods of meditating on God's Word, partaking of the sacraments, prayer, and fellowship with other believers are great goods that we should seek out and not neglect.[14]

A final spiritual blessing is particularly significant near the end of life: the joy of being reconciled to those from whom we have been estranged because of sin. The natural benefits of reconciliation are widely appreciated: lowering of tensions, restored mutual support, and so on. The supernatural benefits are also significant: unity in the faith, the peace of wholeness and not merely the absence of conflict, and a powerful witness to Christ's power. Jesus taught that being reconciled

---

14. See both Section III, "Principles of Application," in the 1988 PCA Report on Heroic Measures and Westminster Larger Catechism 88 on the ordinary means of grace.

to those whom we have offended is more important than making an offering as part of worship (Matt. 5:23–24).

Called to Be Reconciled: God's Word calls us to be reconciled to others whom we have wronged.

Sometimes life-sustaining medical treatment can make it possible for believers to be reconciled before it is too late. That alone may be a great enough benefit to offset the physical and financial burdens imposed by using it.

People who do not know Jesus as their Savior and Lord cannot even imagine the delightfulness of these spiritual goods. They may think that these goods are little different from the gentle thrill they get from asking a false god to prosper their business or the sense of satisfaction they feel when they make sacrifices for others. For all they can see in their spiritually blind condition, Christian devotion is outwardly very similar to pagan devotion. We should not allow their inability to appreciate our delights to keep us from estimating them rightly and including them in our thinking about end-of-life medical treatment. In addition to paying closer attention to the sweetness of these spiritual blessings and giving thanks for them, we need to recognize the spiritual burdens involved in being cut off from enjoying what is spiritually delightful. Failing health is not the only obstacle that can get in the way of these joys. Having Christian friends move away from town or wander away from the faith can complicate or undermine our joy. We can become oppressed by the cares of this world, wallow in unrepentant sin for a season, or make poor choices in our friends. These threats to our spiritual health can arise while we are physically healthy. We also need to recognize that failing physical health can have implications for our ability to enjoy spiritual goods. More than that, the medical treatments used to fight physical difficulties can involve limitations that deprive us of access to spiritual goods. Whatever compromises our ability to enjoy spiritual goods must be counted as a spiritual burden. Spiritual goods are great benefits; spiritual deprivations are great burdens.

No Obligation to Suffer Merely to Live Longer

The Bible teaches that we should be ready to suffer for the sake of Christ. More than that, Paul teaches that our suffering somehow "fill[s] up" Christ's suffering (Col. 1:24). We may even be called to suffer in order to live long enough to fulfill the responsibilities we have, or to fulfill promises we have made. But in all that the Bible says about suffering for righteousness or for the cause of the gospel, God's Word does not say that we are required to suffer *merely in order to* live as long as possible. Certainly we may not squander our lives or take steps to end them, but we are not called to suffer simply to live longer. Even though his eye was "undimmed, and his vigor unabated," Moses was allowed to die rather than watch Israel pass into the promised land (Deut. 34:7). Paul in Philippians 1:19–26 asserts that he would prefer to die and be with Christ rather than to go on living; he is willing to live to serve Christ, but he is not required merely to live.

> **Not Obligated to Suffer Only to Stay Alive:** God's Word does not say that we are required to suffer *merely in order to* live as long as possible.[15]

The suffering that the Bible calls us to endure is always a necessary part of some other calling that God has given us—as an evangelist, as a parent, as a soldier, or as a martyr (see Matt. 5:11–12; Phil. 1:29; 1 Peter 4:12–19).

> **Called to Suffer for Christ's Sake:** God's Word calls us to suffer for the name of Christ if persecuted, or to testify to Christ's lordship.

The suffering imposed by life-sustaining medical treatment may not serve any purpose other than keeping us alive. In that case, we may still

---

15. The 1988 PCA Report on Heroic Measures finds that "life is not [to] be abandoned simply on account of suffering. . . . Yet, there is no reason to believe that extraordinary means that extend life only by increasing suffering and dependence are

choose to accept the burdens involved in life-sustaining treatment, but we are not required to accept them.

To illustrate: Consider the case of Mary, a 69-year-old believer who "beat" breast cancer ten years ago but has recently been diagnosed with stage 4 pancreatic cancer. Mary's oncologist says that Mary's prognosis is grim. Although Mary was in good health before her first bout with cancer, she is now too weak to do much more than watch TV and have short visits from friends. Because of her experience with breast cancer, she knows firsthand what chemotherapy would involve for her: prolonged nausea, greatly diminished ability to concentrate, and incontinence that would make it embarrassing to entertain guests. Mary has learned that she is eligible to participate in an experimental trial of a treatment that might extend her life by as much as nine months. The side effects of the trial, however, are likely to be even more intense than those that Mary experienced with her previous cancer treatment. If Mary declines to participate in the trial, humanly speaking she is likely to die within the next two months. She can be kept more comfortable than she would be with the experimental treatment, but she will probably die much sooner without it. Taking both physical and spiritual goods into account, we see that the Bible does not require Mary to participate in the experimental trial. She may choose to participate, but she may also choose not to.

Although the Bible requires us to protect our own lives and the lives of others, it does not require Mary to suffer simply for the purpose of living longer. Pain and suffering are part of the curse, an ongoing consequence of Adam and Eve's rebellion in the garden. Pain-management techniques can limit some of the effects of the fall, but not all of them. Sometimes pain can be part of a broader effort to resist the effects of the fall. The pain involved in physical therapy, for example, is accepted as part of restoring healthy function.[16] In Mary's situation, the physical

---

always to be chosen as means of glorifying God" (§ II).

16. The word *proportionate* is sometimes used to describe a burden worth bearing. Pain that is a key part of achieving full health is proportionate pain. Burdens that do not serve a clearly superior end are *dis*proportionate burdens. The concepts of the *proportionate* and the *disproportionate* are central to Roman Catholic moral theology. In

and spiritual burdens that would come with participating in the experimental trial would be great. If the only gain would be a bit more time of pain and isolation, Mary may decide that the experimental-trial option would be excessively burdensome.

At times we may be called to suffer for the sake of the gospel. When that happens, the suffering is not excessively burdensome; the end realized is superior to the burdens endured. Paul reasons this way in Philippians 3 about the hardships he experienced on his missionary journeys. We may be called to a physically difficult mission field or to physical persecution in order to advance the gospel. But Mary's pain would not advance the gospel. Participation in the experimental trial would mean living her remaining days in pain and discomfort. Her interactions with her family, church, and friends would be greatly limited. Her enjoyment of spiritual goods would also be significantly diminished. The spiritual goods of corporate worship, reading the Word of God and hearing it preached, taking the sacraments, and prayer all depend on a certain level of physical vigor. A person who is too sick or confused to enjoy these delights is cut off from the most valuable goods that this life affords. Medical treatment that seriously compromises Mary's access to these ordinary means of grace is medical treatment that imposes a great burden.

Although the world does not see it, being deprived of these goods is spiritual suffering comparable to being deprived of pain relief, clarity of mind, and social interaction. Non-Christian doctors may struggle to understand this kind of burden, and even some Christian doctors may be uncomfortable in asking people to think about them. It is not that these Christian doctors are ashamed of the gospel; it is rather that their medical training has focused on the physical implications of medical treatment. One important way that we can help fellow Christians who are facing difficult choices about medical treatment is to gently raise questions about spiritual benefits and burdens.

Reformed discussions of God's law, these concepts are usually called the *ordinary* and the *excessive*. See *Ethical and Religious Directives for Catholic Health Care Services* (Washington, DC: United States Conference of Catholic Bishops, 2009), part 5.

Ineffective Medical Measures

Especially near the end of life, medical treatment can become ineffective. Medical knowledge has made remarkable advances in the last few decades, but medicine remains limited in what it can accomplish. When medical treatment will not be effective, we are not biblically required either to start using it or to continue using it.

Treatment may be ineffective even when it extends physical life a bit and reduces discomfort. Spiritual goods can be more important than physical comfort and slightly longer physical life. Just before Jesus was nailed to the cross, he was offered "wine mixed with myrrh" (Mark 15:23). The purpose of this drink is not explained. It may have been a mocking ritual of false compassion. It may have been intended to prolong the dying process (and thus the spectacle) by deadening some of the pain. Myrrh was expensive, so it likely had some purpose, and it was used in genuinely benevolent contexts as a painkiller.[17] Whatever the Romans' purpose, Jesus rejected the offer. While it may have been effective in giving temporary relief from thirst and some of the pain, and may even have extended his life somewhat, it was inconsistent with the spiritual task that Jesus had taken on. Jesus demonstrates here that God's law does not require us to use every means possible to limit pain or to extend our lives as long as possible.

Accepting that medicine has reached the limit of its effectiveness can be difficult. Medical knowledge has advanced so rapidly in our lifetimes that we have come to expect that there is *always* something more that medicine can do. When we are facing our own death or the loss of a beloved family member, we are zealous to find some way to stop death's advance. Years of being amazed at medical advances can make it really hard to believe that the very best that medical skill can do is to keep us comfortable. Between our desire to hold on to life and our confidence in medical technology, we struggle to think clearly

17. The Gospel authors may also have intended to allude to the magi's gift offered to Jesus as a king. For more on myrrh and to see recent questions about myrrh as a painkiller, see Erkki Koskenniemi, Kirsi Nisula, and Jorma Toppari, "Wine Mixed with Myrrh (Mark 15:23) and *Crurifragium* (John 19.31–32): Two Details of the Passion Narratives," *Journal for the Study of the New Testament* 27, 4 (2005): 379–91.

about our remaining medical options, and we may lose sight of the great blessing we have in being kept comfortable in our final hours.

Making end-of-life choices is like being in the midst of a storm. It is hard to see clearly and even harder to appreciate the good things that aren't flying away. Peace in the midst of a medical tempest is the work of the Holy Spirit, who accomplishes his work through both natural and supernatural means. Among the natural means are pain-management techniques and doctors and nurses who give careful explanations of what medicine can and cannot accomplish. Among the supernatural means are ears that hear even when we are frightened and godly counselors who give biblically sound advice in a way that we can understand. Together, these natural and supernatural means may rightly recommend focusing on comfort and doing less than everything else medically possible near the end of life.

Westminster Larger Catechism 136 and the Sixth Commandment

The suggestion that we may aim for comfort while saying no to aggressive life-sustaining treatment may seem to run contrary to pro-life convictions. Christians today who are serious about God's Word are appropriately zealous about defending the sanctity of life. We lament how commonly abortion is used to take the lives of unborn children. Our hearts ache for those who take their own lives, and we deplore changes in the law that make abortion and suicide more likely. Appropriate regard for the preciousness of human life is at the heart of Westminster Larger Catechism 136, which details the sins forbidden by the sixth commandment. When the framers of the catechism included "the neglecting or withdrawing the lawful and necessary means of preservation of life" among those sins, they were thinking of willful murder or suicide by choking or starving someone. In the seventeenth century when the catechism was written, machines to keep heart and lung function going had not been invented. The "lawful and necessary means" for keeping someone alive were all effective, and none of them imposed a great burden on the recipient in order to work.

The 1988 PCA Report on Heroic Measures notes WLC 136 on its way to concluding that the Bible permits us to decline ineffective and excessively burdensome treatment. The report does not reject the counsel given in WLC 136. What the catechism says was clearly true at the time it was written, and its zeal for the sanctity of life is biblically sound today. The report's conclusion implicitly finds that WLC 136 does not address the biblical appropriateness of declining ineffective or excessively burdensome treatment near the end of life. WLC 136 assumes that the "lawful and necessary means" are both effective and not excessively burdensome. Making this assumption explicit, WLC 136 correctly teaches that it is sinful to neglect or withdraw the lawful, necessary, *effective, and reasonably burdensome* means of preserving life. Declining ineffective or excessively burdensome treatment does not violate WLC 136, it is not a violation of the sixth commandment, and it is not sinful.

DECLINING TREATMENT IS NOT A FORM OF SUICIDE

How we describe things affects how we feel about them. "She dug her nails into his forearm until he cried" suggests something very different from "She held him so tightly as he cried that it left marks on his arm." Not all descriptions are helpful, and sometimes even honest attempts to describe an event distort what is happening. "Mr. Smith's daughter is helping him commit *suicide* by asking the doctors to turn the ventilator off" is a poor description of what is happening if the ventilator is not helping Mr. Smith recover consciousness and his daughter is accurately expressing his wishes. Suicide is the sin of willfully and wrongly *taking* one's own life. Mr. Smith is not taking his own life if the ventilator is not effective treatment. Disease or loss of function is killing Mr. Smith. Mr. Smith is not killing himself, and neither his daughter nor the physician and nurses who withdraw the ventilator support are killing him. So it is neither accurate nor helpful to describe the withdrawal of the ventilator as *suicide*. It is even less helpful to use the term *suicide* when talking with Mr. Smith's daughter as she is trying to decide what her father would want done.

For someone convinced that we are obligated to do everything medically possible to extend physical life, the word *suicide* might seem appropriate. Turning off the ventilator likely means that Mr. Smith will die; so if Mr. Smith turns off the machine, he will be *doing something likely to end in death*. That might seem like the very definition of *suicide*. Using the word *suicide* to describe turning off the ventilator would tilt the discussion steeply in favor of continuing the use of the machine. While Mr. Smith's daughter might be moving toward withdrawal of the ventilator too quickly or without adequate grounds, using the word *suicide* doesn't help anyone think about the decision clearly. Suicide is more than just taking steps that end in death. If that were enough, then every martyr for the cause of Christ was a suicide, and Christ himself committed suicide on the cross. In order to see that the withdrawal of ineffective or excessively burdensome treatment is not suicide, we must consider the biblical data on suicide.

Suicide in the Bible

What the Bible says about self-murder must begin with what God's law says about murder. Genesis 9 makes it clear that human life is precious as the image of God. No human has the authority to take human life without clear permission from God. Genesis 9:5–6 gives that permission in order to punish murderers. Exodus 20:13 forbids murder. Numbers 35:9–34 sets aside cities of refuge for those who take life unintentionally. Deuteronomy dictates the evidence necessary for legitimate execution (Deut. 17:6). Private citizens do not have the authority to take someone else's life except in self-defense. None of us as individuals has the authority to take the life of a person unless that person is trying to kill us.[18] God's Word has not given us that authority.

> **Prohibition against Taking Life:** God's Word forbids us as private citizens to take steps that intentionally end someone's life.

---

18. Here I am passing over the subject of protecting the lives of others. We are authorized to use sufficient force to protect our family members as well. See Exodus

Looking to God's Word for guidance about suicide is crucial because American culture today assumes that we each have the authority to dispose of our own lives however we wish. Not only does the surrounding culture believe that we each may choose our values, our life projects, and even our identity, it also believes that we have the authority to kill ourselves. As a practical matter, most people have the *ability* to end their own lives. Yet having the practical ability to do something is not the same thing as having the moral authority to do it. Only God has the authority to take human life; we do not. Suicide is forbidden, but concerns about God's law are rarely central when someone is thinking about taking his or her own life.

For people whose lives are dominated by the loss of loved ones, mobility, physical comfort, or purpose, bringing death quickly may seem like a solution. People considering suicide as a solution need comfort and the gospel far more than they need to have their thinking corrected. Our answer to people who are suffering should not be mere resignation to God's demands. Instead, we should draw close to them and make the goodness of life more evident, highlighting the opportunities they still possess to walk with Christ and serve him. In our fallen world, taking delight in this life is often difficult. The gospel alternative to resignation is not insisting that life is great. The alternative is walking by faith: opening our eyes to the spiritual goods that we can enjoy now and trusting God's promises about our future. We need also to acknowledge that even people of faith grow weary of this life. The solution is not denying the brokenness of the world. It is facing that brokenness and walking with Christ.

The desire or attempt to take one's own life is mentioned only a few times in Scripture, but many of them are well known. After he had betrayed Jesus and handed him over to the Pharisees, Judas Iscariot killed himself (Matt. 27:5). When the Philistine army had him surrounded, Saul took his own life by falling on his sword, as did his armor-bearer (1 Sam. 31:4–5). Abimelech (Judg. 9:50–57) also

---

22:2–3 and the discussion of self-defense at "The Biblical View of Self Defense," http://www.biblicalselfdefense.com/.

had his armor-bearer kill him, lest anyone say, "A woman killed him." Ahithophel (2 Sam. 17:21–23) hanged himself after David rejected his advice. Zimri (1 Kings 16:15–20) burned himself along with the palace when he saw that all was lost. All these people had turned against God, and while the act of taking their own lives is not singled out as a separate sin, the act of self-destruction is treated as consistent with (or flowing from) a heart at enmity with God. Moses, Elijah, Jonah, and the Philippian jailer were not enemies of God, but out of anger, exhaustion, selfish frustration, or fear, each man asked God to take his life (Num. 11:10–15; 1 Kings 19; Jonah 4; Acts 16). Not only did God deny their requests, they were told to carry on with the difficult work that God had called them to do.[19]

A few biblical heroes take steps that they know are likely to lead to their own deaths and yet are praised for it. Samson uses his divinely restored strength to bring down the temple of Dagon, killing those inside and himself with them (Judg. 16:25ff.). John the Baptist calls Herod to repent of taking his brother's wife and ends up with his head on a platter (Matt. 14:1–12). Stephen testifies to Jesus' lordship and is stoned to death (Acts 6–7). James is executed for his profession (Acts 12:2). And Jesus goes willingly to his own execution. Jesus, however, is God; as he says, he has the authority to lay his life down and to take it up (John 10:17–18). Samson, John the Baptist, and Stephen were not *seeking to die*. For them, death was a cost of serving God with all they had. Taken together, these passages of Scripture teach that we as mere creatures do not have the authority to take our own lives intentionally.

Suicide is not permitted by God's Word. It follows from this that "physician-assisted suicide" is not biblically justified, either. Physician-assisted suicide is taking one's own life by using drugs, devices, or instructions prescribed by a physician. The physician's role is to provide a way for the suicide to be "humane and dignified,"

---

19. For a clear and helpful discussion of suicide in the Bible, see Robert Barry, "The Biblical Teaching on Suicide," *Issues in Law & Medicine* 13, 3 (Winter 1997): 283–99.

usually meaning minimizing the pain of the person dying and the distress of the loved ones who remain.[20] Until as recently as 2009, a physician in the United States faced the loss of his or her medical license and criminal prosecution for assisting in someone's suicide. Starting with Oregon, states have been adopting laws that allow physicians to assist people in dying under certain conditions. Common requirements to qualify for physician assistance in dying are that the person seeking to die be diagnosed with a terminal illness, not be clinically depressed, and be able to give informed consent to the doctor's fatal orders.

Advocates for these laws argue that people who are going to die anyway (terminally ill) should be allowed to die in a "humane" way, meaning at a time and in a manner of their choosing. To deny them the freedom to control their own deaths, they argue, is to deny them the dignity and respect they deserve. It is an insult, they contend, for the law to punish people for taking their own lives by imposing the penalty of voiding their life insurance policies or invalidating their wills. Current thinking assumes that each of us "owns" our life, and that we thus each have the authority to protect or destroy it as we wish. More than that, our culture assumes that it is cruel for the law to prevent the people with the skill to minimize the pain and inconvenience of dying from giving badly needed assistance. Prohibiting physicians from helping people to do what they want in an efficient way is just another way of imposing society's values on people who are already dying.

It is tempting to dismiss physician-assisted suicide with the conclusive observation that its central assumption is wrong. We do not have the authority to take our own lives. While this is sufficient to show that physician-assisted suicide is biblically prohibited, we should resist the temptation to make condemnation our first response. The reasons that advocates give for allowing physicians to ease people out of life painlessly are biblically wrong, but according to the reasoning

20. The phrase "humane and dignified" is taken from the Oregon law allowing people with terminal illnesses to seek a physician's assistance in ending their lives. The official phrase repeated through the 2015 version of the statute is "to end his or her life in a humane and dignified manner." See ORS chapter 127, https://www.oregonlegislature.gov/bills_laws/ors/ors127.html.

of our day they are not silly. These advocates' position rests on a false assumption, but it is motivated by a laudable desire: to help people deal with the prospect of being forced to live on when life has become a great burden. When Christians use the Bible to show that our lives are not ours to destroy, people who do not know Jesus are likely to think that Christians must be heartless. Non-Christians will too easily conclude that Christians do not care about the suffering of others, and that Christians care more about being right than we do about loving people. The reasons that people want to end their lives ought to matter to us. We should want to say more than "No" to their cry for help, both to non-Christians and to Christians who live in states that permit physician-assisted "death with dignity."

Pain Is a Real Burden, Calling for Compassion and Nonlethal Relief

The three most common reasons given by people for wanting to die "with dignity" (by suicide) are that:

- They no longer see a point to being alive;
- They do not want to be a burden to others; and
- They do not want to suffer with unmanageable pain.

These reasons are very different, and so need to be treated separately when we have the opportunity to walk with people through their pain.

People who are eager to die because they see no point to their lives need the gospel. Followers of Christ who feel this way need to be reminded of Christ's love for them, of the advance of his work in making all things new, and of his call for us to labor as faithful stewards of our resources. They do not need to be chastised for losing sight of the splendor of the gospel, since spiritual depression by itself is not sinful. Westminster Confession of Faith 18.4 reminds us that our assurance of salvation may be "shaken, diminished, and intermitted . . . by some sudden or vehement temptation [or] by God's withdrawing the light of His countenance, and suffering even such as fear Him to walk in darkness and to have no light." Our first impulse should be to treat struggling believers with compassion, sharing in their distress as fellow broken sinners. We can communicate the point to life by loving them as Christ loves them.

Those who do not know Jesus and cannot see a point to being alive also need the gospel. In the midst of their despair, everything is dark. Humanly speaking, the truth of the gospel is simply foolishness. Insisting that they need only to think hard about the ultimate goodness of life will not be helpful. Thinking harder won't help. Apart from Christ, there is no ultimately satisfying reason to live. Their reasoning ability may be working just fine. They see that nothing under the sun is worth living in pain, and they are drawing the right conclusion if this life is all there is. Calling them stupid or condemning them as wicked will only convince them that we don't really care about them. What they need is to learn the amazing truth that Jesus saves sinners, and that even in pain it is fulfilling to live for him. Suffering unbelievers are spiritually blind to these realities. But they may be able to see what is visible to earthly eyes: our love for them and our confidence that Christ is worth living for even through difficulty.

Not wanting to be a burden to others seems like a noble goal. It is not just Americans who are horrified at being a burden. It is a universal human temptation, fueled by unbiblical ideas about the importance of staying in complete control of our lives and the nature of real love. Adam and Eve's first sin was an expression of their desire for autonomy. They trusted themselves more than anyone else, including God. Pride in being the absolute master of our fate is crucial—we think—to self-respect. In the grip of this lie, we can too easily believe that loss of independence is a fate worse than death. It isn't. Dependence gives others the opportunity to care for us. We were designed to flourish in community, sometimes caring for others and other times being cared for. People who doubt that anyone would want to care for them should be connected to churches that are eager to show Christ's love by caring for the brokenhearted.

Finally, those who are facing unmanageable pain deserve to be treated with compassion as well. Pain-management techniques are making rapid advances, but there are still diseases and conditions involving pain that cannot be controlled. Living with pain that cannot be managed is horrible. Many people suffer in pain that they did nothing to bring on themselves. We may not assume that those in pain somehow deserve it. The world is broken. It also has a Savior, but Christ's final victory is still in the future. Until then, pain is all too real, and we should not try to convince people that it isn't so bad or that it will be somehow made up for by heaven. Those who seek to end their lives in order to avoid living and dying in pain are bearing the effects of the fall more acutely than other people. Biblically permissible pain management should be aggressively used. Luke 8:43–48 tells of a woman who presumed to touch Jesus to get relief, and Paul used his Roman citizenship to avoid a flogging (Acts 22:22–28).

> **Faithful Relief from Pain:** God's Word permits us to seek relief from pain in ways consistent with being a faithful steward of our resources and our witness to the gospel.

People dealing with pain are likely also suffering from loneliness, loss of delight in earthly joys, and anxiety that the pain will lead them to do something shameful. Even when we cannot help with the physical pain, we should look for ways to limit the other parts of their suffering. We can be present and attentive; we can look for things that are still delightful, such as shared memories or experiences; and we can give assurance that even when the pain is depriving them of control, we will not leave them.

Not much can be done directly to persuade someone who loves autonomy more than anything else. Those who insist that they are the absolute masters of their lives are unlikely to see the good in mutual dependence with loved ones or the joy of serving a loving Savior. When they are in pain, we should still be reaching out to them in love. We will not win an argument about the wrongness of suicide. By drawing near, praying, and bearing whatever we can of their suffering, we can have Christ's love for us spill over into their lives. They will suffer less, and they may even ask us why we haven't abandoned them in the way they expected.

Jesus and the Martyrs Are Not Suicides

God's Word clearly gives Jesus and the martyrs the moral authority to allow death to overtake them in their pursuit of great spiritual goods. This is pivotally important as we work to apply God's Word to decisions about the use of life-sustaining medical treatment. Nearly every death that is mentioned in Scripture involves someone who did not want to die being killed by someone or something that the person could not stop. Human killers such as enemy soldiers or treacherous friends could be stopped only by more powerful defenders or by God's direct intervention. Old age, disease, and the forces of nature (drowning, being attacked by wild animals, or being struck by a falling tower) are all unwanted and unstoppable causes of death. For most of human history, only God could stop these forces. No one who dies from unwanted, unstoppable forces is guilty of self-murder.

Jesus and the martyrs are important examples because they *could* have stopped their own deaths, chose not to, and are not guilty of suicide. Jesus had the power to stop his own death at any point and chose to accept it. Martyrs for the gospel sometimes had the power to stop oppressors from killing them by renouncing Christ. They also chose to allow death to overtake them. We can conclude, then, that Scripture does not prohibit every instance of allowing death to come even when we have the ability to stop it. With Jesus and the martyrs, we know that death is part of realizing a great spiritual good.

Letting Die Is Not the Same as Killing

One of my first attempts to join in a discussion about God's law and medical practice brought me into conflict with a Christian physician. I was young, arrogant, and—I now know—wrong. To the physician's credit, he was patient with me. He did not let on that I was being a pill. In conversation after church, I had overheard the physician say that a decision to turn a machine (a ventilator) *off* should follow the same reasoning and principles as a decision whether the machine should be turned *on* in the first place. It seemed to me at the time that this was monstrous. Deciding whether to turn a machine on or start a course of treatment involves all kinds of uncertainty about whether the treatment will work. Once a machine had been turned on, I imagined, if it was doing any good at all it should be kept on. With it running, any uncertainty about effectiveness had been removed, and surely starting a treatment brought with it the obligation to keep using it if it was helping. This seemed to me especially true if the treatment was keeping someone alive. In that case, turning the machine off seemed to be the same thing as killing the person. Thirty years ago, this reasoning seemed unassailable to me.

Before we had machines that could force air in and out of the lungs of people in a coma, it was usually impossible to do anything to keep death from happening when someone had to fight to keep breathing or had stopped breathing altogether. The only option was to wait for whatever was killing the person to run its dismal course. For example, when someone died of pneumonia—until recently a very common cause of death—no one asked *who* did the killing. Lamentation was appropriate, and no person was to blame. Now we have machines or techniques that can forestall death. These medical options are truly marvelous, but they tempt us to think that there is always someone to blame when death comes. Having the medical means of sustaining life tempts us to think that we are killing someone if we do not make physical life last as long as medicine allows. But the Bible does not say that we must do everything possible to extend physical life. It teaches that sometimes it is permissible to let someone die without being guilty of killing the person. God's Word teaches that *killing* and *letting die* are not the same thing.

Declining Ineffective Treatment Is Not Taking Someone's Life: God's Word permits us to decline ineffective or excessively burdensome treatment, so declining treatment is not forbidden, and thus it is not intentionally ending someone's life.[21]

21. The 1988 PCA Report on Heroic Measures finds that it is morally wrong to bring about death in order to relieve suffering, but that withdrawing or withholding ineffective treatment is *not* morally wrong. Withholding CPR (or authorizing a DNR order) is thus permissible, and may be best if CPR would be only minimally effective (§ III.6, 11).

Consider Simeon the prophet, whom Luke describes as recognizing the baby Jesus as the Messiah. Simeon responds with prayer: "Lord, now you are letting your servant depart in peace, according to your word; for my eyes have seen your salvation that you have prepared in the presence of all peoples" (Luke 2:29–31). Simeon was not asking to die. He was saying that he was content, rejoicing that he had lived to see God's promise fulfilled. Death was not far away, and he was ready for it. Assured, somehow, by God that he would not die until he had seen the Messiah, he was acknowledging that the promise had been kept. None of us doubts that God had the power and authority to keep Simeon alive or to take him home. Simeon's prayer shows us, however, that it can be righteous to say to the Lord, "I am ready to die; I have lived long enough." The 90-year-old believer today who has lived a full life and whose unmanageable pain has him longing for heaven can righteously say, "Lord, I'm just dying to die." It would be wrong for him to kill himself, and it would be wrong for anyone to poison or suffocate him. But neither he nor anyone else is biblically obligated to extend his pain by attaching him to a machine merely to keep him alive. We may let this servant of the Lord depart in peace, killed by disease or infirmity and not by those who declined ineffective or greatly burdensome treatment.

PRAYING FOR HEALING WITHOUT PLANNING ON A MIRACLE[22]

Both Christian and non-Christian doctors are dismayed when the families of people who are gravely ill ask to have "everything" done "to give God time to work a miracle." The non-Christian doctors are often dismayed because they think that a family is using prayer and the prospect of a miracle as ways to avoid facing what is happening. Even though the non-Christian doctors are usually trying to understand

---

22. Although it is common to use the word *miracle* only to refer to supernatural acts of God that confirm the Word of the Lord, I use *miracle* in a looser sense to fit with typical Christian usage today. Unless otherwise noted, *miracle* means "supernatural act of God." For more on the precise meaning of *miracle* as confirming the Word of the Lord, the reality of supernatural healing, and the continuing possibility

what the family is going through, because they are sure that miracles don't happen, they see prayers for supernatural healing as wishful thinking. Just when the family should be confronting reality, prayer provides a good reason to put off making hard choices. If family members persist in saying that they want everything done while they pray, non-Christian doctors will struggle to be patient with them.

Christian doctors are also frustrated by families who say, "Do everything while we pray for a miracle," but not because the doctors doubt the power of prayer. Christian doctors know that God can and does heal the sick in answer to prayer, at times even acting apart from natural means. When a family is using prayer to avoid dealing with hard choices, Christian doctors typically join with the non-Christian doctors in asking the family to focus on the medical facts. Even knowing that God *can* heal supernaturally, they want the family to make decisions on the basis of what is *medically* likely. This can lead to a feeling of abandonment by family members who expect a Christian doctor to be on their side. Often, this deepens their resolve to maintain all the medical treatment, regardless of the burden that it is imposing on their sick loved one.

Christians zealous to pray for their sick loved ones are following clear biblical teaching. The problem with insisting on "doing everything while we pray" is not in the desire to pray. It is in the belief that God needs us to do something in order to make his supernatural work possible. God's Word calls us to pray for healing, but it does not call us to use medicine to give God more time. While we are praying for supernatural healing, we should be making medical decisions on the basis of medical, natural likelihoods. Both non-Christian and Christian doctors want families deciding on the basis of what is likely *humanly speaking*. The Christian doctors will also be praying that God will work healing, either through their skill with the natural means or by acting above or without natural means.

---

of *wonders*, see Sinclair B. Ferguson, David F. Wright, and J. I. Packer, *New Dictionary of Theology* (Downers Grove, IL: InterVarsity Press, 1988), 433–34; B. B. Warfield, *Counterfeit Miracles* (New York: Charles Scribner's Sons, 1918), 25–28.

God's Word Calls Us to Pray for Healing

The Bible says directly in James 5:13–18 that we are to pray when we are sick. Referring to the efficacy of Elijah's fervent prayers first for drought and then for rain, James calls us to gather the elders to pray for the sick to be healed, anointing them with oil. Along with the elders, all the rest of God's people are encouraged by Scripture to intercede for those who are physically ill. Genesis 20:17 recounts how Abraham prayed and Abimelech was healed. The Psalms contain numerous prayers asking God to heal (35:11–14; 41:1–4; 88:3–17; 102:1–11) or praising God for healing in answer to prayer (103:3; 116:3–4, 8–9). Jesus heals people who are brought to him by others (the paralytic, Matt. 9:1–8; the boy with seizures, Luke 9:37–43). He grants requests for healing by loved ones even when the sick person is not present (the servant of the centurion, Luke 7:1–10; the daughter of the Canaanite woman, Matt. 15:21–28). God's Word also shows us that we are to pray for our own healing. Hezekiah prays that he will be delivered from death, and God lengthens his life by fifteen years (2 Kings 20:1–11). And Jesus heals many people when they cry out to him (Bartimaeus, Mark 10:46–52; lepers, Luke 17:11–19; etc.).

God's power to heal is evident throughout the Scriptures, and yet it is not always God's will to heal. David fasts and calls on the Lord to heal his first child by Bathsheba (2 Sam. 12:15–23). The child dies, and David is nonetheless at peace. Mary and Martha urge Jesus to come quickly to keep Lazarus from dying, but Jesus chooses to delay, and Lazarus dies (John 11). Jesus later raises Lazarus from the dead, but he will do the same for all those who die in the Lord. The immediate answer to Mary and Martha's prayers was not healing. God's purposes were served by Lazarus's death. The same may be true when we pray that God will heal us or our loved ones.

What We Pray about Medical Needs

Scripture assures us that God can heal in answer to our prayers, but not that he will heal. These things are also true about our prayers that the medical team will be skillful, careful, and diligent. We are to ask in prayer for all our needs (Phil. 4:4–7). God's Word tells us that God is the giver of all the natural talent and honed skills that doctors, nurses, and other members of the medical team have. Exodus 36 says explicitly that God gave Oholiab the skill he would use to make the furnishings for the tabernacle, and Jesus' parable of the talents (Matt. 25) indicates that all our abilities are from the Lord.

> **Called to Pray for Healing and All Our Other Needs:** God's Word calls us to pray for all that we need, both supernatural—such as wisdom, peace, and healing—and natural—memory, skill, professional judgment, and healing.

Because of this, it is appropriate that we pray that God would grant surgeons, anesthesiologists, radiologists, and nurses especially steady hands and clear judgment when they are caring for our loved ones. God's Word does not promise to supply skill and good judgment every time we ask for them in prayer, but our prayers are among God's appointed means for giving them when he wills.

As much as we desire healing, we can rejoice that God's Word promises that he will give us other things that we need even more. James 1:5 encourages us that if we lack wisdom, we are to ask for it. God will give us wisdom if we trust his provision when we ask. (The warning against "doubt" in the following verses is a warning against asking in a way that puts God to the test. If we ask in trust that he will provide, we are not doubting in the way James has in mind.) Peace is the same: God promises to grant us peace when we ask (Phil. 4:6–7). Sometimes we resist the Holy Spirit and talk ourselves out of being at peace, but our prayers for peace are still answered according to his promise.

How We Pray Matters

When we pray, we pour out our hearts to God. We are assured that the prayers of God's people are precious to him, and the Psalms show us that our prayers can include bewilderment, lamentation, righteous anger at the brokenness of the world, and even dismay. Psalm 88 ends with "my companions have become darkness." Guided by the Holy Spirit even in our groaning (Rom. 8:26–27), we have the privilege of being candid about our fears and our pain. We ask for what we desire, but we ask knowing that both our knowledge and our desires are fallible. God knows what is best, for our loved ones, for ourselves, and for his glory. So as our prayers make it clear what we would do if we had God's power, we acknowledge that it is best that *his* will be done. If we desire our own will to be done more than we desire God's will to be done, then we are putting God to the test. God's Word warns against expecting such prayers to be answered (James 1, 4), and such prayers deprive us of the comfort of resting in God's loving wisdom about what is best.

Having open and trusting hearts is essential whenever we call on the name of the Lord in prayer, whether in private or together with others. When our prayers are heard by others, we must be careful to make our trust in God evident in our words as well as in our hearts. Both for our own sake and for the sake of those who are listening, we need to use words that display hope rather than despair. Non-Christians who hear (or even overhear) our prayers need to know that Christians have the privilege of asking God for exactly what we want. They should also hear that we know the difference between asking God to keep his promises (to grant wisdom and peace) and asking God to exercise his power if it is his will.

We know from Scripture that we have access to God's presence in Christ (Heb. 4:16) and can confidently approach him with our requests. We know that we are loved by the Maker of all things. We know that he is fully able to heal and give skill if that is best. Most precious of all, we know that he has promised his presence in wisdom and peace and that his promises are all "Yes" in Jesus (2 Cor. 1:18–22).

Our spoken prayers must take into account their impact on those who can hear us. When we ask boldly, confident in God's power and love, and eager for his name to be glorified, others come to see a vital part of what it means to belong to Christ. Fellow believers are encouraged as we put into words the faith that they have. Non-Christians hear what it means to serve a risen and loving Savior instead of being either entirely alone or living under the forbidding rule of a distant potentate. Our prayers do not diminish God in their eyes; they make his glory and majesty more striking to ears that dimly recognize the music of heaven as delightful even as they rebel against God's rule.

God Doesn't Need Our Help

So we should by all means pray for healing, skill, wisdom, and peace. We should even pray aloud, trusting God to use humble prayers to advance his work in the hearts of others. But we should not imagine that God needs our help in order to answer our prayers. As Paul pointed out to the philosophers on a hill in Athens, "The God who made the world and everything in it, being Lord of heaven and earth, does not live in temples made by man, nor is he served by human hands, as though he needed anything, since he himself gives to all mankind life and breath and everything" (Acts 17:24–25). God does whatever pleases him (Ps. 115:3), and one thing that pleases him is caring for us (Ps. 115:9–13).

It is tempting to think that we must contribute something in order to deserve God's attention and power. We find it easy to believe that God's healing power somehow depends on the intensity of our faith. Yet God's Word says that even if our faith is tiny, our enormous requests may be answered (Matt. 17:20). It can also seem to us that God is waiting to see whether we are serious enough to deserve his healing power. But God is the *Author* of our faith. The Holy Spirit works faith in us even as we are (from our perspective) striving to work out our salvation (Phil. 2:12).

Just as God does not need us to find the faith to unlock his power to heal, God does not need us to buy time for him to find room in his schedule or to recharge his batteries. God's wisdom, love, and power are beyond what we can imagine. Paul in Athens puts it plainly: God is not "served by human hands, as though he needed anything" (Acts 17:24–25).

God Does Not Need Us: God's Word does not call us to use medical means to give God time to heal.

God knows better than anyone else how sick our loved one is. It can be a hard truth to hear, but if God is not healing our loved one *right at this moment*, then it is not God's will that our loved one be healed right now. Healing may be only moments away; it may come after a long wait; and it may never come in this life. Decisions about how to handle a loved one's care should be based on our best understanding of God's *ordinary* providence even as we pray for God to intervene in an extraordinary way.

We Should Not "Use" Medical Technology to Give Time for a Miracle to Happen

When someone we love is in need, we are eager to find *something* that we can do to make a difference. This eagerness is even more intense if we suspect that we have been lax in caring for the sick person. Knowing that God can heal and has healed people when medical experts could see no earthly hope, it can seem that we can serve God's purposes by asking for medical technology to be used to "keep Mom alive while we pray for God to work a miracle." This request is neither wise nor kind. We should pray for God to heal by whatever means necessary, including the wisdom and skill of the doctors and nurses; and we should make decisions about the use of life-sustaining medical devices in light of what our loved one would want and the ordinary way the world works.

> **Against Planning on a Miracle:** God's Word calls us to pray when we are sick or in distress, asking God to work a wonder according to his will; but we are called to submit to God's will, making plans that do not depend on God's working a miracle.

If our loved one would have wanted life-sustaining treatment and the burdens that come with it, we should ask for it and pray that the burdens will be small as God uses natural and supernatural means as he sees fit either to restore or to have death come gently.

When we have good evidence that our loved one would want even burdensome life-sustaining treatment used, we should insist on it even if others try to persuade us that it is pointless. But the evidence needs to be strong. Most people—and certainly most Christians—would rather *not* die in the hospital while hooked up to machines and unable to make decisions for themselves. Whether from a desire to maintain control of their own lives or a readiness to go home to be with Jesus, most people would choose not to have technology used to keep them alive unless it was part of restoring them to health and life outside the hospital. People who are unconscious or unable to direct their own care are often dealing with medical problems that ordinary means cannot fix. If they were able to speak for themselves and would decline life-sustaining measures, we would be sad, but we would follow their instructions. We would trust them to decide that the burdens involved were not worth a few more days of life if they cannot enjoy the goods that this life affords. We would also support the decision even as we prayed together for God to heal.

The decision to use or not use life-sustaining treatment should be based on the best information about what our loved one wants and what is naturally likely. This is how wise choices are made in every other area of life, and especially by those who know that God is the Author of nature and has the power to act above or against what is naturally likely. In Luke 14:25–33, Jesus praises those who count the cost before committing to a plan. He is ultimately talking about the cost of following him, but he is assuming that it is wise to count the ordinary or natural costs. Jesus does not say, "A wise person starts to build a tower and prays that God will provide enough money to finish it." He says that a wise person estimates the ordinary costs and makes sure that the resources are in place before starting. The wise person *also* prays while the tower is being built that God will bless the venture.

When we are making decisions about a loved one's care, we are accepting both the potential benefits of a longer life and the likely burdens of pain and isolation. The physical and social implications are important, but the spiritual benefits and burdens are even more serious. When we make choices that our loved one would not make, and when those choices impose burdens that are not biblically commanded and that the person would not have chosen, we are making the wrong choices. Justifying these decisions by saying that we are showing our faith that God will provide doesn't make them right. Too often, we push for treatment because *we* are not yet ready to lose our loved one.

When that happens, we are putting our needs ahead of our loved one's wishes. Instead, we should pray for God to provide what only he can give (wisdom, faith, relief, and healing) and then make choices on the basis of what our loved one would want among the options that the medical team is offering. If either all the available treatments are ineffective or our loved one would consider them excessively burdensome, then we should pray for God to intervene in a marvelous way even as we decline the life-sustaining technology.

KEY TERMS

advance directive
benefits and burdens
decisional capacity
martyr
suffering
suicide
suzerain
vassal

STUDY AND *DISCUSSION QUESTIONS

1. What moral principles does the author derive from Matthew 25?
2. What does it mean to say that bearing the image of God makes us part of God's ambassadorial team?
3. Why would ancient kings send visibly infirm image-bearers?
4. How is the image of God used to connect the imperatives that follow from *both* the parable of the talents and the division of the sheep and goats in Matthew 25?
5. *Respond to the following: "People who are physically or cognitively challenged bear the image of God only dimly. They do not reflect God's rationality and other properties as clearly as other humans do."
6. What is the biblical foundation for a person's authority to make medical decisions for him- or herself?

7. What conditions must be met in order to be treated as decision-ally capable?

8. What does it mean in practice to be decisionally incapable?

9. What is the biblical justification for giving children the authority to make choices for their parents?

10. *Is the standard legal hierarchy of surrogate decision-makers the same as the hierarchy assumed by Scripture?

11. When the Bible refers to "life," what is the most common *kind* of life that it has in view?

12. *How should we answer a sincere believer who says, "The Bible is not a textbook for science, and medicine is a science. So we should not be looking to the Bible for norms for medical decisions"?

13. Describe some of the physical, psychological, social, and financial benefits and burdens that commonly come with life-sustaining medical treatment.

14. Describe the spiritual benefits and burdens that commonly come with CPR, mechanical ventilation, and tube-feeding.

15. *Why is it difficult to describe a situation in which someone has a clear biblical *obligation* to suffer physically solely for the purpose of living longer?

16. How might Westminster Larger Catechism 136 appear to oppose the claim that discontinuing ineffective life-sustaining medical treatment is biblically permissible?

17. *If someone believes that the Bible permits declining life-sustaining medical treatment, is he or she obligated to take exception to WLC 136? Why or why not?

18. Can people who commit suicide go to heaven?

19. *It is surprisingly common for young people who were raised in a Protestant church to believe that all suicides are condemned to hell. Why do they believe this?

20. *Where does the Bible condemn suicide as a sin?

21. Is it suicide for a martyr to accept death rather than deny that Jesus is the Christ, the only Mediator between God and man?

22. Give an example of a situation in which it is sinful to let someone die by failing to do something.

23. Give an example of a situation in which it is *not* sinful to let someone die by failing to do something.
24. *Many Bible-believing Christians believe that they should use all the life-sustaining medical treatment available to keep a loved one alive. Why is this a common belief?
25. What should be said to someone who says, "I need to keep the machines on to give God time to work a miracle"?
26. What things should we pray for when someone is gravely sick?

FOR FURTHER READING

Barry, Robert. "The Biblical Teaching on Suicide." *Issues in Law & Medicine* 13, 3 (Winter 1997): 283–99.

Biro, David. *The Language of Pain: Finding Words, Compassion, and Relief.* New York: W. W. Norton & Company, 2010.

Caplan, Arthur. "Little Hope for Medical Futility." *Mayo Clinic Proceedings* 87 (November 2012): 1040–41.

———. "Not My Turn." *Lancet* 380 (2012): 968–69.

Douma, Jochem. *The Ten Commandments: Manual for the Christian Life.* Translated by Nelson Kloosterman. Phillipsburg, NJ: P&R Publishing, 1996.

Ferguson, Sinclair B., David F. Wright, and J. I. Packer. *New Dictionary of Theology*, s.v. "miracle." Downers Grove, IL: InterVarsity Press, 1988.

Frame, John M. *Medical Ethics: Principles, Persons, and Problems.* Phillipsburg, NJ: Presbyterian and Reformed, 1988.

Garr, W. Randall. *In His Own Image and Likeness: Humanity, Divinity, and Monotheism.* Leiden: Brill, 2003.

Jones, David Clyde. *Biblical Christian Ethics.* Grand Rapids: Baker, 1994.

Kaiser, Walter C., Jr. "How Can Christians Derive Principles from Specific Commands of the Law?" In *Readings in Christian Ethics*, edited by David K. Clark and Robert V. Rakestraw, 192–201. Grand Rapids: Baker, 1994.

Koskenniemi, Erkki, Kirsi Nisula, and Jorma Toppari. "Wine Mixed

with Myrrh (Mark 15.23) and *Crurifragium* (John 19.31–32):
Two Details of the Passion Narratives." *Journal for the Study of
the New Testament* 27, 4 (2005): 379–91.

Meilaender, Gilbert. *Bioethics: A Primer for Christians.* 2nd ed. Grand
Rapids: Eerdmans, 2005.

————. *Neither Beast nor God: The Dignity of the Human Person.* New
York: New Atlantis Books, 2009.

Middleton, Richard. *The Liberating Image: The Imago Dei in Genesis 1.*
Grand Rapids: Brazos, 2005.

VanDrunen, David. *Bioethics and the Christian Life: A Guide to Making
Difficult Decisions.* Wheaton, IL: Crossway, 2009.

Warfield, B. B. *Counterfeit Miracles.* New York: Charles Scribner's
Sons, 1918.

*The Westminster Confession of Faith and Catechisms as Adopted by the
Presbyterian Church in America with Proof Texts.* Lawrenceville,
GA: Committee on Education & Publication of the PCA, 2007.

3

END-OF-LIFE TREATMENT DECISIONS: CHALLENGES

Christians should be among the first to acknowledge that medical efforts cannot forestall pain and death forever. We know that in a fallen world, death awaits all of us (Heb. 9:27) unless Jesus returns first (1 Thess. 4:13–18). We need not cling to this earthly life as though death were the utter end, and because there is "now no condemnation for those who are in Christ" (Rom. 8:1), we can look forward to being at peace with God forever when we die. Because we have this sure and certain hope, it is hard to explain why Christians often use painful and expensive medical treatment merely to keep themselves alive when they are unconscious or permanently confused. As long as the medical treatment is effective—likely to maintain or restore the normal functioning that will enable them to pursue the tasks they have been given as image-bearers—use of the treatment is part of faithful service. But when the medical treatment is ineffective, Christians should be ready to acknowledge that medicine has reached its limit and that they are ready to go home to be with Jesus.

This chapter works through the kinds of medical choices that people are most likely to face near the end of life. The organization of the chapter follows the pattern most common in state-approved forms for expressing wishes about end-of-life treatment. These forms separate questions about conditions from questions about treatment. This is a helpful division of the issues, since it reduces the nearly infinite number of possible treatment decisions to a very small number by grouping all the medical challenges (conditions) and all the medical options (treatments) into only a few kinds of each. The legislators who crafted the Tennessee Advance Care Plan did an especially good job of grouping the possibilities, boiling them down into four kinds of conditions and four kinds of treatments. Most of the decisions that we are likely to face are anticipated by these groupings, making this approach helpful for showing the biblical principles that we may need to consider when making end-of-life decisions.

THE CONDITIONS THAT FORCE HARD CHOICES

Between 2004 and 2010, state legislatures across the country took steps to increase the likelihood that people would leave instructions about the kind of medical care they wanted as they approached death. The states acted in response to a growing problem. The power of medical technology to keep people alive in the hospital was growing too fast. For people who could recover from their afflictions, this increase in the availability and efficiency of life-sustaining methods allowed doctors to support people's lives while they recovered. Many of these people would have died from their injuries and diseases only a few years earlier; the life-sustaining treatments made their recovery possible.

Supporting recovery was not the only outcome made possible by the new technologies. These life-sustaining treatments could also be used to keep people alive in the hospital even when recovery was not humanly likely. By the year 2000, these treatments were being recommended for people who could not make decisions for themselves. An unconscious person with no medical likelihood of ever regaining consciousness might have his or her life maintained by machines in the hospital for months before finally dying. Very few people who see someone being maintained on a breathing machine in an intensive care unit say, "I want to die like that." Most people, when asked to describe how they would like their death to happen, respond that they would rather die at home than in the hospital. Very few say that their preference is to die in a hospital, hooked up to machines and unable to interact with others in the room.[1]

Before 2000, it was legally difficult to leave instructions that doctors could follow without significant legal risks. Without a document drawn up by an attorney clearly identifying someone's choice of agent to speak for him or her or what the person wanted done in the specific situation that had arisen, the doctors and hospital could not run the risk of being sued for wrongful death if the medical team did less than "everything." As the "everything" that medicine could do expanded, the number of people being maintained on machines increased. It was hard to believe that most of these people wanted it, and the legislators recognized the value of changing the law to make it easier for people to have their wishes honored when decisions were made about life-sustaining treatment.

The forms that the fifty states adopted have some differences, but they are especially valuable in what they have in common. Legislative research identified patterns in the decisions that people or their agents regularly faced near the end of life. The most important pattern is the connection between medical *conditions* and a desire to do less than everything medically possible. For example, few people want the aggressive use of life-sustaining treatment if they are unconscious and never going to wake up again. When asked what they want done if they are likely to recover and return to a normal life, most people say that they want everything done. That makes sense, and it means that an official form that simply asked, "Do you want everything medically possible done if you cannot decide for yourself?" would be confusing and hard to answer. It would depend on what condition the person was in. Because of this, all state forms first ask about the conditions under which we want life-sustaining treatment to be limited in some way. This chapter first describes the four conditions most likely to force us to make decisions about limiting treatment. The remainder of

---

1. See, for example, Barbara Gomes, Natalia Calanzani, Marjolein Gysels, Sue Hall, and Irene J. Higginson, "Heterogeneity and Changes in Preferences for Dying at Home: A Systematic Review," *BMC Palliative Care* 12, 1 (2013): 7–19.

the chapter considers the four types of treatment that might be limited and explains biblical principles that can guide the decisions that we or our agents may have to make.

Permanent Unconsciousness

The condition most likely to raise questions about limiting treatment is *permanent unconsciousness*. All the state forms ask about it, and it is easy to see why. When people imagine a sad ending in the hospital, it probably involves someone who is unresponsive, in a sterile hospital bed, connected to multiple machines, and surrounded by monitors. When the person's body is too weak to continue despite all the mechanical assistance, death is usually a relief to his or her family members and the nurses who have been caring for the person. A decision to turn off the machines and to allow natural death is always emotionally difficult. Family members may be pretty sure that this is not how their loved one would want to live. They may know that their loved one would consider the many burdens imposed by the treatment to greatly exceed the benefit of being alive in this condition. Yet the family may still find it impossible to "give up."

Permanent unconsciousness is real. It is impossible to achieve God's level of certainty that a specific person's unconsciousness is *permanent*. A medical condition is permanent if it is irreversible. Because God has the power to reverse every physical setback, including death, no condition is absolutely irreversible. So when a doctor says that someone is "permanently unconscious" or that someone's loss of heart and lung function is "irreversible," the doctor is saying that as far as medical science is concerned, consciousness or heart-lung function is never going to return. Both Christian and non-Christian doctors make these kinds of medical judgments weekly. A Christian doctor who declares a condition irreversible is not doubting the power of God to do something wonderful that confounds the medical establishment. Doctors make judgments about what is medically likely, humanly speaking. Our prayers should be for God's will. Our decisions should be based on what is likely if God does not intervene supernaturally.

Doctors are fallible. It is prudent to get a second medical opinion when a decision rests on a pivotal judgment, such as the judgment that someone is permanently unconscious. Most doctors are not offended by a request for a second opinion if it is asked for by someone who clearly wants to make sure of the situation before making a decision. Requests for a second or third opinion that appear to be delaying making a decision at all, or requests that betray skepticism about the doctor's knowledge or character, are not appreciated. Asking a nurse for help in wording the request is a good idea. The nurse will find out how the specific doctor involved would want to be asked. Doctors are people, too. They know that a judgment about what is permanent will have big consequences. Friendly requests will make sense to them.

If a judgment about permanence is confirmed by a second opinion, the chances that the medical situation will change are exceedingly small. A few times a decade, someone regains consciousness after doctors have said that the condition is irreversible. The story is worldwide news precisely because it happens so rarely. We should not use these few cases as proof that doctors can't be trusted or that we should make choices on the basis of the tiny number of extraordinary cases. We are called to make decisions on the basis of a careful consideration of the best information we can get. If two doctors independently determine that unconsciousness is medically permanent, that is the best information we are going to get. We know from Psalm 103 that God has the power to heal all our diseases. This general truth about God's power is not a good reason to discount what the doctors are saying. Acting on the doctors' judgment will not prevent God from healing directly if that is God's will.

Medically permanent unconsciousness is a biblically sound basis for limiting medical treatment. People who are unconscious are unable to enjoy spiritual goods in the ordinary way. They are unable to use their talents and other resources to pursue God's purposes in the world. They are no longer acting on decisions about being faithful stewards of their time and opportunities. They are unable to enjoy the earthly goods of interaction with family and friends, of sharing meals together, of sharing past joys and sorrows, or of looking ahead to what God will do when all things are made new. The losses of these good things are all significant burdens, and the physical burdens imposed by the machines maintaining a person's bodily function are added on top of these spiritual, social, and psychological burdens. Even if the financial burden of keeping the machines running does not matter at all, it would be reasonable to think that these burdens greatly exceed the benefit of having the person's bodily functions maintained.

We are not biblically required to start or continue to use medical treatment that is excessively burdensome. We may choose to start or continue its use when we believe that doing so is part of faithful stewardship of our resources, but we are not obligated to bear excessive medical burdens in order to stay alive. For this reason, we may also decide in advance that we do not wish medical means used to extend our lives when we are permanently unconscious. In chapter 5, I will recommend directing those empowered to speak for us to limit treatment when we are permanently unconscious. If the medical personnel know that we are Christians, these instructions will probably surprise them. They will think that limiting treatment is wise, but they may ask why a Christian would think so. We should be ready to explain why we think it is part of faithfully serving our Savior.

Permanent Confusion

Some state forms ask specifically only about permanent unconsciousness. That condition most commonly calls for decisions about limiting treatment in the hospital setting. *Permanent confusion* is more likely to be an issue in long-term care facilities, and concerns about giving up too quickly on those with trouble thinking led some lawmakers to omit explicit mention of permanent confusion from the official forms. In a culture increasingly comfortable with the death of people who are inconvenient, these concerns are reasonable. Christians should be careful to keep the dignity of image-bearers firmly in mind, but we should not shy away from thinking through what medical treatment we will want if we become permanently confused. As image-bearers, we have the task of using our time, talent, and other resources to pursue our Master's purposes. Permanent confusion does not eliminate our usefulness as Christ's servants, but it does alter it. Medical treatments that impose significant burdens on top of the other burdens that come with permanent confusion may greatly exceed the benefits gained by those treatments. In that case, we are biblically permitted to limit medical treatment. With our instructions made clear in advance, our agents are also biblically permitted to choose to limit medical treatment as they speak for us.

Permanent confusion can be part of many health challenges, and especially of challenges common to those who have already lived a full life. *Dementia* is an umbrella term for a range of problems with memory, thinking clearly, and focusing attention. Alzheimer's disease and vascular dementia are two common problems, and there are many other kinds. All forms of dementia come in degrees, usually moving from mild memory loss or brief disorientation to severe impairment that looks like the absence of connected thought. Most forms of dementia involve a gradual decline of overall mental abilities. The rate of decline may not be consistent, and may include periods of reversal and short recovery of previous abilities.

Confusion is not precisely defined, but it is at heart the inability to think clearly. What it means to think clearly is set by what was normal when we were healthy and in the prime of life. For most people, normally clear thinking has few memory lapses, only brief periods of disorientation about time and place, and a constant ability to see solutions to practical problems. Being confused means struggling with these abilities. All sorts of things can cause confusion, and the condition is often reversible. A mild head injury or concussion may leave us temporarily confused. Some medications cause confusion. Diseases such as diabetes can bring on confusion. Being confused is reversible when the cause of confusion can be removed or sufficiently reduced.

Permanent confusion is trouble thinking clearly that cannot be reversed by medical means. Confusion from an incurable cause typically gets worse over time, reaching a point at which it is impossible to make decisions. The description of *permanent confusion* in the Tennessee Advance Care Plan form is particularly clear and helpful because it explains the condition in practical terms:

> [I am permanently confused when] I become unable to remember, understand, or make decisions [or when] I do not recognize loved ones or cannot have a clear conversation with them.

This description is given in the first person (what it will seem like to *me*), but it highlights abilities that others can assess as well. This is important because when people really are permanently confused, they no longer have the ability to determine whether they are or not. They probably also lack the ability to explain to others in a connected way their reasons for thinking they are permanently confused.

Our task as image-bearers is more than faithful stewardship of our resources. We also bear the image as objects of honor, a part of the task that persists even when our mental abilities are profoundly impaired. People reduced to the point that they don't even recognize themselves are still people who fully bear the image. In the absence of instructions from them or loved ones empowered to speak for them, we are biblically obligated to honor them with attention, medical care to alleviate pain, and serious efforts to provide them with protection, food, and clothing. When our mental abilities are compromised, we become difficult to care for and inconvenient to our loved ones. The difficulty or inconvenience that permanent confusion imposes on loved ones is not a biblically adequate basis for caregivers to decide that medical treatment should be limited. But permanent confusion can be a biblically sound reason for us to request *for ourselves* that medical treatment be limited if the condition arises. This is not because the life of a permanently confused person is no longer valuable. It is because we have the authority to determine that some medical treatment options are a poor use of our resources. Medical treatment can become excessively burdensome when we are permanently confused.

We are biblically permitted to decide in advance to limit treatment if we become permanently confused. The same reasons that supported permission to limit treatment in advance for permanent unconsciousness apply to permanent confusion. Because we are not obligated to ask to have treatment limited, I will explain how this reasoning goes for myself: If I were to become permanently confused, the social and spiritual burdens imposed by aggressive life-sustaining treatment would be great. Confusion would drastically reduce the social benefits of time spent with my loved ones and neighbors. The fragments of memory that I retained would likely cause distress as I vainly struggled to connect my thoughts and to appreciate the moment. My ability to enjoy the great spiritual goods of meditating on God's Word, worshiping with God's people, and prayer would be less than that of a child. If I lost the ability to discern the body, it would become unwise to give me communion. The loss of all these joys would be a burden that greatly exceeded the benefit of still being alive. If I were permanently confused but briefly restored so that I could assess my situation and decide what I would want, I would judge that aggressive treatment to keep me alive (CPR, ventilation, and even tube-feeding) would be excessively burdensome when I became permanently confused again. I am biblically authorized to make such a choice, and thus I am authorized to make that decision in advance and leave the instructions for those who will speak for me.

The social and spiritual burdens imposed by aggressive medical treatment for someone permanently confused would be great for any believer. For people whose earthly work depends on trained mental abilities—teachers, researchers, analysts, craftsmen, and so on—permanent confusion would also include the burden of not being able to serve others with their mental talents and training. The loss of these abilities does not make their lives meaningless, valueless, or pointless. Their value always was and continues to rest in their importance in God's eyes as his image-bearing servants. They continue to serve his purposes by being objects of honor. Permanent confusion does not change their value. But it may impact their assessment of the faithful use of their resources and the benefits and burdens that would come with aggressive medical treatment. We are not required to limit medical treatment when we are permanently confused, but we are biblically allowed to decide that aggressive treatment will not be a part of the faithful use of our resources.

Terminal Illness

Terminal illness is a common category on state forms and in discussions about end-of-life treatment options. It is easy to give a rough idea of what it means for a condition to be terminal (death isn't far away unless something surprising happens). It is much harder to make the meaning of *terminal* precise. When physicians say that a condition is "terminal," they mean that if the disease or dysfunction runs its usual course, even with the best medical attention death will happen *in a relatively short time*. If they are pushed to be more specific than "relatively short time," most physicians will give an estimate, but they will usually say that it is a rough guess. Insurance companies want better than rough guesses. In order for someone to be "terminal" for insurance purposes, a physician must certify that death will occur *within six months*.

Physicians go along with the insurance companies' request for precision, but in their own thinking they do not make decisions based on the six-months estimate. This gap between the medical meaning of *terminal* and the insurance meaning of *terminal* makes it difficult to use the word confidently in advance directives. A doctor's judgment that my condition is terminal may play a legitimate role in my end-of-life choices, but the term is too vague to use in instructions that I leave for others who will speak for me when I cannot.

Here an example may help. A person with stage 4 pancreatic cancer is in trouble. The five-year survival rate for this condition is very low. If the cancer is not detected until it has progressed to stage 4, the chances that it has spread to other vital organs is high, and the chances that chemo- or radiation therapy will be effective is low. It would be ordinary for an oncologist to judge that the person's condition was terminal, and it would be biblically appropriate for the person to include the likelihood of death in the near future in decisions about the use of aggressive life-sustaining treatment. If the person's kidney function collapsed, it would be biblically permissible to say no to starting kidney dialysis. It would be reasonable to think that the burden of adding that kind of treatment greatly exceeded the benefits involved.[2] The decision to decline

2. The 1988 PCA Report on Heroic Measures says that a person may refuse "heroic measures" if he or she has an incurable illness and "God is clearly drawing [life] to a close" (III.18).

the treatment would not be based on being in a terminal condition. It would be based on the burdens and benefits specific to kidney dialysis. Someday, when kidney dialysis is a simple, painless, in-home procedure, it will be hard to call it an excessively burdensome option. Knowing that the condition is terminal might inform the benefits-and-burdens judgment, but it would not in itself determine the outcome.

A person's being diagnosed with a terminal condition all by itself is not a sufficient reason to limit aggressive medical treatment. Someone else with a similar stage 4 pancreatic cancer diagnosis and compromised kidney function may decide that the most faithful use of his or her talents and opportunities means putting up with the burdens of starting dialysis in order to use the remaining days well. All sorts of factors can make a difference: age, a project nearing completion, the need to be reconciled to someone who was wronged, or even the desire to share in an important family milestone. Having a terminal diagnosis is a legitimate consideration in making end-of-life decisions. It is not a conclusive consideration.

An advance directive that limits life-sustaining treatment simply on the basis of a terminal diagnosis runs a needless risk. Some people with a terminal diagnosis continue to have remarkable talents and the opportunity to use them faithfully. As long as we are able to make our own treatment decisions, we will be able to judge whether the benefits of life-sustaining treatment are sufficiently large. If we leave instructions to limit treatment if we are in a terminal condition and we become *temporarily* unable to make decisions, our agents may feel compelled to decline life-sustaining treatment that we would have wanted. As it is currently used, the word *terminal* is too vague to use in a biblically careful advance directive.

Dependence for Daily Living

A fourth and final condition that raises questions about the use of aggressive end-of-life medical treatment concerns our ability to care for our basic daily needs, referred to as our *activities of daily living*. The description used in the Tennessee Advance Care Plan is clear and practical:

I am Dependent in all Activities of Daily Living means that I am no longer able to talk or communicate clearly or move by myself. I depend on others for feeding, bathing, dressing, and walking. Rehabilitation or any other restorative treatment will not help.

This is a degree of dependence that none of us are eager to experience, but by itself it is not a biblically adequate reason to limit life-sustaining medical treatment. As with being in a terminal condition, it is important to imagine this condition without the presence of permanent unconsciousness, permanent confusion, or even significant pain-management problems. To help narrow the focus so that only this kind of dependence is in view, consider the case of Gloria.

Gloria is a quiet, 77-year-old Christian woman. She and her husband, Fred, still live in the house in which they raised four rowdy sons. Three of the boys live out of town, but the youngest, Earl, lives in the house next door. Gloria is morbidly obese, and two attempted knee reconstructions have failed. Between her bad knees and her weight, Gloria cannot get from the bed to her wheelchair without assistance. Prolonged inactivity has left her with poor muscle tone in general. Her husband is not strong enough to transfer her from her motorized chair to the toilet, so she needs the help of either a nurse or her son to go to the bathroom or to get into bed. Since suffering a stroke five years ago, Gloria has struggled to put together whole sentences. She follows the conversations around her, and when others are patient, she can contribute to them. It is evident that her thinking is somewhat impaired, but not dramatically diminished. She just finds the words hard to put together.

Until last week, a nurse visited every morning to help Gloria bathe and dress. During the rest of the day, she went to the bathroom without leaving her chair, with her husband taking care of her intimate hygiene needs. Earl cooked for all three of them and helped Gloria get into bed. Fred and Gloria are financially secure, and when the time comes, they will hire the nurses necessary to help with Gloria's care. Gloria is conscious and not confused. Her condition is fragile, but not terminal. She is not in pain. Although Gloria is dependent in all her activities of daily living, she is not dying. If Gloria's kidney function started to fail, it is likely that someone would ask her whether she wanted to use dialysis as a life-sustaining treatment. Despite her limitations, Gloria should accept the dialysis. The treatment would have the prospect of restoring and maintaining her ability to use her talents and other resources to serve God's purposes.

Many today would doubt that Gloria has an obligation to use dialysis in her condition. It is now commonly believed that our lives are ours to dispose of as we wish. On top of that, too many people think that being a burden to others is either selfish or hateful. For someone convinced that death is better than being a sad inconvenience to loved ones, it may seem that the benefit of longer life that the dialysis option gives to Gloria is overshadowed by the burden of imposing on others in a selfish and shameful way. Our culture loves independence and entertainment, so dependence and boring hard work are offensive. We may have to wipe our own children's bottoms, but wiping any adult's bottom is work for people who either are desperate or lack the skills needed to find a less disgusting job. Dependence in the activities of daily life is unacceptable in today's culture because caregiving is not valued.

The Bible rejects the idea that dependence is shameful and that caregiving is only for losers. Instead, the Scriptures call for us to honor the elderly as sources of wisdom even when they are frail, and to praise caregivers as noble gifts from God. The Bible treats dependence and caregiving as two sides of the beautiful, loving relationship that is found in healthy families. As family ties have grown weaker over the past century, the tasks of caregiving have been increasingly outsourced to paid strangers. Those dependent on hired caregivers can easily conclude that they are nothing more than a financial burden. They may even be embarrassed and angry to find themselves being treated like children.

Against these cultural trends, Christians should embrace the Bible's valuing of the dependent and the caregivers. Romans 12:10 calls us to "outdo one another in showing honor." Philippians 2 urges us to imitate Christ, who humbled himself for our sake. Among all the things that we are to do as Christ's servants, serving those in need is surely one of the most important. In order for us to bear one another's burdens, those with burdens must allow their burdens to be borne. The world may say that those who are "dependent in all activities of daily living" are a drag and should not impose on people they love. We must reject that notion. People in need of our help give us the opportunity to serve our Master by serving each other. Depending on others should not be counted as a burden. Matthew 9:1–8 tells of a paralytic who allows his friends to carry him to Jesus for healing. Jesus commends the faith of all of them. The biblical principle is thus:

> **The Privilege of Being Cared For:** God's Word discourages us from treating dependence on others when we are sick or infirm as a great burden.

In 1991 Gilbert Meilaender generated a lively response with an article in *First Things*, "I Want to Burden My Loved Ones."[3] His thesis was simple and countercultural: to be a burden to each other is what it means to be part of a family. This is true of families formed by biology and adoption. It is even more true of the church as a family. Scripture calls us to "bear one another's burdens, and so fulfill the law of Christ" (Gal. 6:2). Declining life-sustaining medical treatment merely to avoid being a burden to loved ones is to reject God's design for our life together. The culture will not understand what we are doing. We may even struggle to resist the world's way of thinking about it. People are called to be stewards of their resources. Devoting those resources to caring for the weak and being cared for when weak is stewardship that pleases Christ.

TREATMENT OPTIONS

The state forms for recording end-of-life instructions typically separate questions about the "conditions" that would trigger some limiting

---

3. Gilbert Meilaender, "I Want to Burden My Loved Ones," *First Things* (March 2010), http://www.firstthings.com/article/2010/03/i-want-to-burden-my-loved-ones.

of options from questions about which treatment options to limit. The remainder of this chapter discusses the biblical principles that can inform choices about each of the four kinds of treatment options commonly used in American hospitals in 2017. Christian reflection on biblically appropriate end-of-life treatment only a century ago would not have foreseen the challenges posed by medical technology today. The advice in this chapter will probably need to be updated in the future. God's Word does not change, but applying it to changing technology will likely require further reflection.

The four categories of end-of-life treatment options are CPR, life support (especially mechanical breathing assistance and dialysis), treatment of new conditions, and artificial nutrition and hydration. It is assumed that treatment for medical conditions that was ongoing when life-sustaining treatment became an issue will continue. As the burdens that come with maintaining life mount, questions may also have to be answered about whether the burdens from the ongoing treatment are excessive.

CPR (Cardiopulmonary Resuscitation)

It is really bad to have your heart stop beating. Before 1960, it meant that you were dead. No one had to ask, "Do you want us to try to restart your heart if it stops?" The question wouldn't make sense, because no one knew a way to try. Now all sorts of people are trained in CPR, and many public buildings and private offices have AED (automatic electronic defibrillator) machines available. We now think that every time someone's heart stops, the obvious thing to do is to try to restart it. In part because of this widespread expectation, most people think it is obvious that CPR should be attempted if someone's heart stops while the person is in the hospital. The hospital has the best equipment and people with excellent training, so if it makes sense to attempt resuscitation in a public place, it must make sense to attempt it in the hospital.

This line of thinking would be reasonable if heart attacks in public places were medically similar to someone's heart stopping while the person is in the hospital. For mostly healthy people who are at the hospital for routine procedures, administering CPR is clearly the thing to do. The value of CPR for people nearing the end of life is much less obvious. Most TV and movie depictions of CPR make it hard to see why its value is limited. Dramatic portrayals of resuscitation attempts suggest that the physical benefits of CPR (chest compressions, electrical defibrillation, injections of heart drugs, and mechanical devices to assist breathing) clearly outweigh the physical burdens imposed in the attempt. The benefits seem to outweigh the burdens because soon after the emergency procedure is performed (in screen time), the person whose heart had stopped is walking out of the hospital. He or she returns to a normal life and is completely recovered. The physical benefit (a normal life) of recovery in these depictions "costs" only a short flurry of activity by doctors and nurses, with little physical burden imposed on the person in the bed.

While the dramatic portrayals are exciting and advance hopeful plotlines, a resuscitation attempt on screen is very different from what happens in real life.[4] (An easy way to annoy a doctor or a nurse is to suggest that you know what a *full code* is like because you have seen one on TV or in a movie.) "Chest compressions" start with forcefully pounding the chest of the person whose heart has stopped. A nurse once told me that when he was taught CPR, he was told, "If you aren't breaking ribs, you aren't doing it right." "Electrical defibrillation" is the jolt from charged paddles that causes the person's body to bounce on the table. Everyone near the person receiving the jolt needs to stand clear, since the hefty electrical charge could find its way to the ground through a bystander's merely touching the intended recipient. The drugs that are pushed into the system of the person being "coded" are "uppers," artificial adrenaline that speeds up the body's systems. The devices to assist breathing very likely include inserting a tube down the throat and into the lungs (intubation). All these measures are invasive and uncomfortable, leaving injuries that will be painful long after the resuscitation attempt even if it succeeds.

---

4. The American Heart Association has a simulated resuscitation attempt at https://www.youtube.com/watch?v=eXmAzsRQi9I. This is still only a simulation.

What counts as a *successful* attempt depends on the goal. If someone's heart stops while the person is in the hospital and the attempt begins right away, then it is likely that the heart will be restarted. Death will be forestalled for a time. Most people hope for more than that. They want their hearts restarted as a necessary step toward getting well enough to leave the hospital and return home. Almost no one wants to die in a hospital bed while hooked up to machines. So a successful resuscitation attempt is one that staves off death *and leads to leaving the hospital and living a life similar to the one known before going to the hospital.* That would be a physical benefit clearly great enough to outweigh the physical burdens that come with a resuscitation attempt.

If a successful resuscitation attempt means restoration to life outside the hospital, then very few attempts are successful. Even in the most favorable conditions in an advanced hospital, fewer than 10 percent of resuscitation attempts lead to the person's being discharged from the hospital. The most likely outcome is that the attempt fails. In those cases, no benefit is gained but all the burdens are imposed. The only joke I know about medicine rests on these grim likelihoods: Where do you want to be if you need CPR? Answer: On television. Any CPR attempt imposes a great physical burden on the recipient's body. People who say, "I believe that a CPR attempt would impose burdens that greatly exceed the benefits likely to follow from the attempt" would not be saying something crazy. Near the end of life, they are probably saying something that is reasonable and biblically permissible.

A vivid story should help us to see how this can be so. Mindy is frail, but until recently led an active life. Both her heart and her kidneys are weak. She receives dialysis once a week and carefully follows her doctor's instructions about diet and exercise. Mindy has never married. She is at peace with God, has numerous friends, and has used her artistic talents to make a living and serve the church. Mindy is now in the hospital with a serious infection. She is on constant dialysis, but the antibiotics are not keeping up with the infection. She is getting weaker, and the cardiologist is concerned that her heart might quit. The physician overseeing Mindy's care asks whether she wants a resuscitation attempt if her heart stops beating.

In this situation, God's Word permits Mindy to say *either* yes or no. She can say yes if she believes the benefit of living longer is worth the burdens that would come with the resuscitation attempt. Mindy could ask the physician what would probably happen if the attempt succeeded in restarting her heart. The physician might say, "You would certainly be in the hospital for quite a while if we got your heart restarted. You would be likely to wake up on a ventilator to support your breathing, and we still don't know whether your infection can be controlled. It is not looking promising right now, and we are using the most powerful antibiotic in our arsenal. So you may not live long afterwards. In your current condition, the chances that you'll ever leave the hospital if your heart gives out are under 1 percent." Hearing all of that, Mindy would be biblically justified in saying, "I want you to attempt CPR. I have ideas for art projects that I'd like to pursue if I can get out of the hospital. The odds may be long, but I want to try to get there." Mindy knows that it is unlikely that she will be able to do more with her talents and opportunity if her heart stops. Her desire to do more is righteous, and it is up to her to decide whether the benefit-burden balance is acceptable.

Saying yes to the CPR question here shouldn't be controversial. It is important to consider the yes answer in order to see why the no answer would also be biblically permitted. God's Word does not require Mindy to endure great pain in order to pursue the slim chance of doing more with her talents. She may think the way Paul does about his own death in Philippians 1:20b–23. Paul knows that his own death may be near. He is not afraid to die; his chief desire is that

> Christ will be honored in my body, whether by life or by death. For to me to live is Christ, and to die is gain. If I am to live in the flesh, that means fruitful labor for me. Yet which I shall choose I cannot tell. I am hard pressed between the two. My desire is to depart and be with Christ, for that is far better.

Mindy is facing a choice like the one Paul is describing. In Mindy's case, the choice is about authorizing CPR that has very little chance of restoring her ability to engage in "fruitful labor." She may say no to the CPR attempt if her heart stops, saying, "My desire is to depart and be with Christ." Neither Paul nor Mindy has the authority to take his or her own life. Both have the authority to say no to things that may prolong their lives. Paul doesn't say what his choice would involve. Mindy's choice is between accepting or declining medical treatment that is burdensome and unlikely to restore her to fruitful labor. God's Word permits her to decline the treatment as excessively burdensome.[5]

The judgment that the burdens involved are excessive is ultimately Mindy's to make, and when possible Mindy should be seeking help in making it. The implications of her decision are clearly grave. Her physical condition could easily be diminishing her ability to think through the problem completely. And the facts surrounding her situation are complex. Along with needing a physician to explain her medical conditions and the likely outcomes for her options, financial and spiritual consequences are involved. Mindy's righteous eagerness to be with Jesus may lead her to overlook vital facts or to weigh the implications incorrectly. The final decision is hers, and in the situation described she is biblically permitted to choose either to accept or to decline CPR if her heart stops. If the situation were only somewhat different, however, deciding to decline CPR could be hasty, or even unfaithful. Mindy should ask for help in making the decision.

The chances that emergency CPR will restore Mindy's ability to engage in fruitful labor are slim because her heart is weak, so it is hard to see how a minor change to her situation would make it *sinful* for Mindy to decline CPR. Minor changes might make the decision to decline CPR reckless. To see how this might happen, it is necessary to talk about Mindy's age. In the story so far, her age has not mattered. A 22-year-old with a weak heart, compromised kidney function, an uncontrolled infection, and a possible heart attack is facing as grim a prospect as an 80-year-old in the same condition. Reducing any of those threats could easily make Mindy's age important. If, for example, the treatment she was receiving was making sustained progress against

5. 1988 PCA Report on Heroic Measures, § III.3, 11.

the infection and Mindy was 22 years old, CPR might be likely to lead to her leaving the hospital and resuming her work. If she were 80, CPR would probably still not be *likely* to restore her to that point. Even with the many burdens that CPR would impose, wise counselors might urge 22-year-old Mindy to accept CPR if her heart were to stop. If, further, Mindy had spiritual projects needing attention (being reconciled to someone she had wronged, for example), her counselors might have even more reason to encourage her to accept CPR.

The authority to determine that proposed medical treatment is excessively burdensome is not unlimited. CPR to restore heart-lung function is always a great physical imposition, and it is never guaranteed to work even under ideal conditions. Yet it is sometimes a valuable and appropriate option, able to get someone past a brief crisis and returned to faithful service. In that case, declining it can be faithless if the only burdens in view are physical. Financial concerns may make the burdens great (see chapter 6), but when a return to faithful service is the likely outcome, accepting CPR should be seriously considered. Yet if doctors are asking about a DNR order (declining CPR), return to faithful service is not likely. So if a trusted doctor is recommending against CPR, it is probably best to accept the recommendation.

Ventilator, Dialysis, or Other Mechanical Maintenance

CPR is an emergency procedure. It is the most commonly discussed end-of-life treatment option in the hospital because the risk of a heart attack is often high for people sick enough to be hospitalized. Deciding in advance whether to start CPR enables the sick person's family and the medical personnel to be on the same page about what to do if the sick person's heart stops. Instructions about CPR are all about whether the resuscitation should be attempted at all. If CPR is attempted and succeeds in restarting heart-lung function, then the CPR event is over. The second category of end-of-life treatment options covers machines and techniques that support vital functions in a long-term way. Mechanical ventilation and kidney dialysis are the two most common treatments of this kind.

The biblical principles guiding choices about these kinds of life-support options are the same as those that apply to CPR. Mechanical breathing (ventilation) can be needed for only a short time while the person struggling to breathe recovers from an infection, but it may also be used as a long-term measure that ends only with death from some other cause. The benefits and burdens involved depend on a host of factors, with the burdens accumulating with long-term use. The same is true of dialysis. As a short-term measure to support recovery from a temporary loss of kidney function, the burdens are small and the benefits great. When it is used as a long-term means of maintaining renal function, the relative benefits and burdens can shift significantly. A person's medical prognosis and the goal in view in the use of the treatment make a big difference. To see how much the prognosis and goal matter, consider the case of Bonnie and questions about continuing the use of a ventilator.

Bonnie is a 45-year-old Christian mother of two and a career nurse. She and her husband are on the lake in their boat when another boat loses control and smashes into them at high speed. Bonnie's husband is killed, and Bonnie is flown by helicopter to a good local hospital. When she arrives at the hospital, Bonnie is unconscious. Her neck is broken and her mouth and nose are mangled, but the EMTs have immobilized her back and kept her breathing all the way to the hospital. In order to make sure that she is able to breathe, the emergency staff at the hospital open a hole in Bonnie's neck and insert a tube connected to a ventilator. The ventilator does the breathing for her: pushing air in and pulling it out.

After two days, Bonnie opens her eyes. She is groggy and does not remember the accident. While she was unconscious, the doctors kept her immobilized in her bed to minimize movement in case she had sustained a concussion. Once she awakens and seems to understand that she shouldn't try to move, they ask her to wiggle her toes. She can't. On examination, they learn that Bonnie is paralyzed from the neck down. The doctors are not sure whether the paralysis is permanent. The injury to her spinal column is serious, but it is possible that it is not severed. They will need to run tests and watch her carefully.

The doctors are pleased to discover that Bonnie is able to understand what they are talking about. She is on high doses of painkillers and is still trying to come to grips with her situation. The injury to her face makes it impossible to talk, but her eyes follow the doctors when they move and light up when they talk about the details of her condition. When the nurse in the room mentions that Bonnie is herself a nurse, one of the doctors says, "Blink once if you can understand me." Bonnie blinks once. Using one blink for "Yes," two blinks for "No," and three for "Please ask that another way," they are able to determine that she does not want CPR if her heart stops. Bonnie knows all too well the trauma of *doing* CPR, and the doctors estimate that she would have only a tiny (under 2 percent) chance of being revived. Judging that the burdens would greatly exceed the foreseeable benefits, she says yes to a DNR order.[6]

One of the doctors asks whether she wants to have the ventilator turned off. It was started when she was unconscious, and the doctor knows that legally Bonnie has the authority to have it turned off if she doesn't want it. Bonnie blinks three times. The doctor then says, "Do you want the ventilator left on?" Bonnie blinks once. Her injuries make it impossible for her to explain why she wants it, so the doctors start guessing what her reason is. Early on, one of the doctors asks, "Do you want it continued while we run tests to find out more about your prognosis?" Bonnie blinks once immediately. She knows that if her paralysis is reversible, she is likely to heal sufficiently to leave the hospital, go home with her children, and maybe return to nursing. The benefit of making all that possible makes it easy to bear the burden of being hooked up to the ventilator.

In Bonnie's case, the doctors and nurses happily agree with her choice. Their driving passion is seeing people restored to the life they knew before a disease or an injury, and because Bonnie did nothing to bring on her injury, their sense of justice adds to their professional

---

6. Statistics on success rates for CPR attempts depend greatly on how the data is studied. For an account that is clear about its assumptions, see Swati Singh et al., "Evaluation of Cardiopulmonary Resuscitation (CPR) for Patient Outcomes and Their Predictors," *Journal of Clinical & Diagnostic Research* 10, 1 (2016): 1–4.

zeal. They all hope that the further tests show that her restoration is medically likely. Waiting for more data is clearly a wise thing to do. Bonnie not only has the biblical permission to continue the use of the ventilator, but may even be biblically obligated to use it. A faithful servant looks for ways to return to service.

Given the extent of her injuries, though, they should all brace themselves for discouraging test results. If that happens, Bonnie will face the same set of medical decisions, and a dismal prognosis will change Bonnie's biblical obligations. Suppose, then, that the tests show that Bonnie's injuries cannot be repaired by surgery and that she will never be able to leave her hospital bed. Even after consulting other experts, as far as the doctors can tell, Bonnie will remain paralyzed and will always need the ventilator in order to stay alive.

No matter what else she decides, Bonnie and everyone else should be praying for her recovery and her peace. God may surprise the doctors and heal her. She should not plan on healing, since God may will otherwise, but she should be praying for what she wishes and acknowledging her trust in God's wisdom.

As Bonnie thinks about her options, she should be encouraged to remember that it is a wonder that she survived the accident in the first place, and that if it had happened nearly anywhere else on earth or in history, she would already be dead. Bonnie may also need help seeing that her present affliction is not a punishment for something she did or didn't do. Jesus paid for all her sins, past, present, and future. She is suffering because the world is broken, not for her own sins. The medical skills that have kept her alive thus far are great blessings, not part of a cruel or indifferent plan.

Bonnie will have to decide whether she wants the ventilator support to continue or be turned off. Financial costs will have to be considered (see chapter 6), and she clearly has biblical permission to use the ventilator to support her life as part of her efforts to serve Jesus faithfully. If the life-sustaining treatments, pain-management methods, and financial resources allow her to enjoy spiritual goods and serve others in prayer, she might be reminded that the medical devices may allow her to delight and serve through her limitations.

But it is hard to insist that she is biblically obligated to continue the use of the ventilator as the many burdens it imposes grow. Ultimately, Bonnie is the one bearing the burdens. If she judges that the burdens imposed by the medical devices would greatly exceed the benefit of being kept alive, she would have biblical permission to discontinue their use. She would not be giving up on life. She would not be killing herself. Bonnie would be choosing to allow her injuries to finally run their course.

Treatment for New Conditions

A person unable to direct his or her own care and in a condition (such as permanent confusion) for which the person wants medical treatment to be limited may develop further medical challenges. When this happens, the person will have to decide what to do about the new challenges. New conditions can range from bedsores to urinary tract infections to newly discovered cancers. No matter what decisions are made, medical personnel will always take the steps necessary to maintain comfort. Family members should not hesitate to ask for aggressive pain management. The issue with new conditions is the steps that should be taken beyond managing the pain they cause. Many treatments for newly discovered cancers increase pain and discomfort in order to fight the malignancy. Some new conditions call for surgery and then rehabilitation. Decisions will have to be made about whether to incur the increased pain and struggle. To see what may be involved when new conditions arise, consider the cases of Max and Neville.

When Max was 67, he became a Christian after a life of chasing worldly "success." His wife had become a Christian after they had been married for fifteen years, and Max credits her patient endurance through a losing fight with cancer for showing him the power of the gospel. He gave his life to Christ only a month before she died. Together they shared the peace of Christ as she went home to be with Jesus. Max has three children, all of whom love the Lord. Now 87, he has lived a full life, surviving a heart attack when he was 74. After the bypass surgery, Max's activity level decreased. His food habits remained the same. Now his body is breaking down. Max is significantly overweight, and he has developed diabetes that he struggles to manage. On top of this, Max is experiencing the early stages of dementia. His thinking is still clear enough to understand what is happening, so he knows that he is likely to lose his ability to make decisions for himself. The diabetes and creeping dementia have been a source of worry for Max, but he has a sunny disposition and is resigned to a slow decline.

Then Max falls and breaks his hip.

When he has been moved to a bed and given adequate pain medicine, Max is able to discuss his options with his private physician, Dr. Brown. The doctor says that Max is a decent candidate for hip-replacement surgery. Because of Max's previous heart attack and poor physical condition, the surgery itself has some risks. Physical therapy after the replacement is also likely to be lengthy and painful. But if Max does not have the surgery, he will be limited to a wheelchair, probably for the rest of his life, no matter how careful he is. Moving from his wheelchair to his bed or toilet (or back to his chair) will be difficult and somewhat dangerous. Max could fall again, with even more dire consequences. Dr. Brown has talked with both an orthopedic surgeon and a palliative-care specialist about Max's situation. The orthopedic surgeon is sure that the surgery will work, and thinks that the surgery is probably necessary to keep Max comfortable. The palliative-care specialist is sure that Max's pain can be controlled without surgery, and that the pain management will allow Max to think as clearly as the dementia allows. The assurance about pain management encourages Max, but he still doesn't like his options.

To help in making the decision, Max enlists the aid of his two closest friends. One is an elder in Max's church, and both have been his prayer partners for years. Talking and praying through Max's situation, the three come to the conclusion that the Bible allows Max either to accept or to decline the surgery. Max's age, his poor health, and the likely increase in his dementia are major considerations. His friends believe that if Max were younger, more healthy, and not losing his ability to think clearly, he might be obligated to endure the surgery and recovery in order to make full and faithful use of his time and talents. Because his dementia is increasing, surgery and rehab followed by a return to serving others is not one of Max's options. Even if he survived the surgery and the rehab, it is likely that by then his other health challenges would have worsened. Max's options both involve pain and risk. The surgery could well be effective, but the burdens that come with it are big: he could die during surgery, and he would face a long and painful rehabilitation dominating his last days of clear thinking. The burdens that would come with declining the surgery are also real, but the assurance about effective pain management makes those burdens less terrible.

Max is biblically permitted to say either yes or no to the surgery. After praying for guidance with his two friends, he decides to decline it. He has lived a full life. His children are walking with the Lord, and he has seen his children's children. Many of his friends have died, as has his wife. He is reconciled to everyone. By declining the surgery, he can spend his remaining days of lucidity talking with his children, serving others through prayer and encouragement, and taking delight in worship and other good things.

When Max tells his doctor what he has decided, the doctor does not argue. Working with a pain-management specialist, Max's doctor takes steps to ensure comfort and as much mobility as possible. Max hires nurses to help him in and out of his wheelchair. Although it takes all day to pull off the logistics, Max is able to attend worship and a Bible study until he becomes too confused to understand what is happening. A year after breaking his hip, Max's heart fails him and he ends his earthly race.

Max was able to make all the crucial decisions before his dementia made him decisionally incapable. The case of Neville shows that the decisions might be made earlier: Neville's physical and spiritual conditions are identical to what Max's had been when Max was only 83. Neville is an 83-year-old believer, a widower with a past heart attack, weight problems, advancing diabetes, and a family history that makes some kind of progressive dementia likely. Aware that a hip fracture is possible if he falls, Neville wants to leave instructions declining hip-replacement surgery if his hip breaks and he is unable to make decisions for himself. Even though his hip is not broken, his reasons for declining hip replacement can be just like Max's. Out of a desire to make faithful use of all that Christ has given him, Neville can decide in advance that if dementia would prevent him from deciding for or against the surgery, then the burdens that would come with the surgery would greatly exceed the benefits involved.

In order to ensure that his instructions are as helpful as possible, Neville completes the advance directive form approved for use in his state. He is careful to name the child most likely to understand and honor his wishes as his agent. In the section of the form about treatment wishes, he ensures that it states that if he becomes permanently confused, he does not want medical treatment that is not necessary for keeping him comfortable. To be extra careful, Neville also writes in that he does not want hip-replacement surgery if his pain can be managed without it. He then takes the steps that his state requires to make the form legally executed, makes copies, and puts them where they will be found if they are needed. As the last (and very important) step, Neville sits down with his children and explains what he means by the wishes he has expressed with the form.[7]

Neville's children do not enjoy the conversation. Later, though, when their father's dementia appears and he breaks his hip, they will be very glad to have it. Knowing of the existence of the form and what their father intends by it, the child named as his agent will be able to tell the doctors that Neville wants to be kept comfortable and that if surgery is not necessary for his comfort, then he doesn't want to have it. The child's authority to make this decision comes from Neville, whose authority to make it comes from Christ.

The existence of the advance directive proves to be especially helpful in Neville's case. When at 87 he falls and breaks his hip, his children find the document, but they disagree about whether to attempt the surgery. The child named as Neville's agent correctly remembers that Neville does not want to have the surgery under these circumstances. The other two children don't remember the conversation in any detail, but they are both sure that their father would want whatever the doctors recommend. These two know that the

7. For more on the process of completing an advance directive, see chapter 5 below.

orthopedic surgeon is absolutely convinced that the surgery is needed. Based on that confidence, they believe that their father would want the surgery. Armed with the advance directive, the child named as the agent speaks for Neville and declines the surgery.

It is important to note that even with advancing dementia and other health challenges, both Max and Neville have the biblical authority to choose the hip-replacement surgery. Max could have judged that the benefit of a longer life was worth the burdens that would come with the surgery. Neville could have written his advance directive so that even if he had lost the ability to make the choice himself, his agent would have approved the surgery. If we are seeking to use all we have to serve Christ faithfully, we have the authority to determine which burdens are excessive and which are not. The decisions that Max and Neville made about hip-replacement surgery could be made using similar reasoning about cancer treatment, a heart-valve replacement, or any other treatment that may be needed for a new condition that is diagnosed near the end of life. Our task with every medical decision is to use our resources to serve Christ well.

TUBE-FEEDING (ARTIFICIAL NUTRITION AND HYDRATION)

The prospect of losing the ability to make decisions because of dementia makes vivid the importance of leaving instructions about our wishes to loved ones and medical personnel. Many other age-related health challenges can critically diminish decisional capacity, so even people with a family history free of dementia in its various forms should not assume that they will always be able to make medical choices for themselves. Christians, especially, should be eager to take the steps necessary to relieve family and doctors of the awful responsibility of guessing about what we would want as our physical bodies are reaching their limits.

The choices that Max had to make,. and that Neville made in advance, were focused on whether to get hip-replacement surgery. Their actual or looming dementia figured prominently in their treatment decisions, but the immediate problem was whether to accept treatment for a condition that was not killing them. Most advance directive forms ask for instructions about a fourth kind of treatment that may arise when someone is unable to decide for him- or herself. This fourth category concerns decisions about artificially delivered nutrition and hydration (ANH), sometimes called *tube-feeding*. Food and water seem clearly different from "other treatments" such as hip replacement and chemotherapy, and decisions about medically "pushed" food and water are more likely to be needed than for any other kind of treatment. So it is appropriate and helpful for advance directive forms to raise the issue separately even though it could be included among the "treatment for new conditions."

The Terri Schiavo Case and Its Impact

Before considering cases that focus on the decision challenges, I need to mention reasons why this issue—tube-feeding—must be handled carefully. The first reason is the 2005 Terri Schiavo case that grabbed national attention and embroiled Christian leaders and others in heated public battles. From the media to the courts to the bedside, Terri Schiavo became the rope in a culturewide tug-of-war. Christians over the age of 30 today (in 2017) probably remember the case, and the most likely "lesson" that they learned was that it is always wrong to take out a feeding tube. This is not the place to replay the case, but it must be mentioned because for many Christians, their beliefs about feeding tubes were formed by the coverage of the case. It wasn't only in the news. YouTube was a brand-new medium at the time. Ms. Schiavo's parents used YouTube to post short videos showing her smiling and following objects with her eyes. Even as the courts were giving Ms. Schiavo's husband permission to withdraw the feeding tube, people could see that she was clearly in need of feeding. Sermons were preached on our culture of death and its willingness to starve a woman to death.[8]

8. For a medical account of the case, see Joshua E. Perry, Larry R. Churchill, and Howard S. Kirshner, "The Terri Schiavo Case: Legal, Ethical, and Medical

When the Schiavo case first hit the news, I was teaching bioethics to Covenant College students. We followed and studied the case in some detail, and I was among those who came to the conclusion that withdrawing a feeding tube was a particularly cruel way to kill someone. I was surprised, then, to learn that my solidly pro-life Christian friends with medical degrees did not agree. My own doctor—an elder at my PCA church, a member of the Christian Medical & Dental Society, the chair of Memorial Hospital's ethics committee, and an active volunteer in the antiabortion movement—assured me that withdrawing tube-feeding is often biblically appropriate and clearly what is best for someone whose body is no longer processing food.

A surgeon friend of mine who had been a career medical missionary agreed with him. They did not think the coverage of Ms. Schiavo's case was helpful, since it left out crucial medical details and was more interested in large political matters than in what was best for her. Together they convinced me to examine tube-feeding more carefully and urged me to look at what happens when someone's body is shutting down. Pushing food and fluids into someone who does not want food and whose body will not process it increases the pain (from bloating) without giving any benefit. They were confident that a pro-life doctor would recommend removing a feeding tube only when the physical burdens seriously outweighed the physical benefits. These pro-life physicians had withdrawn feeding tubes, and they urged me to follow any pro-life doctor's recommendation to remove one.

Other doctor friends who had seen the videos of Ms. Schiavo's seeming to respond to her environment said that the video clips were inconclusive even if they had not been edited. These doctors had worked with stricken people who looked and acted as Ms. Schiavo did even when they were not aware of anything at all. The autopsy after Ms. Schiavo died found a brain that could not have been aware of her

---

Perspectives," *Annals of Internal Medicine* 143, 10 (November 15, 2005): 744–48. The ethics of the case from a Roman Catholic perspective are discussed in John J. Paris, "Terri Schiavo and the Use of Artificial Nutrition and Fluids: Insights from the Catholic Tradition on End-of-Life Care," *Palliative & Supportive Care* 4, 2 (2006): 117–20.

surroundings for a very long time. I'm now confident that her parents sincerely believed that she was aware, that the many doctors who examined her were seeking to be honest but still ended up conflicted, and that the whole sad story is a poor basis for reaching any conclusions about the biblical appropriateness of withdrawing tube-feeding.

The Importance of Food

A second reason that tube-feeding should be discussed apart from treatment for other conditions such as chemotherapy is the physiological necessity of eating. Our bodies need food in order to remain healthy and to give us the strength to glorify and enjoy God. Refusing to eat is an act of rebellion (1 Sam. 28:20–25):

> **The Duty to Care for Ourselves:** God's Word does not permit us to reject food that is offered in the ordinary way when we are hungry.

This principle needs to be explicitly stated because influential voices on end-of-life choices are advocating that people who live in states that do not allow physician-assisted suicide should simply starve themselves to death. In *A Better Way of Dying*, the authors recommend that people who are tired of life discontinue eating as a relatively painless "exit" opportunity.[9] They recommend self-starvation because it is unlikely to be detected by loved ones and because it will lead to pneumonia and a gentle end. Most Christians will see that this is not a biblically permissible plan, and as this line of thinking gains acceptance, we must resist it.

A final reason for discussing tube-feeding separately is the psychological, social, and spiritual importance of food. Love is expressed through providing food. A baby's first experience of love is being fed by its mother. The welcome of a stranger is made palpable by inviting

9. Jeanne Fitzpatrick and Eileen M. Fitzpatrick, *A Better Way of Dying: How to Make Choices at the End of Life* (New York: Penguin, 2010), 115–57. This book should not be recommended to anyone facing end-of-life decisions. The first third of the book conceals its goal of hastening death by our own choices.

the person to share a meal. Families and close friends renew their ties over food, and especially over feasts. Jesus draws near to us in a profound and mysterious way in the Lord's Supper. Scripture commends feeding loved ones (Mark 5:43), those in need (Mark 6:37), and even our enemies (Rom. 12:20).

> **The Duty to Show Love by Feeding:** God's Word calls us to feed our loved ones when they are hungry and to give them drink when they are thirsty.

On the other hand, purposely depriving someone of food expresses malice, or even hatred. For a healthy body, dying of starvation is agonizing. It is a kind of death that no one would choose for a loved one. Most of us have some experience with being very hungry or thirsty. The thought of having that feeling only grow until we pass out is terrible. Because we can imagine being hungry and we know the power of food to communicate love, we should always find it difficult to stop delivering food and water.

The Realities of Feeding Tubes

This does not mean that it is always wrong to remove a feeding tube. As long as a feeding tube is providing its benefits and the burdens that it is imposing are small, it is best to keep the tube in place. Sadly, however, the benefits shrink dramatically if one's body stops wanting nutrition. The burdens, on the other hand, get larger the longer a feeding tube is in place. The best use of a feeding tube is to provide nutrition to someone who cannot take food by mouth while recovering from an illness. When used for this purpose, the feeding tube is only a temporary measure. It is part of a larger plan of recovery and will be discontinued when returning to eating in the ordinary way becomes possible. At first, this was the only way in which feeding tubes were used. Today they are used as long-term, permanent ways of delivering nutrition, even for people who are unconscious and have no humanly likely chance of recovering.

Long-term use of feeding tubes usually imposes burdens that only grow over time. Preventing infection at the site of insertion can be difficult. The threat of aspiration (food getting into the lungs) continues even though nothing is going down the throat. Eating by mouth has pleasant associations—the feel, the taste, and the social affirmation of sharing a meal—and those pleasures are lost when food is delivered by tube. For a person who is unconscious or permanently confused, the feeding tube prolongs a condition of spiritual deprivation. The tube is keeping his or her physical body alive, but the person is no longer enjoying the ordinary means of grace in the ordinary way. Even when the body is making some use of the food that is being delivered, this benefit can be overwhelmed by the physical, social, and spiritual burdens imposed.

Even knowing all of this, I continued to believe that it was always wrong to remove a feeding tube. I could not get past the very great burden that would be experienced by someone starving to death or dying of thirst. No matter how hard it would be to drift sideways socially and spiritually, it had to be better than dying from starvation. When I finally stated this objection out loud, Christian doctors and nurses walked me through the physiology of hunger and thirst. Thirst is experienced when one's mouth is dry. If the mouth is kept moist, a person will not feel thirst even if the body needs water. Even more importantly, when our bodies are shutting down from disease or old age, we lose the desire to eat. We stop reaching for food. If food is pushed into our bodies, it isn't processed. When our bodies stop processing food, we are not hungry. Getting food can even be painful; not getting food is not agonizing.

No Duty to Force-Feed: God's Word does not require us to force food or water on our loved ones by mechanical means if the burdens of those means greatly exceed the benefits involved.

Doctors trained in end-of-life care or palliative care will know when this point has been reached. If the mouth is kept moist, removing a feeding tube under these conditions will not increase the person's suffering.

Mechanically delivering food and water is very different from urging someone to eat or drink by mouth. Administering artificial nutrition and hydration as a humane medical option has been possible for less than the last hundred years, since it depends on the use of plastics. As a medical treatment, food and water can be delivered through a tube down the nose or mouth into the stomach. A tube through the nose is an NG (nasogastric) tube. A tube through the mouth is an OG (oral-gastric) tube. Food and water can delivered directly into the stomach through a surgically implanted PEG (perienteric gastric) tube. These are the most common means used. It is also possible to introduce food and water directly into the intestines or directly into the bloodstream, but these are typically only short-term measures because the risks of complications are high.[10]

Cases for Application

The mechanical details are important here because they underscore the vast difference between providing food in the ordinary way as part of the affirming ritual of sharing a meal and providing food through tubes. Tube-feeding requires sophisticated equipment and trained medical personnel. It is complicated medical treatment, far more like kidney dialysis than it is like putting on a bandage or removing a splinter. The mechanical devices push food into the body even if the body doesn't need or even want it. The decision to start using a feeding tube should be thought through very carefully, since it is emotionally much more difficult to discontinue its use than never to start it. With all this in mind, consider the cases of Tina, Sally, Rhonda, and Paula:

Tina is 84 years old and has been serving Jesus since she was 13. Her husband died eleven years ago. She has severe rheumatoid arthritis, which makes it painful to do even simple physical tasks, and she is showing signs of what her doctors believe is early Alzheimer's disease.

---

10. Most Roman Catholic bioethicists, including the American Catholic Bishops, now permit limiting the use of tube-feeding in some cases. See David M. Zientek, "Artificial Nutrition and Hydration in Catholic Healthcare: Balancing Tradition, Recent Teaching, and Law," *HEC Forum* 25, 2 (June 2013): 145–59.

Further complicating her situation, Tina also finds swallowing difficult. It is uncomfortable, and if she is not careful, her food goes down the wrong pipe and into her lungs. The coughing fits that follow can be intense. Tina is nonetheless a cheerful presence in the assisted-living facility that is now home. Her two children and five grandchildren live nearby, and they visit often to hear her stories and sing songs. Recently, Tina's interest in food has dwindled. She eats a bit when others join her at meals, but her children are alarmed to discover that on her own she rarely seeks out food. They think that maybe forgetting to eat is one of the effects of her Alzheimer's disease. Whatever the cause, she is losing weight and her clothes are now baggy.

At the children's request, Tina meets with the children and Tina's doctor. It is a "good" day for Tina's ability to think clearly. The doctor says that if she doesn't do a better job of eating, he will recommend that she be placed on a feeding tube to make sure that she gets nutrition. Tina objects. She claims that she never feels hungry, but that she will try to eat more. No matter what, though, she does not want to be put on a feeding tube. She watched her father linger for months, unconscious and physically deteriorating in a hospital bed. His heart had been strong at first, and the PEG tube kept pushing food in even after he stopped processing and eliminating the waste. He finally died when the bloating put too much pressure on his heart. She says that she does *not* want to die that way or make her family watch her die that way.

Neither her children nor her doctor likes this answer. Even so, it is a choice that is biblically permissible for Tina. She must try to eat more, and she has promised to do so. She will have the staff cut her food into very tiny pieces or puree it. She will take very tiny bites to keep from aspirating it. And she will endure the coughing fits when they come. For their part, her children promise to join her more often for these long meals and to urge the staff to help her remember to eat.

Refusing the feeding tube is not choosing to commit suicide. It is choosing not to force food into her body. Tina is responsible to make faithful use of her resources. She knows that her mental abilities are slipping away. She doesn't know how fast it will happen, but her time is limited. She also knows that her opportunities for service are limited by her rheumatoid arthritis. Tina has been faithful in prayer for the people in her church, for missions efforts, and for justice to be done in the world. Pain prevents her from writing or typing, but she calls people to offer words of encouragement. She will continue to do these things as God gives her strength. While a feeding tube may prolong her life, it would likely be a life of confusion and continuing pain. As part of her effort to serve Christ well, Tina is biblically permitted to determine that the feeding tube would involve burdens that greatly exceed the benefits gained.

Declining a feeding tube seems more drastic than deciding against hip-replacement surgery, but Tina's decision follows the same biblical line of reasoning as Max's decision about hip-replacement surgery. Both decline treatment that is excessively burdensome. Neither seeks to die. Neither refuses to suffer for the sake of the gospel. Serving Christ does not obligate us to suffer merely in order to stay alive. So long as she makes a serious effort to eat when she is hungry, Tina can decline the feeding tube.

Because she knows that her children do not like her decision, Tina asks an elder at her church for help in writing an advance directive that will make it clear that she does not want a feeding tube started when she loses the ability to make her own medical decisions. The elder has known Tina for over forty years. She was his third-grade Sunday school teacher, and she has been a constant source of encouragement to him. He also knows and likes Tina's children, and he is reluctant to conspire against their wishes. He agrees to help her with the document, but urges her to name one of her children as her agent for health care decisions. Tina agrees to name as her agent whichever child promises not to put her on a feeding tube.

When the four of them meet to write the advance directive, they pray for guidance in filling out the document and for the courage to do what is right. All of them have done some research on feeding tubes, and the children listen patiently as Tina gives her reasons for wanting to avoid tube-feeding. The children know that their grandfather's passing was slow and troubling, but they have not heard the details that Tina now adds.

Tina also listens carefully as her children explain their reasons for wanting her to have a feeding tube. Their reasons are simple: they do not want to lose her, and they do not want her to starve to death. It takes two hours, but by the end of the conversation they all agree that her pain issues and her advancing Alzheimer's make tube-feeding needlessly burdensome. Both children promise to decline tube-feeding, and the advance directive is completed and on file by the end of the week. Tina has the biblical authority to accept or decline the tube-feeding both when it is offered by her doctor and in the future through the advance directive. When her Alzheimer's has progressed and she stops eating, the children speak for her and decline the feeding tube. It is hard to carry through on their promise, and it is hard to have her die not long after relaying her choice. The difficulty, though, is from losing her, not from doing something contrary to God's Word.

Although it is heartbreaking to lose a loved one, Tina spared her children a lot of anguish by making the decisions herself while she was still able. To see what can happen if the decisions are not made when it is possible, consider the case of Sally, who is a believer in the same situation as Tina (painful arthritis, creeping Alzheimer's disease, little desire to eat, etc.). Unlike Tina, however, Sally takes no further steps after declining the feeding tube when it is first offered. Sally's two children also disagree with the decision at the time. She has given them her carefully worked-out reasons for turning it down, but they haven't really listened, and they conclude that her pigheadedness is one of the effects of the Alzheimer's. Sally has never written an advance directive.

When Sally's memory and mental abilities have slipped to the point that she cannot make decisions for herself, the doctor again recommends the feeding tube. The children quickly approve, hoping that better nutrition will improve her cognitive status. But the NG tube does not work well. Whether on purpose or by accident, Sally often pulls it out. The children decide that she cannot know what she is doing, so they agree with the doctors who think she should have a PEG tube surgically implanted and steps taken to keep her from pulling it out. Simply covering the insertion site doesn't stop her, so eventually Sally has to be strapped down so that the tube can feed her. Her children are determined that she receive nutrition. She is not going to starve to death under their care.

When Sally's children see her under the restraints and exhausted from fighting against them, they ask for help. A friend from church who is also a nurse meets them for coffee to talk about what is happening to Sally. The friend asks whether Sally has ever talked about what she would want if she was in this condition, and the children work together to reconstruct the reasons she gave when she declined tube-feeding months before. The friend helps the children understand the feelings of thirst and hunger and the importance of keeping Sally's mouth moist. Together they decide that even if Sally has not been clawing at the tube because she is trying to pull it out, they can still be confident that she would not want it. The children know they have the legal authority to speak for their mother and remove the tube. The friend assures them that they have the biblical authority to speak for her as well. After praying together about what it means to honor Sally and God's law, the children sleep on the matter. The next day they ask the doctor to remove Sally's feeding tube.

As heart-wrenching as it must have been for Sally's children to ask for the tube to be removed, their situation was less agonizing than it might have been. Consider Rhonda, whose situation is like Sally's. Rhonda's Alzheimer's has advanced so quickly that she is not decisionally capable when the feeding-tube recommendation is first made. Because Rhonda cannot speak for herself, the medical staff look to her children to make the decision. Appalled at the prospect of losing their mother so quickly, the children have an NG tube ordered for Rhonda. Like Sally, she pulls it out. When the doctor asks whether they want a PEG tube used instead, they ask for help. Rhonda has a close Christian friend who has visited her regularly in the nursing home. She tells the children that Rhonda had often said that she would not want to be kept alive on a feeding tube if she could not interact with her family and fellow believers. Rhonda's friend has also heard Rhonda tell the story of the long death process of Rhonda's father. The friend is confident that Rhonda would not want to be kept alive by tube-feeding.

When the children approach the doctor to decline the PEG tube option, they are surprised when the doctor pushes back. Do they have anything in writing saying what Rhonda would want? Do they remember her saying anything to *them* about it? The doctor says that he needs better evidence before he accepts their judgment as speaking for Rhonda. A young nurse who is nearby exclaims, "Are you trying to kill your mother?!" The doctor says to ignore the outburst, and the nurse apologizes; but the children are shaken.

Since a decision is needed very soon, they agree to the PEG tube's placement. It takes some time to find others who know their mother well enough to have an opinion, but eventually they decide that she would not have agreed to it. When they approach the doctor at the beginning of the next month, he agrees to their request. The PEG tube is removed. The children have the legal and biblical authority to speak for Rhonda. It would have been better for all of them if Rhonda had left instructions about what she wanted before she lost the ability to choose for herself.

These cases all end with the feeding tube being discontinued. This may leave the impression that feeding tubes should be avoided, but that would be a serious mistake. Feeding tubes as a short-term measure to support other healing efforts are a great blessing. They can be a life-saving long-term source of nutrition for people who cannot safely swallow, or who cannot swallow at all. The cases above concentrate on situations in which feeding tubes have only a minimal physical benefit and impose great burdens. Even when the burdens are great, the Bible permits us to use them as part of our attempt to serve Christ faithfully. And when someone's wishes are not known at all, our obligation to protect the least of these may call us to start or maintain a feeding tube even in a situation in which we would not choose it for ourselves. Consider one final case:

Paula's situation is like Rhonda's, but she has no living children. Her Alzheimer's has progressed faster than anyone expected, and when a feeding tube is recommended, she is no longer able to make medical decisions for herself. All her close friends have either died or cannot be reached, and her pastor is called in to help decide whether to place a feeding tube. The pastor is sure that he himself wouldn't want a feeding tube keeping him alive in a permanently confused state. He is also sure that the nursing home is hoping that he will decline the feeding tube on Paula's behalf.

Despite these things, the pastor chooses the feeding tube for her. He does not know Paula's thinking on the matter well enough to speak for her. He cannot in conscience claim that he is speaking *for* her. The pastor has been asked to help, and what he can do is to seek to protect her. He asks whether Paula ever reaches for food. She does. One of her nurses reports that she lights up when food commercials come on the television. And he learns that she still needs to use the bathroom. Convinced that she is among the sick and hungry that he should feed, he says that he thinks the feeding tube would be best. He does not have the biblical authority to speak for her, but he has the biblical authority to help her get food if her body will use it.

KEY TERMS

activities of daily living
artificial nutrition and hydration (tube-feeding)
CPR
DNR
permanent confusion
permanent unconsciousness
terminal illness/condition
Terri Schiavo

STUDY AND *DISCUSSION QUESTIONS

1. What laws did states pass between 2004 and 2010 that changed the landscape for people making end-of-life decisions?
2. What conditions must be met for the *medical* judgment that a condition is "permanent"?
3. Are all people who are permanently confused afflicted with Alzheimer's disease?

4. *Are people who are permanently unconscious or permanently confused still image-bearers of God?

5. *Under what conditions is it biblically permissible to discontinue life-sustaining treatment for someone who is permanently unconscious?

6. What does it take for a condition to be judged "terminal" by a doctor?

7. What is meant by *activities of daily living*?

8. Gil Meilaender argues that he wants to be a burden to his family. What reason does he give for this claim?

9. *What should a pastoral counselor say to someone who would rather die than be a burden to his or her family?

10. What happens when CPR is administered in the hospital?

11. Where do you want to be if someone is going to perform CPR on you?

12. What do the initials *DNR* stand for in the hospital context?

13. What should be said to someone who says, "I don't want a DNR order; it really means 'do not care'"?

14. *Describe a situation in which it would be biblically permissible to say no to a doctor's recommendation of heart-valve surgery.

15. Why is feeding so important to our sense of community?

16. Explain why the Terri Schiavo case attracted so much attention in the mid-2000s.

17. *Describe a situation in which it would be biblically permissible to say *either* yes or no to a doctor's recommendation to insert a feeding tube.

18. *If someone is pro-life about abortion, must that person also *always* be in favor of inserting or maintaining a feeding tube to maintain life?

FOR FURTHER READING

Abernathy, Amy, and David C. Currow. "Letters: Time-Limited Trials." *Journal of the American Medical Association* 307, 1 (January 4, 2012): 33–34.

American Heart Association. "Simulated Resuscitation Attempt." https://www.youtube.com/watch?v=eXmAzsRQi9I.

Berlinger, Nancy, Bruce Jennings, and Susan M. Wolf. *The Hastings Center Guidelines for Decisions on Life-Sustaining Treatment and Care near the End of Life.* 2nd ed. New York: Oxford University Press, 2013.

Fitzpatrick, Jeanne, and Eileen M. Fitzpatrick. *A Better Way of Dying: How to Make Choices at the End of Life.* New York: Penguin, 2010. Note: The recommendations advanced by this book are not all biblically sound.

Paris, John J. "Terri Schiavo and the Use of Artificial Nutrition and Fluids: Insights from the Catholic Tradition on End-of-Life Care." *Palliative and Supportive Care* 4, 2 (2006): 117–20.

Pence, Gregory. *Classic Cases in Medical Ethics: Accounts of Cases That Have Shaped Medical Ethics, with Philosophical, Legal, and Historical Backgrounds.* Boston: McGraw Hill, 2004.

Perry, Joshua E., Larry R. Churchill, and Howard S. Kirshner. "The Terri Schiavo Case: Legal, Ethical, and Medical Perspectives." *Annals of Internal Medicine* 143, 10 (November 15, 2005): 744–48.

Singh, Swati, et al. "Evaluation of Cardiopulmonary Resuscitation (CPR) for Patient Outcomes and Their Predictors." *Journal of Clinical & Diagnostic Research* 10, 1 (2016): 1–4.

Zientek, David M. "Artificial Nutrition and Hydration in Catholic Healthcare: Balancing Tradition, Recent Teaching, and Law." *HEC Forum* 25, 2 (June 2013): 145–59.

4

PUTTING BIBLICAL PRINCIPLES INTO PRACTICE: TRUE STORIES

Even a little experience with end-of-life choices is helpful. Most people face them for the first time when a loved one is gravely ill. It is not a good time for working out what biblical principles should apply or how to connect principles and choices. Thinking through choices that other believers have faced is one way to prepare to answer hard questions, whether for your own care, that of your family members, or that of fellow believers who request your advice. This chapter describes six real situations that called for the application of the biblical principles explained in the previous chapters. All the names and most of the personal details (ages, family connections, even some sexes) have been altered, but the questions raised are fundamentally the same as those faced in the actual events described. In order to simulate the task of answering the practical questions as they arise, questions are posed in the midst of each narrative. Readers are encouraged to consider how they would answer these questions before considering the possible answers suggested and my commentary on the merits of the answers proposed.

All the questions described in these cases were hard to answer when they were asked. The answers I actually gave were not always helpful. While my commentary on the possible answers gives reasons for thinking that one is better than the others, the best answer isn't always what I actually said. Sometimes *my* actual answer is listed as one of the *weaker* options. If in places the tone of the commentary seems condescending, the most likely cause is my disappointment that *I* didn't see the better answer at the time it was needed in the actual circumstances. Also, my commentary on the options obscures how often my ignorance of medicine led me to make a distress call to a friendly doctor. Rich Pesce, MD, took my calls at all hours and walked me through the medical details. The medical facts of the cases in this chapter are what happened, but the answers I recommend are sometimes much better than the answers I gave at the time.

STORY 1: DISTRESSING DIALYSIS

Nora has been an active member of your church for over fifty years. She is now 71 years old and divorced, and until the last couple of years she was the most reliable elementary Sunday school teacher the church has ever known. She has two daughters, both of them married. One of them lives overseas, and the other, Miriam, lives in town and has three children of her own. Miriam is also a member of your church. Nora's health has always been an issue for her. Always heavyset, Nora developed type 2 diabetes in her fifties. Just over three years ago, she suffered a mild stroke as well. Since the stroke, she has lived with Miriam, and even with nursing assistance Nora's condition has deteriorated. She grows confused easily, but she is pleasant to have around and allows Miriam and the children to help her take care of herself. She is able to attend church with her family, and it is evident that she enjoys the service even though she doesn't understand much of the sermon.

Recently Nora's doctors have determined that she needs regular kidney dialysis. Her kidney function has dropped to dangerous levels, and her doctors believe that this is contributing to her confusion and occasional paranoia. Miriam's children are all in school, and she takes time off work in order to accompany Nora to the dialysis clinic for her first session. Although Nora is anxious during the four-hour session, she makes it through it. Afterward, it is evident that Nora is much less confused, and she remarks that she looks forward to getting the treatment again. The next session is four days later.

Miriam is not able to get off work for the next session, and one of the church deacons drives Nora to the dialysis clinic on his way to work. Nora's confusion has returned, but she recognizes the deacon and allows him to take her to the clinic. Not even two hours later, Miriam is called at work: Nora has become violent with the staff at the clinic and is refusing the treatment. Miriam leaves work, goes to the clinic, and is able to calm her mother down. The dialysis is rescheduled for the next day, and Miriam hopes to find someone to sit with her mother through it.

The next day, Nora is even more confused. A friend from church takes her to the clinic, but when the technicians try to start the IV for the dialysis, Nora becomes agitated. She accuses the technician of trying to kill her and tries to leave the clinic. The friend from church is not able to calm her down, and in her confused agitation Nora hits her head against a door and starts bleeding. Clinic staff call for an ambulance, and Nora is taken to the emergency room at the local hospital. Miriam is called at work, and she joins her mother at the hospital as quickly as she can.

When Miriam arrives at the emergency room, she finds her mother resting peacefully. For Nora's own protection, the doctor has placed her in restraints and started the dialysis that was impossible at the clinic.[1] It is evident that the dialysis has removed most of the paranoia. She is still confused, but she is not agitated.

Two days after the episode with the clinic, Miriam asks you to help her think through what is best for her mother. Miriam has talked with Nora's doctor, who said that the situation is difficult. Nora needs the

---

1. Most clinics are not permitted to use physical restraints. Psychiatric facilities and most hospitals can use them with a doctor's order and close supervision. Their use even in hospital settings is now quite rare, out of concern for protecting the dignity of people under their care and limiting exposure to liability. For more on the use of restraints, see A. E. Kleinmann et al., "Systems-Level Assessment of Interobserver Agreement (IOA) for Implementation of Protective Holding (Therapeutic Restraint) in a Behavioral Healthcare Setting," *Journal of Developmental and Physical Disabilities* 21, 6 (2009): 473–83.

dialysis. Her kidney function is compromised to the point that without regular dialysis, she will decline rapidly, dying in a matter of weeks. As long as she is at home in familiar surroundings, her confusion will not turn into paranoia, and she has never been aggressive or violent when at home or in church. Nora's health is not good, but if a way can be found for her to receive dialysis, she is likely to live for nine months to a year longer.

The problem is Nora's reaction to the dialysis. She cannot be dialyzed at home.[2] At the clinic, the combination of confusion and strange surroundings makes her so fearful that she will not accept the treatment. The clinic is not legally permitted to restrain her, even for her own good and even with her daughter's permission. Nora could be given a strong antianxiety drug on the day before and the day of receiving dialysis at the clinic. Use of the drug would probably mean that she would accept the treatment, but it would also mean that Nora would be lethargic and largely unaware of her surroundings most of the time. The dialysis needs to be administered every three or four days, so the drug's effects would be felt most of the time.

The hospital would be permitted to restrain Nora during dialysis, but that would mean admitting her to the hospital every few days. The expense would be very high, and even then it would mean forcing Nora to endure what would seem to her like torture. Every few days she would be strapped to a bed with a needle in her arm, and she would never understand why.

The doctor has described three options for Miriam, and all of them have problems:

- Option 1: Dialyze Nora in the hospital.
- Option 2: Prescribe a strong antianxiety drug to keep Nora calm during dialysis at the clinic.
- Option 3: Discontinue the dialysis.

---

2. In-home dialysis systems are now available, but they are not financially or practically feasible for Nora. See https://www.kidney.org/atoz/content/homehemo for more on in-home hemodialysis.

After describing these options, Miriam says to you, "I don't see how we can choose option 3. It would be like a death sentence. My mother would die sooner rather than later. I have been pro-life as long as I can remember. Surely the Bible says that we should do whatever it takes to keep my mother alive as long as possible."

Question 1A: What Should You Say to Miriam about These Three Options?

Answer (a): "Oh, that she would allow the clinic to do the dialysis! This is all happening so quickly. It is hard to imagine doing anything but fighting for a longer life. But I don't think the Bible commands us to do whatever it takes to live as long as possible. Being pro-life doesn't mean that life is more important than everything else. It means that we should protect life and not cheapen it. Choosing a shorter life without dialysis is still choosing life."

Answer (b): "I'm so sorry that you have been put in this position, Miriam. The Bible makes it clear that only God can give life, and so only God should take it away. Stopping the dialysis would mean taking your mother's life away. I will help you oppose any option that amounts to killing your mother."

Answer (c): "What an awful trial for your faith, Miriam! Option 3 is there to tempt you to put your own needs ahead of your mother's. Giving up on dialysis completely would mean that you were rid of both the inconvenience and the expense of getting the treatment that your mother needs. We should pray right now that you will have the strength to resist this temptation."

Commentary on the Answers to Question 1A

Miriam's cry for help was only about option 3, and all three of these answers focus on the third option. If Miriam had asked what you thought of all three options, it might be better to talk through the pros and cons of each of them. Making sure that the consequences of the choice are clear would help both you and Miriam work through a difficult situation.

Answers (b) and (c) both contain important truths, but answer (a) is the best of the three. While only God may take life directly, Miriam would not be *killing* her mother by discontinuing the dialysis. Nora's physical condition is frail. Her body is racked by diseases and dysfunctions that are killing her. The dialysis allows her body to fight those problems more effectively, but the dialysis comes at a very high cost to her. Contrary to answer (b), agreeing to option 3 would not mean that Miriam was killing her mother.

Answer (c) contains the truth that Nora's condition has been putting a significant demand on Miriam's time. None of the options will diminish Miriam's task of honoring and caring for her mother in the short term. It would be wickedly selfish for Miriam to look for a way to have her mother die quickly, but a temptation to selfishness is not lurking in option 3. Similarly, worries about financial costs are not the central issue here. Most importantly, Miriam did not mention money in her cry for help. Injecting that into the discussion does more harm than good.

The merits of answer (a) require some explanation. The Bible is consistently on the side of life, not death. It would make sense to think that being pro-life means being antideath to the point of using all means necessary to delay death as long as possible. But the Bible does not say that we must delay death as long as possible. As bad as death is, it is not the worst thing. Disobeying God's law is worse than death. Moreover, because ordinary communion with God and the fellowship of the saints are such great blessings, it may be a great burden for Nora to go on living without being able to enjoy these things.

Miriam's question here is about whether option 3 (discontinuing the dialysis) is consistent with her pro-life principles and her desire to honor God's law. God's Word permits Nora to decline medical treatment that is excessively burdensome. Options 1 and 2 would impose on Nora great physical and spiritual burdens: being routinely tied down to endure a procedure that she could not understand or being too disoriented to enjoy time in worship or with her family. Option 3 would mean choosing a shorter life with the spiritual good of worship and the earthly good of time with her family *over* a longer life without those goods. Nora is not able to understand the choice well enough to make it herself, but Miriam can speak for her. Miriam needs to know that option 3 is one that Nora could have chosen for herself in accordance with pro-life and biblical convictions. That doesn't yet settle what Miriam ought to do; it just leaves option 3 as viable.

After praying silently sitting side by side with you, Miriam asks:

Question 1B: Which of the Three Options Should I Choose?

Answer (a): "It seems that it comes down to what you want, Miriam. Do you want to invest the time and money into doing what it takes to keep your mother alive, or do you want to find an easy way out? The clinic is not able to help in this case, and even though the time in the hospital will be a burden, that looks like the only biblically sound option."

Answer (b): "I'm not comfortable accepting this doctor's set of options. I think you should seek the advice of another doctor. A Christian doctor would work harder to find a way to get your mother help rather than giving up on her."

Answer (c): "The key question is, 'What would your mother choose, if she could?' You know her far better than I do, but in this case, I think your mother would choose option 3. Although it will mean living only weeks instead of months, it will be weeks of recognizing you, going to worship, and having her grandchildren near her. Either of the other two options will mean giving those things up. I think if she could choose for herself, she would prefer option 3."

Commentary on the Answers to Question 1B

Answer (b) has some merit. Another doctor may see a fourth option that has not yet been discovered. (In the real case on which this story is based, a fourth option didn't occur to any of the four doctors involved over the course of a forty-five-minute discussion.) If either you or Miriam knows of a Christian doctor that you can ask to review the case, it is worth doing. Answer (b) doesn't solve the problem that Miriam will face the next time her mother needs to be dialyzed. It only puts off the difficulty if no other option is found, probably involving another unpleasant dialysis attempt for Nora.

Answer (a) is the weakest of the three, since it heaps guilt on Miriam no matter what happens next. Either she will have to watch her mother suffer medical treatments that terrify (or stupefy) her, or she will always believe that she put her own selfish desires ahead of her mother's needs.

Answer (c) is the best answer, but it solves Miriam's practical problem only if she honestly believes that her mother would choose option 3. Miriam needs to imagine what Nora would choose if she could understand what was being asked, think through the implications, and communicate her choice. This is a complicated *if,* and you can help Miriam work through the central issues by focusing on them one at a time and in a helpful order.

First, you can ask Miriam whether Nora has ever talked about how she imagined her life would end. If Nora has expressed a desire to live as long as possible even if it means being in the hospital away from her family, then Miriam should choose option 1. She will have to sort out the financial implications, but that doesn't have to be done in the next few days. If Nora is admitted to the hospital in order to make dialysis possible, then it will still be possible later for Miriam to reevaluate whether Nora would want it to continue. If concern about money would have mattered to Nora, then it will be appropriate for Miriam to take it into account.

It is likely that Miriam will not be able to remember a time when Nora talked about what she would want near the end of her life. Before concluding that she has nothing to go on, you can encourage Miriam to remember how Nora reacted to the medical circumstances during the last days of one of her friends, a member of the church, or one of her relatives. Even if Nora did not comment directly on the way her parents died, Miriam may remember how she reacted. Those memories may provide some insight.

Second, you can help Miriam think through her mother's attitude about medications that altered her ability to be alert, relate to her family, hear the Bible read, and participate in worship. Both options 1 and 2 will make it very difficult for Nora to continue to enjoy any of these things. Regardless of the financial costs and the logistical difficulties that those options will involve, continuing dialysis will mean dramatically reducing Nora's ability to spend time with her family and worship at church. If the Nora that Miriam remembers cherished those things, then it is evidence that Nora would be slow to agree to either option 1 or option 2.

Third, you will want to talk candidly with Miriam about Nora's relationship with Christ. If Nora is trusting in Christ alone for her salvation and looking forward to being at home in heaven, it will be much easier to believe that Nora would choose a shorter earthly life enjoying certain goods over a longer earthly life deprived of them, and especially if it meant being deprived of the spiritual goods.

Fourth, then, ask Miriam to talk through what she thinks Nora would count as burdens and benefits for each of the options. Encourage her to say what Nora would *think*, not what she would be comfortable having others *hear*. If Nora were able to make this decision for herself, the judgment of her private self would make the difference. Miriam should not imagine Nora as either more noble or more selfish than she knew her. Writing down Miriam's observations about the burdens and benefits will help her take them all into account when the time comes to decide.

It is likely that in the course of reviewing the burdens and benefits, Miriam will achieve clarity about at least one of the options. You do not need to force her to complete the analysis for an option that she knows Nora would reject. If Miriam begins to settle on an option that surprises you, resist the temptation to try to push her away from it. She knows Nora better than you do, and neither of you wants to make a choice that Nora would not have wanted, as long as the option is biblically permissible.

Epilogue

Over the next two days, Miriam talked with friends from church about Nora's situation and prayed for clarity. She also attempted to explain to Nora what was happening. Even though Nora never showed that she understood the options or indicated what she wanted, she did not get agitated or cry.

Before the next scheduled dialysis appointment, Miriam decided that Nora would not want to go through it again. She canceled the appointment and began calling Nora's friends to make sure that they visited her soon. Nora was well enough to receive and to recognize most of her friends before her health failed. She became weaker and weaker over the next three weeks, slipped into a coma, and died at home a few days later. Miriam took time off work to be with Nora during her final days.

STORY 2: PRAYING FOR A MIRACLE

Dave is a 35-year-old believer who has been a member of your church since he came to Christ in college. He and his wife, Hannah, have two children (9 and 5) and have been active helpers in the nursery for years. Dave has been an extreme sports enthusiast, spending what time he could away from his work as an accountant and his time with his family doing acrobatic tricks on his stunt cycle. Three days ago, Dave misjudged a landing and sustained a serious head injury. His helmet had come off in flight, so he slammed his head directly on an uneven concrete surface. You heard about this from a fellow church member on the day it happened. All you have heard since then is that Dave is in "critical" condition.

This morning, Hannah called the church to ask whether someone could come and talk with her about Dave's condition. The pastor calls you to say that he is too sick to go to the hospital and asks whether you can go in his place.

On your way to the hospital, you pray that God will give you wisdom. When you arrive in the ICU, a nurse shows you to Dave's room. Hannah is there, and she is crying.

Question 2A: What Is Your Primary Goal for the Beginning of This Conversation?

Answer (a): To get Hannah to stop crying.

Answer (b): To find out what is making Hannah cry.

Answer (c): To assure Hannah that she is not alone and that you are not in a hurry.

Commentary on the Answers to Question 2A

The best answer is (c). Although you want to find out why Hannah is crying (b) and you want to relieve her distress (a), your chief goal is to make Christ's love for Hannah clear. Being in any kind of hurry to work on solving her problem will show Hannah that you need her to do or be something to please you. Don't do that to her. She is crying because she is grieving over the brokenness of the world. It is brokenness that now touches the very center of her world. Crying is a godly response to her circumstances. Make enough noise entering the room to let her know you are there. Introduce yourself and find a seat. Wait for her to invite you to talk. Don't read or check your phone. Continue praying silently for wisdom, patience, and gentleness.

When Hannah becomes aware of your presence, she asks whether you have been praying. When you say that you have, she says that she has been, too. Her prayer since the accident has had a single focus: that God would work a miracle to heal Dave and return him to his family. She insists that it cannot be God's will for Dave to die so young, and with a family that needs him. She is sure that if God loves her, Dave will be completely healed.

Question 2B: What Should You Say in Response to Hannah's Prayers?

Answer (a): "Hannah, as much as we wish this had not happened, the age of miracles has ceased. Dave was physically strong before his accident, and we can hope that he will have the strength to fight through this injury. But it is wrong to ask God for a miracle."

Answer (b): "Hannah, I'm so sorry this has happened to you. I know it is hard to see why God would want this to happen, but we know that everything happens according to God's will. By faith we can resist the temptation to doubt God's wisdom. Let's pray together now that God will increase our faith."

Answer (c): "Hannah, I'm so sorry. I was praying that God would be with you and Dave now as you face this difficult time. May I pray for you two right now?" (If yes, pray aloud, acknowledging God's love and power, and that God would heal Dave and give Hannah comfort.)

Commentary on the Answers to Question 2B

Even though Hannah's focus on Dave's recovery includes theological difficulties, now is *not* the time to deal with those problems. The best answer here is (c). Hannah is likely only to resent any attempt to turn the hospital room into a classroom (both (a) and (b)). And it would be hard to fault her for resenting it. What she needs now is the assurance of God's love and presence, and you—ministering in Christ's name—are that loving presence.

Affirm every part of Hannah's prayer that you can. Acknowledge that you, too, are praying for Dave's healing. While humanly speaking it is unlikely that Dave will recover, Hannah's prayer for his recovery is biblically warranted. We are to ask for anything consistent with God's revealed will. Wanting Dave to recover is not just permissible; it is a righteous desire. Furthermore, God may, in fact, heal him. It would not be a *miracle* in the technical sense (since it would not confirm the Word of the Lord), but it would be a wonder. And the age of wonders has not ceased.

Finally, Hannah's claim that it cannot be God's will that Dave die is not the conclusion of a theological argument. It is the cry of a young wife facing an awful loss. She is not sinfully distrusting God; she is clinging to her hope in God's love in the midst of her pain. For this reason, (b) is not the best answer. Affirm what is true, and then pray for her and for Dave.

After you pray with Hannah and then sit quietly for ten minutes, a doctor enters the room and asks to speak with Hannah. Hannah asks if you can stay in the room during the conversation, and the doctor agrees. The doctor introduces herself as Dr. Suarez, the chief intensivist, a physician who works full time for the hospital overseeing all the medical care in the intensive care unit.

Dr. Suarez says, "Mrs. Wilson, I have been watching your husband's case carefully since he came to the ICU three days ago. I'm afraid that I don't have any good news to report. The injury that he sustained to his head is so severe that he is never going to regain consciousness. While we can keep his heart and lungs functioning even with a profound brain injury, we can't do anything to reverse what happened to his head. We don't have to make any decisions right now, but later today I will need you to tell me what Dave would want. As his wife, you have the legal authority to speak for him about his treatment. I'm very sorry that it falls to you, but when I return after lunch I'll want you to say whether Dave would want to keep all these machines on. The machines can't do anything to cure him, and it is possible that he would not want to be kept alive in this condition."

Hannah, pale and with a blank expression, says, "Thank you, Doctor." Then she sits down and resumes crying. The doctor takes Hannah's hand, waits a couple of minutes, and then says, "I'm so sorry this is happening. I'll be back in a couple of hours," and leaves the room.

Almost as soon as the door closes, Hannah wails, "I hate that doctor! She has already given up on my Dave." A few minutes later, more calmly, Hannah says, "Will you help me fight to keep Dave alive? I just *know* that God is going to work a miracle. If I give up now, it will show that I don't trust God and don't love Dave."

Question 2C: What Should You Say to Hannah Now?

Answer (a): "How could the doctor be so heartless? I will do everything I can to help you protect Dave. The doctor clearly doesn't care about Dave as a person; she just sees a problem that she doesn't want to deal with any longer than necessary."

Answer (b): "I wish the doctor had stayed longer so that you could ask questions. You and I know how much you love Dave, and that is why it is right for the doctor to ask you to make decisions for him. I know Dave from church, but not as well as I would like. Can you tell me more about him?"

Answer (c): "This is going to be a serious test of your faith, Hannah. The doctor and probably other people from the hospital are going to ask you to allow them to act as if God doesn't have the power to heal Dave. You will have to be strong and push back against their faithless plans."

Commentary on the Answers to Question 2C

Hannah is certainly right that God is able to heal Dave. The doctor is also right that Hannah should be the one to speak for Dave when decisions are needed about his care. Sadly, it is unlikely that Dave and Hannah have talked much about what he would want, so Hannah will need to do her best to imagine how Dave would decide how long to keep his body functioning without a medical reason to think that he will ever regain consciousness. Even though Dave also believes that God can do wondrous things, he may not want the machines left on merely to keep him alive in his current condition.

Right now, though, is not the time to ask Hannah to think through the hardest choices. With more than an hour before the doctor returns, it would be better to get her talking about Dave. The way she talks about him will help both of you get closer to understanding what he would want. Thus, the best answer is (b).

Concerning answers (a) and (c), not enough is known yet about what the doctor needs to have decided or what she will recommend. This means that answer (a) runs too far ahead of the discussion. The same is true of (c), but for a different reason. It is possible that medicine can no longer help Dave, and if God wills that he be healed, he doesn't need anyone to make time or space for him to do it. God also is not hindered by Hannah's faith, whether strong or weak. Praying for healing is appropriate, and Hannah should be encouraged to ask for it.

But she should also be encouraged to ask that God's will be done. It may not be God's will to restore Dave to health. You can help Hannah by gently connecting the request for healing with the desire for God's will to be done.

Prayers for "miraculous" healing in the hospital are common. They are typically a source of frustration for medical personnel, but not because doctors and nurses don't believe that God has the power to heal. Both Christian and non-Christian doctors are dismayed when families focus all their attention on the possibility of a miracle. They are dismayed because too often, focusing on a miracle leads families to withdraw from thinking through all the decisions that the medical team has to make. All doctors are frustrated by things that get in the way of families' helping them choose what their loved one would have wanted. As you pray with Hannah for Dave's recovery, you can also be helping all those caring for him by encouraging her to give a clear account of what Dave would want.

Over the course of the next two hours, Hannah tells you about Dave. You learn about how they met; about Dave's delight in their children; about the pleasure he took in helping others do their taxes; and about his love for physically demanding (and dangerous) recreation. You learn that Hannah had always been nervous watching as Dave performed his stunts, and that she had been dreading an accident just like the one that happened. It appears that Hannah is tempted to blame herself for Dave's condition. More than once she asks, "Would he be lying there if I had told him that he *had* to stop?"

When the doctor returns to talk about what might come next in Dave's treatment, Hannah is clearly tired, but also relieved that the wait is over. Dr. Suarez says, "My review of your husband's condition is not hopeful. The damage to his brain is extensive, and I can find no record of someone with his degree of injury regaining consciousness. Because he was in good shape before the injury, our machines here could keep his heart and lungs functioning for weeks or even months. But I do not believe he will ever wake up. I'm very sorry we cannot do anything more than keep him comfortable. I recommend that you allow us to turn the machines off. We will take care that he doesn't suffer as he passes."

Hannah asks what you think, and you ask both Hannah and Dr. Suarez if you can talk to Dr. Suarez privately. They agree, and you step outside the room.

Question 2D: What Should You Say to Dr. Suarez Now?

Answer (a): "I think you are asking far too much of Hannah right now. Earlier you heard her say that she is praying for a miracle, but your summary of the situation ignored her faith entirely. It must be evident to you that Hannah is seriously pro-life, and yet you are asking her to let you kill her husband by turning off the machines. How can you be so insensitive to her religious convictions?"

Answer (b): "Based on what I know about Dave, he would be able to accept that he's never going to leave this bed. He wouldn't want to cling to his earthly life just for the sake of lying in a hospital bed. He knows that Jesus died on the cross for his sins, so he wouldn't fear death and the judgment that will come to all of us after it. I will help you convince Hannah to approve your recommendation to turn the machines off. You can make it easier for her by showing that you understand that he will be going to be with Jesus."

Answer (c): "Thank you for giving such a clear picture of Dave's situation. It is very sad, but it is also a lot to take in. Is it possible to delay making this decision in order to make sure you are right and to help Hannah accept what is happening?"

Commentary on the Answers to Question 2D

All three of these answers have merit. They all ask the doctor to be more thoughtful about what is happening to Hannah and how difficult it would be for Hannah to agree to turn the machines off so quickly. If Dave were able to speak for himself, it would be biblically permissible for him to agree to turn the machines off. The physical and spiritual burdens that come with staying on the machines are very great, and the medical equipment cannot be an effective means of restoring his ability to choose for himself or enjoy ordinary spiritual and physical goods.

Hannah has the authority to speak for Dave to authorize turning off the machines, but she is nowhere close to making that decision. Centering her thinking on the possibility of a miracle has been an important part of dealing with her grief. The doctor should have seen this and taken it into account. So answer (a) would be truthful. Even so, answer (a) would not help either Hannah or Dr. Suarez. They will need to agree in order to move forward with Dave's care, and rebuking the doctor will not make that more likely.

For a similar reason, answer (b) is not best. Everyone needs to hear the gospel, including Dr. Suarez. If she is a believer, she might find the reminder about Christ's work helpful. If she is not a believer, it might be the first time she has heard the gospel expressed clearly. Either way, she is likely to resent your attempt to use this crisis to force her to listen to you preach. You will probably convince the doctor that she should try to talk with Hannah without your interference. That would not help Hannah.

The best answer is (c), since it gently asks the doctor to help in finding a way to walk with Hannah at a pace she can handle. It is likely that the doctor will recognize that she has the power to give Hannah both time and needed information. The doctor could explain to Hannah what specific evidence they both might be looking for to determine whether there is a medical reason to think Dave will regain consciousness. While you are joining Hannah in praying for a miracle, you can encourage Hannah to allow the doctor to focus her professional attention on what medicine can do. Together, Hannah and the doctor can identify two or three easy-to-read measurements of Dave's condition and set a schedule for checking to see whether those numbers are improving.[3] Periodically meeting with the doctor to check Dave's

---

3. It is likely that the doctor's judgment in Ben's case uses the Glasgow Coma Scale, which assesses eye opening, verbal responses, and motor responses from 1 (no response) to 5 (best). Fully conscious people score a 15. Scores of 8 or less are

numbers and discuss what they mean to the doctor will give Hannah time to adjust to what is happening. The purpose of the pause is not to give God time to work. God will be doing exactly as he wills in Dave's body and Hannah's heart the entire time.

Epilogue

The doctor was relieved to have a way to reset her relationship with Hannah. At their next meeting, the doctor showed Hannah the monitors that she was depending on to tell her how Dave was doing. She answered Hannah's questions about how the numbers on the monitors would change if Dave started to regain consciousness. They agreed to discuss his condition every twelve hours or so. Hannah continued to pray for Dave's recovery, and she did not notice that her confidence in the doctor's judgment was growing. Three days after his accident, Hannah was exhausted, but she no longer doubted the doctor's desire to care for Dave. When the doctor came to discuss the latest numbers, Hannah asked which machines would be turned off if she thought Dave would want it. The doctor explained what the process would involve but did not press the matter. The next day, Hannah had the medical team turn off the machines as she read to Dave from Psalm 116. Dave died a few minutes later.

STORY 3: EVELYN'S HEART

Evelyn is the 72-year-old mother of your best friend, Dan. A believer mature in the Lord, Evelyn lost her husband to a stroke ten years ago. She lives in southern California, as does Dan, her youngest son. Her two other sons live in Alaska. Four years ago, Evelyn began

---

comatose, and those below 7 are unlikely ever to regain consciousness. For a simple description of the Glasgow Coma Scale, see http://www.mdcalc.com/glasgow-coma -scale-score/. While the Glasgow Scale is quantitative, the number is the result of three professional estimates of response. Ideally, the doctor would be able to direct Hannah's attention to numbers generated by the monitors measuring Ben's bodily functions. For more on recovery from coma, see http://www.rainbowrehab.com /pages/understanding-stages-coma/.

to show signs of dementia, and over the last few months her energy and endurance have diminished. The decline of her memory and reasoning ability has been slow and gradual, but now her doctor often thinks she is decisionally incapable. She is sometimes (but not always) unable to give informed consent to her doctor's recommendations. This became an issue when her doctor needed her to make a decision about replacing one of her heart valves.

The doctor recommended the valve replacement because he believed that both Evelyn's loss of energy and her dementia were made worse by poor blood flow. At 72, she is young enough that the valve replacement may restore her strength and cognitive abilities. The doctor and his colleagues estimate that there is a 40 percent chance of "success" for the operation, meaning a clear improvement in both thinking and energy. On the day that the doctor proposed the valve-replacement operation, Evelyn was having a good day mentally. According to the doctor (and the nurse who was in the exam room), Evelyn asked questions that showed that she knew what was being proposed and gave clear consent. The surgery was scheduled before Dan heard anything about it. The procedure would be expensive, and it could even go beyond the "lifetime maximum benefit" for Evelyn's health insurance.

Question 3A: Dan Asks, "I'm Not Sure Whether This Surgery Is the Right Thing. What Should I Do?" What Should You Say Now?

Answer (a): "This is your mother's decision to make if the doctor believes she is able to make it. If you think she is overlooking important considerations, you should find a way to bring them to her attention without suggesting that it should be up to you and not her."

Answer (b): "Your mother's doctor is taking advantage of her. He will get paid for the procedure and she will be financially ruined, all for a slim chance of slight recovery. You should tell her not to trust the doctor and to get a second opinion."

Answer (c): "Your mother has a biblical obligation to have the surgery. Without it, she will continue to decline. The money should be no concern because God will provide it, somehow."

Commentary on the Answers to Question 3A

Even though Dan is eager to make sure that his mother gets all the care possible, it is her decision to make. Answer (a) is the best response. If either Dan or his mother has concrete reasons for thinking that the doctor is giving bad advice for the sake of making money, or if they are unsure what the surgery will accomplish, Dan should recommend getting a second opinion. Second opinions can be valuable when the decision has grave consequences or questions remain. When the questions have been answered, however, a second opinion can complicate matters without shedding any new light. Because Dan has no reason to believe that the doctor is taking advantage of his mother, answer (b) is not best. Answer (c) is the worst option here. Scripture does not say that Evelyn is obligated to get the surgery. She may choose to have the surgery, but she does not have a duty to choose it. The money advice in answer (c) is also misguided. While it is true that God will provide for all of Evelyn's needs, Evelyn is still responsible to make prudent decisions about her resources. She may choose the surgery if she has the resources to afford it, but she must not promise to pay for the surgery and then expect God to provide money that she does not have. In chapter 6, more will be said about the role of money in decisions like the one that Evelyn is facing here.

Dan decides not to question his mother's decision because the doctor has insisted that she knew what she was doing when she approved it. Not long after the surgery, Evelyn's new valve begins to leak. On the one hand, the operation has shown that her dementia was related to her heart function. She quickly regained her ability to reason, remember, and join in conversations after the surgery. And now, as a result of the leak, her dementia problems have returned. On the other hand, the leaking valve has left Evelyn worse off physically and mentally than she was before the surgery. In order to monitor her condition, her doctor admits Evelyn to the hospital. Time in the hospital, it is thought, will enable her to regain enough strength to undergo a follow-up operation to repair the leak. Everyone agrees to focus on the goal of gaining back this strength.

After Evelyn's husband died, she had signed a "Living Will" form. It says that she wants "no extraordinary measures" to be taken to keep her alive. Now the doctors want Dan to get his mother to execute a "Durable Power of Attorney for Health Care Decisions" that names Dan as her agent (the legal decision-maker). The doctors want this form in her medical records so that they can get consent from Dan rather than waiting for Evelyn to have "good" days. They are not looking for a way to go against her wishes. They simply want to be able to act quickly in giving her care, and Dan would be able to give answers right away. The law allows them to go to court to get Evelyn declared incompetent; but the process is long, the judge may not agree, and it is clear that Evelyn trusts Dan to speak for her. Dan knows that his mother will agree if he asks her to sign the document that would make him her agent, but he is troubled.

Question 3B: Dan Asks You, "Why Are the Doctors Asking Me to Do This? Are They Tired of Dealing with My Mother? It Seems They Are Asking Me to Trick Her into Signing Away Her Authority. Would It Be Wrong to Do What They Ask?"

Answer (a): "The doctors want to be able to act quickly if your mother needs it. Their request is driven by their desire to do what is best for her, but only if she would want it. If you are her legal agent, they will know that they can get her consent quickly through you. But you should explain this to your mother and ask her to let you do it for her. No tricking should be needed if you are patient."

Answer (b): "You should not worry about tricking your mother into signing it. Her reasoning ability makes her effectively a child. Just as it is okay to win a child's agreement by telling only the happy part of a story, it is okay for you to get her signature by whatever means necessary. The doctors want you to do this because they know she will trust you. It is for her good."

Answer (c): "The doctors are likely frustrated because they have to spend a long time getting your mother's consent. They want you to get her to sign the power over to you so that they will not have to spend that time. Don't trick her if you can avoid it, but her care will be improved if you get her to sign the form."

Commentary on the Answers to Question 3B

Dan is certainly in a difficult spot here. It is reasonable for the doctors to want to be able to get decisions quickly in order to give Evelyn the best possible care. Dan's fear that the doctors are asking him to trick his mother is misplaced, however. Sometimes hospital personnel forget how strange it is to ask a loved one to give the power to choose to someone else. In their eagerness to make care go smoothly, they can push too hard for the conversation to happen. No one has told Dan to trick his mother into agreeing. Dan is simply afraid that he will not be able to explain things clearly enough, making it necessary to trick her in order to get her consent. Answer (a) is the best response here. Answers (b) and (c) are both inferior. Answer (b) advises Dan not to honor his mother; answer (c) accuses the doctors of a lack of professional commitment to Evelyn without any evidence. Their request that Dan talk with Evelyn about giving him the authority to choose for her is standard hospital practice. If Dan seizes an opportunity when Evelyn is as clear-thinking as possible and carefully explains what he wants and the need, she will give him the authority without being tricked.

It means waiting until the next day, but Dan finds a time when his mother is able to understand what it would mean to sign the form enabling him to make decisions if she cannot. Because he has questioned her doctors about the kinds of decisions that might be needed soon, Dan also talks with Evelyn about the meaning of her living will.

He finds out that "no extraordinary measures" include CPR if her heart stops. It also means that she does not want to be intubated to maintain her breathing unless the doctors are confident that it will be only a temporary measure. If tubes are needed to make her well enough to leave the hospital, she will put up with them.

Encouraged by direct instructions, Dan feels ready to speak for his mother if he is needed. It was hard to start the conversation, but it turns out to be just in time. Evelyn will not have another "good" day mentally. Within hours of their conversation, the doctor asks Dan to authorize a do-not-resuscitate order for his mother. He agrees to it without hesitation. She has told him that it is what she wishes. The doctor also asks about a DNI (do not intubate) order. Dan says, "Not yet." He remembers that his mother said that tubes are okay if their use is temporary.

Over the next two days, Evelyn's condition deteriorates. She develops headaches that can be managed only by aggressive pain medicine. On top of this, she becomes anxious. In her sleep she mutters jumbled words about things that have been lost, and both waking and sleeping she picks at the bedclothes or the tubes from the IV stand. Out of concern that her fretfulness is degrading her chances of recovery, Evelyn's doctor prescribes antianxiety medicine to calm her down. When the medicines for pain and anxiety take effect, Evelyn is finally able to sleep.

Sleep is not enough to turn the tide for Evelyn. In the middle of the third night after her last "good" day, Evelyn's breathing becomes labored. The doctor on call discovers that Evelyn's lungs are filling with fluid. Concerned that her medications are making it harder for her to breathe, the on-call doctor stops them. He leaves a note on Evelyn's chart about this change and orders that she be placed on the ventilator. When the day shift takes over the next morning, Evelyn is confused, agitated, and grimacing in pain. When Dan arrives at the hospital later that morning, his mother's eyes are closed and she is asleep, but the struggles of the night before are still evident on her face. The nurses walk him through what has happened, and he is angry.

Question 3C: Dan Asks You, "What Can I Do to Make Sure the Doctor from Last Night Is Punished for Putting My Mother through All That Pain and Distress? Did This Happen Because I Wasn't Here to Protect Her?"

Answer (a): "It is frustrating that the on-call doctor added to your mother's suffering, but the aim was to help her breathe. Focusing your energy on "punishing" the doctor will not help your mother, and it will only make things worse for you. Your mother is resting peacefully now. Make her the center of your concern. When this is all over, I will help you express your displeasure with what happened last night."

Answer (b): "You can't be here all the time, and we learned last night that the doctors can't be trusted to keep your mother from having her pain increased unnecessarily. I am willing to take turns with you so that someone will always be here to keep an eye on her. I can call you if anyone starts making changes that increase her pain."

Answer (c): "Since it is impractical to transfer your mother to another hospital, we need to make a priority of reporting the on-call doctor to the chief medical officer at this hospital and filing a complaint with the medical executive committee. The other doctors will hear about it and know that they had better avoid a repeat of last night."

Commentary on the Answers to Question 3C

Answer (c) would be appropriate only if the on-call doctor had been drunk, violent, or so incompetent that the nurses were openly questioning the doctor's orders. None of these things happened, so answer (c) is the weakest of the options. Dan is right to be grieved that his mother had such a painful, anxious night. The doctor probably should have known her situation better before making changes to her treatment, but the doctor's aim was Evelyn's good. Dan should plan to express his concerns about the doctor's decision at some later date and as part of an overall assessment of the care that his mother received. In the midst of Evelyn's crises, Dan should focus his energy on managing the next difficulty that will arise. Answer (b) looks noble, but answer (a) is still better. Both you and Dan should be making Evelyn's good the center of your concern. Posting a suspicious guard in the room will not change any doctor's behavior, so it will not improve Evelyn's care. The change in the visitation pattern will not be noticed by the doctor at all, but it will be noticed by the nurses. Making Evelyn's room the one "with the friend looking for mistakes" will make it harder for the nurses to look forward to visiting Evelyn. Adding that complication to the relationship between Evelyn and the nursing staff is not worth the cost. The best answer is (a).

Throughout his mother's time in the hospital, Dan has called each of his brothers every day to give them an update on her condition. Until she was put on the ventilator, all had been hopeful that she would rally and be able to get the leaking heart valve repaired. Now that seems unlikely. Low blood flow has contributed to increased dementia and opened her up to the infection attacking her lungs. With so many things going wrong, the doctors have asked Dan to agree that the goal for her care should change from getting fit for surgery to staying as comfortable as possible in her last days. The doctor cannot say just how much longer she will live, but Dan should expect her physical condition to diminish steadily no matter what is done.

Dan doesn't want to make the decision to alter the goal of his mother's care on his own. He wants his brothers' advice, but he knows they will ask questions that he doesn't know how to answer. Dan's brothers both live on tight budgets, and Dan is sure that they will want to know if they should make plans to fly down to see their mother before she dies. Buying tickets on short notice would be expensive. If they knew she would live for two more weeks, they could schedule flights that were easier to afford.

Question 3D: Dan Asks, "Should I Urge My Brothers to Pay the Extra Money to Get Here in the Next Few Days? Or Should I Just Encourage Them to Get Here Sometime Soon?"

I Doubt Our Mother Would Want Them to Pay a Lot Just to Get Here. Should That Matter?"

Answer (a): "You should tell them to get here as soon as possible, regardless of the costs. Even if your mother would *say* that she didn't want them to spend a lot of money to get here, we should assume that what she would want most is to see them again before she dies."

Answer (b): "You should tell them to get tickets they can afford, if they can afford tickets at all. Your mother is close to death. She would not want them to spend a lot of money, and she probably wouldn't want them to remember her in her current frail, sickly state. Honoring your mother means following what you know she would want."

Answer (c): "You should tell them that while you can't order them to do anything, your advice is that they get to your mother as soon as they feasibly can. Your mother's condition is deteriorating rapidly. The grief of losing your mother will be serious no matter what, but adding regret about not seeing her before she died would make the grieving period more difficult. She would not want money to be thrown away, but she would also want you to recover from her death quickly. Getting here soon is part of what she would want."

Commentary on the Answers to Question 3D

The best response here is answer (c). Dan has indicated that Evelyn would want her sons to see her one more time before she dies. Even if Evelyn had expressed no wishes about their visiting, Dan knows that she would want their grief at her death to be minimal. Seeing her one more time will enable Dan's brothers to make sense of her death as painlessly as possible. Answer (a) is inferior to (c) because Dan knows that his mother would give the cost serious consideration. She would not want the boys to come no matter what it cost them. The weakest answer is (b). It makes the unwarranted assumption that Evelyn wouldn't want her boys to see her in her current sick condition. If Evelyn had told Dan to keep his brothers away for this reason, he would be obligated to consider it. Even then, he should push back. Keeping them away for this reason would hurt her peace as the end approached. It would also deprive the brothers of a last opportunity to honor her and to begin grieving their loss of her.

Dan's brothers drop everything, pay the higher fares, and are scheduled to arrive in southern California late on the following day. Dan asks the doctors whether she will still be alive when they get there. The medical team has just met to review her condition. They are confident that the ventilator will keep her breathing that long, but they can't guarantee that her heart will hold up. They ask whether Dan wants to suspend the DNR order until his brothers get there. They aren't sure that a resuscitation attempt would work, but they are willing to attempt it if that is what Evelyn would want.

Although Dan knows that his brothers would be sad if she were dead when they arrived, he is pretty sure that his mother would not want the traumatic attempt made just so that they could see her. He thinks that she would say no to a resuscitation attempt if she could make the choice. So he tells the doctors to keep the DNR order in place. He continues to pray that it is God's will that she be healed completely. Now he adds the prayer that she not die before his brothers get there.

When Dan makes the decision to leave the DNR order in place, the doctor asks whether Dan has thought about when it would be time to turn the ventilator off. Dan has relayed Evelyn's wish to use "tubes" on only a temporary basis, and the doctor wonders how Dan will know that the ventilator's temporary function has been fulfilled. Dan is perplexed, and before he can respond, the doctor continues, "You don't need to have an answer now. As you think about my question, please consider letting me run a 'time-limited trial' to see if there is a medical reason to think she will recover."[4] Dan doesn't know what the doctor

---

4. See Timothy E. Quill and Robert Holloway, "Time-Limited Trials near the End of Life," *Journal of the American Medical Association* 306, 13 (October 3, 2011): 1483–84. See also Amy Abernathy and David C. Currow, "Letters: Time-Limited Trials," *Journal of the American Medical Association* 307, 1 (January 4, 2012): 33–34 (with reply from Quill and Holloway). The use of time-limited trials was recommended to

is talking about, so the doctor explains that a time-limited trial would involve defining clear numerical signs that the ventilator is allowing his mother to gain strength. The medical team would carefully measure her body's current ability to get oxygen into her blood and to deliver that blood to her vital organs to fight infections and repair damage. All those functions have numbers associated with them. After twenty-four and forty-eight hours, the measurements would be taken again. If the numbers improved to levels that they would define at the outset, they would know that the ventilator is making it possible for her to recover. Dan isn't sure how helpful this approach will be, but he agrees to having them start the process.

When Dan's brothers arrive at the hospital the next day, Evelyn is asleep in the ICU. She is still on the ventilator, but her color has returned and she no longer shows signs of distress. As the brothers talk around her bed, she opens her eyes. The ventilator makes it impossible to speak, but she smiles in a way that shows some recognition. Dan is excited to see her response, and relieved that he can now lean on his brothers when the doctors ask for decisions.

Dan needs his brothers' help right away. Evelyn falls back to sleep just as the doctor comes into the room to discuss the meaning of the measurements taken at the twenty-four-hour point in the time-limited trial. Dan has not said anything to his brothers about the trial approach, and the doctor carefully walks through it with them. The doctor also reports that the data they have just gathered shows no sign of improvement. It is important to wait another twenty-four hours before making any big decisions, but the numbers would have to jump dramatically for the outlook to be hopeful. If the ventilator is not supporting improvement, the medical team will recommend that it be withdrawn.

Over the next twenty-four hours, Dan and his brothers stay at their mother's bedside, talking and praying. Evelyn does not open her eyes again. Instead, she becomes increasingly restless. More than once, the nurses have to increase the drip rate on her pain medicine to decrease

---

me by R. Henry Williams, MD

the signs of pain. The nurses do not say what these changes might mean, but Dan and his brothers don't think that increasing pain is a good sign.

When the doctor comes to discuss the forty-eight-hour numbers, the brothers are not surprised when the news is bad. Dan has told them what numbers the doctor has said would be clear evidence that she is improving. Even without an explanation from the doctor, they can see that the numbers are nowhere near what they need to be. Because Dan has been in the hospital long enough to ask the nurses what the various monitors are for, he knows that some of the numbers the doctors were tracking are on display near his mother's bed. He has been secretly watching to see whether they would approach the target values. Since they have not improved, he is ready when the bad news comes.

The doctor waits for the brothers to absorb the results. Then he turns to Dan and asks whether he knows what his mother would want done now. Dan says that he thinks so, but asks for an hour to talk it through with his brothers to be sure. The doctor agrees to return in an hour or so. After half an hour of crying, praying, and talking through what their mother would want, they are confident that she would not want the ventilator to be her permanent support. They know that once the ventilator is turned off, she will not last long. They don't know whether she will wake up again, but if she does, they want to be ready. They devise a plan that feels right to them, but none of them is sure that it is biblically sound.

Dan wants to know whether God's Word permits him to carry out his plan for the last part of his mother's life. While the medical team is preparing to remove the tube for the ventilator, he and his brothers will read aloud Evelyn's favorite Bible passages: Romans 8 and Psalm 23. As the team withdraws the ventilator, they will sing her favorite hymn, "Beneath the Cross of Jesus." Then they will pray silently as the team determines whether she will breathe on her own. If she fights to breathe, they will stop praying and give soft words of encouragement. If the doctors say that she is not going to make it, they will take turns telling her that they love her and that she should greet Jesus for them when he takes her home.

Question 3E: What Do You Think of This Plan?

Answer (a): It is beautiful.

Answer (b): It shows a lack of faith.

Answer (c): No amount of Scripture-reading and hymn-singing can change the fact that the brothers are killing their mother.

Commentary on the Answers to Question 3E

Answer (c) is the worst because it is cruel, insensitive, and biblically unwarranted. The plan is to discontinue treatment that is excessively burdensome. Evelyn is likely to die—but the complications in her heart and lungs are what will kill her, not discontinuing the treatment. Answer (b) is also deficient. It presumes to know that if Evelyn's loved ones had more faith, then they would have the courage to do something different. The best answer is (a). The brothers are choosing as Evelyn would choose, not only in discontinuing the treatment but also in the way they are going to use the occasion of her last ordeal to worship together. Whatever part of the plan that Evelyn is able to comprehend as they carry it out will delight her. The plan is beautiful because they will be glorying in their shared hope, which is exactly what she would have chosen if she could.

Epilogue

In the small hours of the next morning, Evelyn went to be with Jesus. She left this life hearing her sons singing over her and expressing their own confidence in Christ's work on her behalf. They were sad and emotionally spent when they left the hospital, but Dan had no regrets about the choices he had made. He knew that his mother would have made the same choices if she had been assured that they were biblically sound. He was satisfied that God's Word had allowed every decision he made.

STORY 4: TRIPLETS IN PERIL[5]

Katie and Steve are members of your church. They have been married for four years when they finally succeed in conceiving. It is success in triplicate: they are thrilled to discover that Katie is carrying three boys, identical triplets. The pregnancy develops normally for triplets. Katie is especially sick early on, but once the morning sickness passes, it is simply exciting.

During a routine ultrasound in Katie's eighteenth week, the radiologist determines that one of the boys is no longer developing normally. A more detailed scan is performed. Katie and Steve learn that all three of the boys are in the same sac, so all three share the same amniotic fluid. They also discover that the smallest one is dying. Katie and Steve agree to call this boy Trey, and they begin praying that God will reverse his decline and restore him to health.

The doctor leading the team caring for Katie and the boys schedules a meeting to discuss what should be done next. Katie and Steve ask you to be there for the meeting, and you agree to join them.[6]

---

5. The events described in this story occurred nearly ten years before the publication of this book. The medical options available in 2017 are more extensive than they were for the parents in this story. Advances in neonatal medicine and surgical techniques for children still in the womb may make the advice given to these parents seem too quick or insensitive to the parents' pro-life convictions. At the time the events happened, the medical options were limited to those described. The story is included to illustrate the role that the principles offered in this book can play in extreme circumstances.

6. It would be surprising if Katie and Steve have talked with this doctor before this difficult discussion. The doctor involved is likely to be an employee of the hospital, probably a neonatologist. The doctor who has been overseeing Katie's pregnancy maintains a private (OB/Gyn) practice. Katie and Steve have also been to see a private-practice pediatrician, the doctor who will be caring for the babies after they are born. While the neonatologist will have read the OB/Gyn's notes on the pregnancy, it is unlikely that the private-practice doctors will have visited the hospital or talked by phone with the neonatologist. Medical-payment systems no longer give private-practice doctors a financial incentive to visit people in the hospital. As a result, decisions in the hospital are often made with doctors that the family is meeting for the first time. For more on this aspect of the relationship between doctors and those they serve today, see chapter 7.

From the outset, the tone of the meeting is serious. The doctor has discussed the situation with his colleagues earlier in the day.[7] They have agreed that the situation is dangerous for all three of the boys. They have explained that one baby's death will quickly make the surrounding amniotic fluid they share a threat to the other babies. As far as the medical team can tell, Trey is dying. His decline has been steady since it was first noticed, and the team believes that they can predict within an hour the time he will die. Their current estimate is that it will happen around midnight tonight. As awful as it will be to have Trey die, the doctors are worried about the safety of the other two boys. If the team waits until they are sure that Trey is dead before they take steps to remove him from Katie's womb, they will not be able to get his body out before he makes their shared sac unable to support the continued development of the other two boys. None of the boys has developed far enough to survive outside the womb, so if the team does not act before Trey dies, all three babies are likely to die.

The doctor proposes that the team control the time of Trey's death, removing him before his death in order to keep him from poisoning the environment for his brothers. He concedes that Trey will die when the team removes him, but he believes it is necessary to protect the healthy boys.

The doctor asks whether the situation is clear. Katie and Steve say that they understand, but want to know how soon they will need to decide what they want to do. The doctor replies that they can wait until an hour before the team must know, but that after that, it will be too late to assemble the personnel and equipment needed to remove Trey before he dies on his own.

The doctor leaves to give Katie and Steve time to discuss the

---

7. The team of caregivers that the neonatologist has consulted probably includes some of the advanced-practice nurses involved with the case, along with doctors doing their residency in maternity. For more on the increased role of advanced-practice nurses and physician assistants, see John J. Perry, "The Rise and Impact of Nurse Practitioners and Physician Assistants on Their Own and Cross-Occupation Incomes," *Contemporary Economic Policy* 27, 4 (2009): 491–511.

proposal. At their request, you pray for them, asking God to give Katie and Steve wisdom and peace through this trial, and that even now Trey would be restored to health. After the prayer, Steve looks at Katie, who nods gravely. Steve then says, "We desperately want to have children, and it appears that we must go along with the doctor's proposal if we want to have any."

Question 4: Steve Asks You, "What Do You Think of the Doctor's Proposal?"

Answer (a): "What the doctors are proposing asks you to deny your confidence in God's goodness. They say they are sure that Trey will threaten his brothers, but they can't *know* that. We ought to wait for Trey to die on his own and then act as quickly as possible to remove his body. Otherwise, we will be authorizing an *abortion*, and surely that can't be what God wants."

Answer (b): "What a heavy burden you are being asked to bear here, both of you! I think if we could ask Trey what he would want, he would say that he would rather die an hour earlier than have his brothers die also. I can't speak for Trey, but as his parents you can. The doctors aren't asking if you want them to kill Trey. They are asking you whether you think Trey would approve of their proposal. If you think Trey would approve if he could understand the proposal and speak, then I think you can approve of the plan."

Answer (c): "Steve, it appears that you are making an idol of having children. You are willing to kill one of your children in order to feed the idol of parenthood. I can understand that you are afraid to be childless, but God clearly condemns putting your own desires ahead of obeying his commands. We should only be trusting God to heal Trey. If it is God's will for you to have children, he will deliver them through this crisis. Let's pray together again that Trey will be healed and tell the doctors that we are trusting God rather than human 'wisdom.'"

Commentary on the Answers to Question 4

Humanly speaking, Trey is going to die within the next few hours. God certainly has the power to heal him immediately; and if it is God's will that Trey's condition should turn around dramatically, it will also be God's will that the change is made evident to the medical staff. No matter what else is happening, it will be appropriate to continue to pray that Trey might be spared. In this case, as in many other circumstances, fervent prayer can be accompanied by taking steps to act prudently if God does not supernaturally intervene.

One part of answer (c) is that Steve, Katie, and you continue praying. That part of the answer is correct. The focus of answer (c), however, is a rebuke, and that part is inappropriate at this point in the crisis. It is possible that Steve and Katie are excessively in love with the idea of having children. Their love for the idea may even be a kind of idolatry, making a genuine good (children) into an ultimate good.[8] But Steve's admission that he and Katie are "desperate" could only be a righteous cry of anguish. A desire for children is biblically sound; their hearts would have to be made of stone *not* to be broken by Trey's imminent death and the threat to the other boys. Answer (c) overreads what Steve is saying and only adds further grief to a sad situation.[9]

Seizing on Steve's cry of despair as the key to the choice they are facing is a mistake. But that does not mean that it would be biblically *wrong* for Steve and Katie to reject the doctor's proposal. Praying fervently for Trey's recovery is biblically praiseworthy. Choosing not to hasten Trey's death—even by an hour—and praying in faith that God will protect Trey's brothers is also consistent with biblical teaching. If, in the end, Steve and Katie do not experience the beginnings of peace about the doctor's proposal, you can give them biblical comfort that God's love and care for them and their children is beyond anything

8. For a biblical description of idolatry as excessive love of something good in itself, see Timothy Keller, *Counterfeit Gods: The Empty Promises of Money, Sex, and Power, and the Only Hope That Matters* (New York: Penguin, 2011).

9. It is permissible for Steve and Katie to be angry and hurting. For practical (and concise) advice about caring for people facing loss, see Barbara M. Roberts, *Helping Those Who Hurt* (Colorado Springs: NavPress, 2009), especially 93ff.

they can imagine. Together you can wait to see what the Lord will do as you all watch and pray. I did not think this the best answer at the time, but I am confident that it would have been a biblically permissible response to the doctor's proposal.

Answer (a)'s use of the word *abortion* will only make it more difficult for Steve and Katie to deal with this crisis—both now and every time they look back on this dark hour. While it is technically correct that the doctor is proposing to "abort" Trey's development, that proposal is significantly different from the abortions that pro-life people such as Steve and Katie know to be contrary to God's law.[10] Attaching the label *abortion* to the doctor's proposal ignores all those important differences, forcing Steve and Katie to see themselves as killers if they agree to the proposal.

The doctor is not asking Steve and Katie to *initiate* Trey's death, or to treat Trey as less than a person made in God's image. If that were the proposal, then using the term *abortion* might force everyone to see things in the proper light. The proposal would ask Steve and Katie to violate God's law. That is not what the doctor is proposing. Steve and Katie have done nothing to bring Trey close to death, and if Trey posed no threat to his brothers—if he were simply in a separate amniotic sac!—then they would be fighting to keep him alive as long as possible. It is not helpful to use *abortion* to describe what the doctor is proposing.

Answer (b) is the best of the three, although it doesn't remove all the pain and grief. Even though it is biblically permissible for Steve and Katie to approve the doctor's proposal, they are not biblically obligated to approve it. Steve and Katie are facing a situation in which more than one course of action is biblically permitted. They have more than one way to honor God's law, and it is important for you as their spiritual shepherd to help them see this.[11] When we are not facing a crisis, it is

10. For a clear description of the medical meaning of *abortion*, see Harvey Marcovitch, *Black's Medical Dictionary* (London: A&C Black Publishers, 2009), 3: "Abortion is defined as the expulsion of a fetus before it is normally viable, usually before 24 weeks of pregnancy."

11. The existence of situations in which more than one path is biblically permitted without any one of them being obligatory is discussed by David Clyde Jones, *Biblical*

usually easy to see that we can keep God's law in more than one way. For example, we can choose to spend disposable income either on a vacation or on concert tickets. If a well-meaning Christian friend said that we had to figure out which use of the income God's law *required* us to choose, we would know that our friend was confused. When we face a momentous choice, however, we more easily believe that God's law must forbid all but one option. Steve and Katie are facing a very serious choice, and it will needlessly add to their burden to suggest that they need to search out God's *one* option when in fact there are many ways to be obedient to Scripture.

Steve and Katie can honor God's law by declining the proposal and waiting, prayerfully depending on the Lord. But that is not their only option. They are also biblically permitted to agree to the proposal on Trey's behalf. To see that this is so, consider an analogous case:[12] Suppose that Trey and his two brothers were adult soldiers, taking shelter in a foxhole when a live grenade landed at their feet. Suppose, further, that Trey's brothers were healthy and that Trey was suffering from the end stages of a terminal illness. If Trey were to throw himself on the grenade, smothering it and taking all its lethal shrapnel in order to save his brothers' lives, we would recognize it as an act of heroism. Trey's action would not be suicide, even though his action hastened his own death. Instead, it would be the highest expression of righteous love that the Bible commends: "Greater love has no one than this, that someone lay down his life for his friends" (John 15:13).

The grenade in the analogy threatened to kill all three of them. Trey was already dying from something else. By diving on the grenade, Trey chose to save his brothers. It was a choice that he was biblically permitted to make, but it is not a choice that he was *obligated* to make. Each of the boys could have righteously focused on saving only himself.

Christian Ethics (Grand Rapids: Baker, 1994). Jones's treatment of God's law is both thoughtful and deeply committed to the inerrancy of God's Word.

12. The pros and cons of considering analogous cases to gain insight into a difficult case are discussed in chapter 1. On the place of casuistry (moral inquiry by considering cases) in medical ethics, see Robin Downie, "Guest Editorial: A Personal View: Health Care Ethics and Casuistry," *Journal of Medical Ethics* 18, 2 (1992): 61–66.

What Trey did in the foxhole analogy was not forbidden, and it was not obligatory; it was simply permitted. His action would be heroic because he made a sacrifice that he was not required to make.[13]

Trey in his mother's womb is in a similar situation. The main difference is that Trey himself is the grenade. If he dies before he is removed from his mother, he will become the bomb that threatens his brothers. If there were a way to ask Trey what he would want, it would be permissible for Trey to volunteer to die a little earlier in order to save his brothers. It would also be permissible for Trey to decline. Trey is neither obligated nor forbidden by Scripture to fall on the grenade for his brothers.

Of course, there is no way to ask Trey what he would want. He is not old enough to understand the proposal that the doctors are making. He is not even old enough to talk. Even if he understood what was being asked, he would not be able to express his wishes.

But Trey is not voiceless. Both the Scriptures and the American courts permit parents to speak for their children.[14] Every state in the United States makes clear provision for this, especially regarding medical treatment. Doctors are required to obtain informed consent before performing any procedure. For children too young to give consent on their own, parents must give the consent. The doctor's proposal in this case will mean invasive medical procedures for both Katie and Trey. Katie can give consent for what will happen to her, and Katie and Steve together can give (or decline) consent for Trey. Just as it would be biblically permissible for grown-up Trey to choose to hasten his own death to protect his brothers from a grenade, it is permissible for Steve and Katie to make the same choice *on Trey's behalf* in this case.

---

13. Stories about self-sacrifice are common in discussions of ethical theory. On the specific problem of self-sacrifice for another, see M. David Litwa, "Self-Sacrifice to Save the Life of Another in Jewish and Christian Traditions," *Heythrop Journal* 50, 6 (November 2009): 912–22.

14. The biblical appropriateness of parents' speaking for their children is discussed in chapter 2. For a recent discussion of the legal power of parents to speak for their children, see Clare Huntington and Elizabeth Scott, "Children's Health in a Legal Framework," *The Future of Children* 25, 1 (2015): 177–97, http://www.jstor.org .ezproxy.covenant.edu/stable/43267768.

Under the pressure imposed by the doctor's request for a decision within one hour, it is likely that Steve and Katie will not be able to come up with the foxhole analogy. It is also unlikely that they will recognize their opportunity to speak for Trey, affirming his almost certain desire to make the sacrifice in order to save his brothers. A spiritually trustworthy friend, however, can help them to see their righteous options more clearly in the midst of a dark situation.

Epilogue

It is the custom in Steve and Katie's church to mark the birth of a covenant child by placing a vase with a single red rose on the lectern next to the worship leader on Sunday morning. Five months after Steve and Katie were presented with the doctor's proposal, the vase on the lectern contained three roses: two red and one white. The red roses were for Trey's brothers, born as healthy identical twins the previous week. The white rose was for Trey, who had given his life an hour early in order that they might live. The congregation had known that Steve and Katie were carrying triplets, and they had been told when Trey died five months earlier. When anyone in the congregation asked what had happened to the third child, Steve and Katie would say, "At twenty weeks, he was dying. His last act was to give up his life for his brothers' safety. We had to tell the doctors for him, and we knew it was what he would want."

STORY 5: PASTOR WITH PARKINSON'S

Sharyl is the oldest daughter of Bruce, a 77-year-old retired PCA pastor. Bruce had to resign his pastoral position three years ago because of his health. Although he is still mentally sharp, he is too weak to do much away from home. The problem that forced him to step aside was the onset of Parkinson's disease. Before that, Bruce had soldiered on through a weak heart (from angina) and difficulty breathing (from emphysema). When the Parkinson's tremors started, he had to resign from his pulpit ministry. Bruce's wife died soon after he retired, and since then he has lived with his daughter Sharyl. A nursing service sends someone every morning and evening to help Bruce with his hygiene needs and to plan his meals for the day. Sharyl does the shopping and takes him to the doctor for his appointments. Bruce keeps busy editing his sermon notes for publication, praying for his former flock, and listening to sports on the radio.

Bruce's doctor has told him how he is likely to die. As the tremors get worse, he will eventually swallow something the wrong way, have a coughing fit that overtaxes his heart, and die from heart failure. While that isn't a pleasant idea, Bruce doesn't want to die in the hospital hooked up to machines. He completed an advance directive asking not to be resuscitated and put the signed document in a prominent place on his desk so that Sharyl could easily find it. The advance directive names Sharyl as his agent for health care decisions, so he is confident that his wishes will be followed.

As it turns out, Bruce's plan does not work. Three months later, he loses consciousness when some friends from church are visiting. Sharyl isn't home; the nurse is not there; and the visitors call 911. The ambulance arrives before the visitors can contact Sharyl, and the EMTs do what they are trained and required to do: Bruce is resuscitated on his living room floor and taken by ambulance to the hospital. Before he can make sense of what is happening, Bruce is admitted to the ICU for observation. He has had a heart attack, but he did not die. Three miserable days later, he is released from the hospital. Physically he is weaker, but he resolves never to return. His doctor estimates that if he is resuscitated again, even if he regains consciousness in the hospital, he will never again be strong enough to return home. He will die in the hospital.

Since that trip to the hospital, Bruce has been enrolled in a hospice service. The change to hospice has not affected his care routine much, but now he sees a clear way to make sure that he won't be taken to the hospital again. His plan is simple, but he isn't certain that it is biblical. He wants to get his family to promise that they will *not* call 911 if he collapses again. More than that, he wants them to practice calling the hospice service instead. Besides Sharyl, Bruce has two other children who live in town, and together they have five grandchildren who are old enough to call an ambulance in an emergency. Their ages are 7, 10, 13, 18, and 22. He wants them to take turns practicing calling the hospice service *and not calling 911* if they find him unconscious. He wants to pretend to be on the floor unconscious and for each of them to show that they know how to check to see whether he is breathing and has a pulse, and then to call the hospice service hotline number no matter what they find. The hospice service has agreed to have someone answer the hotline number to play along with the drill.

In addition to having his family practice calling hospice instead of 911, Bruce wants to ask every visitor to read back to him a short promise that he or she will not call 911 if Bruce collapses while the guest is there. He is worried that even if his family is doing what he wants, a visitor might use a cell phone to call an ambulance. As a final safeguard, Bruce has asked his doctor to fill out an order that can be shown to any EMT saying not to perform CPR or attempt to resuscitate him. (Most states now have forms that are in force even outside the hospital or nursing home. EMTs are trained to follow the orders on these forms if they are shown them in time. Most are called either a "POST" form—for Physicians Orders Scope of Treatment—or a "POLST" form—for Physicians Orders for Life-Sustaining Treatment.[15])

Question 5: Bruce Asks, "Is This Plan Biblically Sound? Is This a Cruel Thing to Do to My Family? Is It Asking Too Much of My Guests?

Answer (a): "The plan is sinful for more than one reason. You are giving up on life when you are still able to do good; and you are asking your family, friends, and doctor to help you kill yourself."

Answer (b): "The plan is biblically permissible, but it is unwise to ask the younger three grandchildren to go through the practice drills that you have in mind. None of these children will be left alone with

15. If there is no legally recognized doctor's order, EMTs are required to resuscitate and stabilize any person they can, regardless of clear oral instructions from family members or written instructions from the person who has collapsed. For a helpful state-by-state listing of these forms, see https://www.everplans.com/articles/state-by-state-polst-forms.

you in your state of health. So having them pretend to find you dead will only distress them and make it harder for them to cherish life in the way God's Word tells us to do. Also, while it is a good idea to anticipate good intentions and cell phone use, it is unkind to force visitors to make a promise as a condition of their visit."

Answer (c): "The plan is sound as it is. You have good reasons to avoid going back to the hospital again. The Bible allows you to decline heroic medical treatment if you are so very close to death anyway. Your family should want to help you keep from having another awful trip to the hospital, so they should be willing to go through the practice. The same is true for any real friends you have, and it is the professional duty of your doctor to write the order if that is what you want."

Commentary on the Answers to Question 5

The best answer is (b), and it means that you will need to help Bruce modify his plan in two big ways. Bruce's desire to eliminate the possibility that someone will call an ambulance is understandable, but his plan imposes significant burdens on his younger grandchildren and his houseguests. Answer (a) is the weakest of the responses, since it calls sinful what the Scriptures permit (declining ineffective or excessively burdensome treatment) and it wrongly asserts that anyone who refrained from calling an ambulance would be *killing* Bruce. Answer (c) is promising, but overlooks the ways that the plan adds needless distress to grandchildren and guests. Answer (c) also overstates the doctor's professional duty. Bruce's doctor should write orders that conform to Bruce's wishes, but only if the doctor believes that those wishes are medically appropriate. In this case, Bruce's general wish (to be spared another resuscitation attempt and death in the hospital) is medically appropriate, but answer (c) says that the doctor is professionally obligated no matter what Bruce wants. That goes too far.

Epilogue

Bruce's doctor agreed to fill out the POST form, and Bruce pinned it to the wall next to the door that any ambulance crew would use to enter the house. In consultation with two trusted church elders, he prepared a short statement expressing his longing for heaven and his request that hospice be called if it looked like he needed medical attention. He e-mailed the statement to everyone likely to visit him and asked what they thought. Nearly everyone responded with some form of sad agreement and committed to pray for his comfort and healing.

The one practice session he conducted with his children and two oldest grandchildren was a grim affair, but he had not expected it to be festive. Sharyl went first, and even though she had helped him plan the event, she broke down crying when she came into the room where he was lying on the floor in his pretend collapse. Through her tears she checked his vitals and slowly dialed the hospice hotline, saying the numbers aloud as she read them from the sign next to the phone. At first, the person who answered thought it was happening for real and started barking orders. Sharyl snapped into the drill mode that she had been rehearsing in her head and calmed the hotline worker down. After that rough beginning, the rest of the practice runs went smoothly. The grandchildren were especially somber as they went through the steps they had seen their parents, aunts, and uncles take before them. When it was over, Bruce ordered pizza and they watched an especially silly comedy together.

Bruce died just over a month later, and in just the manner that his doctor had predicted. When his heart gave out, the only person in the house was a nurse from the hospice service. She knew not to call an ambulance, keeping him comfortable while she called for a doctor to come and determine whether anything might be done. Then she called Sharyl. The doctor was there when Sharyl arrived, and her father was dead. She was glad that he had given such clear instructions about what he wanted done—and she already missed him.

STORY 6: TAMMY'S HEART AND LUNGS

Kevin and Joanna Shaw adopt Tammy from Kazakhstan when she is 17 months old. Tammy joins their family as the youngest of five children; the other four are 13, 11, 7, and 5. She is curious, shy, and often sleepy. At her first careful medical examination after joining the family, it is discovered that Tammy has only two chambers in her heart (rather than the usual four). Because of this, blood flow to her lungs is low, limiting her energy and making it harder for her body to fight infections. The Shaws are told that open-heart surgery on Tammy should be able to reconstruct her heart and achieve a nearly normal blood flow. Only a few hospitals in the country could do it, but the prospects for success are strong if the surgery is scheduled as soon as possible.

Repairing Tammy's heart will be expensive. Kevin and Joanna locate a surgical team in Minnesota with extensive experience in the kind of heart reconstruction that Tammy needs. One or both parents will need to be with Tammy during the three-week period of testing, surgery, and recovery; and when they return home, the follow-up regimen will require further assistance from skilled caregivers. While the Shaws are financially comfortable, the expenses involved are daunting. When Joanna tells the women's Bible study at church about Tammy's condition and the possibility of surgery, one of the older women in the group says, "You shouldn't worry about the money, dear. I will pay for whatever your insurance won't cover. We've been praying for Tammy since the beginning of the adoption process. She feels like one of my own grandchildren." So for Kevin and Joanna, money will not be an issue.

The Shaws are told that with the surgery and strict attention to the aftercare program, Tammy will have a 60 percent chance of living a long life with only minor limitations on her activities and physical development. Without the surgery, she has little chance of living into adulthood and will be both physically and cognitively delayed.

Question 6A: Kevin and Joanna Ask You, "What Does the Bible Say about Whether We Are Obligated to Schedule the Surgery on Tammy's Heart?"

Answer (a): "Tammy's life is a gift from the Lord, but you need to think about your other four children as well. Even though the surgery option won't cost you money, it will take an enormous toll on your time and the energy you have to give to your other children. *Everything* will be about Tammy for a very, very long time. You can encourage your children to help you love Tammy in her challenged condition as she grows, but you should not pursue the surgery. Let's pray now that God will give you peace and allow you to see all your children's needs."

Answer (b): "Tammy is your child. You are biblically obligated to do whatever you can afford to provide all that she needs. Without the surgery, she will never realize her potential. She will almost certainly die much sooner than she would with the surgery. It would be biblically wrong to deny Tammy this chance at living a normal life. Let's pray together that God will give you the energy to walk this long road for Tammy's sake."

Answer (c): "Tammy is a gift to you and your family from God. Surgery would likely be a good thing for her, but no one can guarantee that it will work. The Bible does not obligate you to schedule the surgery, and the Bible does not forbid you to schedule it. If you have sought the Holy Spirit's guidance together in prayer and agree about what you should do, you should move in that direction confidently. Let me pray now that God will direct your steps."

Commentary on the Answers to Question 6A

Although it may feel like a cop-out, answer (c) is the best response. The Bible does not require Kevin and Joanna either to pursue the surgery or to reject it. Many of the considerations offered in answers (a) and (b) are true and helpful. The problem with (a) and (b) is the assertion that Kevin and Joanna are *obligated* one way or the other. Between (a) and (b), answer (b) is better because money is not an issue in this decision. All parents with multiple children must find a way to use their time and energy to meet the needs of all their children. In every family, some children need more from their parents than others. Tammy's need would be great with the surgery, but Kevin, Joanna, and the rest of the family would bear that burden together. The choice they are facing is hard, and they should pray, weep, and seek unity about what should happen next.

The Shaws are of one heart about what they need to do: they schedule the surgery for Tammy. Over the next few weeks, they work through the logistical details of getting Tammy to Minnesota, lining up people to watch their children when they will both be with Tammy, and following the surgeon's preoperation instructions. The time goes by quickly, and their other children are eager to spend as much time with Tammy as they can.

When Kevin, Joanna, and Tammy arrive in Minnesota, Tammy is exhausted from the trip. The low blood flow to her lungs has resulted in acute respiratory distress syndrome. The surgery will have to wait until she is strong enough for it. For four days the medical team gives her constant attention, using fluids and suction first to stabilize her and then to build up her strength.

During her fifth night in the hospital, Tammy's heart and lungs stop working. The medical team does everything to resuscitate her. After an unusually long time—a *long code*—they are able to restore heart and lung function. Because the surgery has been scheduled for later that day, the team assembles quickly, and Tammy is taken to the operating room to do the reconstruction she needs.

As Kevin and Joanna wait in suspense for more than six hours, the surgical team works on Tammy. During the long open-heart surgery, Tammy's heart-lung function stops five different times. She is resuscitated each time. The operation ends with her heart reconstructed, and she is moved to a recovery room. She is taken off the ventilator, breathing shallowly, and goes to sleep.

Because things have moved so quickly from the long code to the end of the surgery, it is never possible to stop and assess how Tammy's other physical systems are holding up. She has gone extended periods without heart or lung function. Much of the time, her breathing has been through a tube into her lungs. Until the surgery is over, no one can assess what has happened to her brain and her lungs.

When she is stable enough to run tests, the news is not good. Although Tammy can move her limbs voluntarily and fix her attention on her mother, her lung function is critically weak. The medical team decides to wait to scan her brain function until they know more about her heart and lungs.

Then Tammy's heart and lungs stop working again. The team resuscitates her, but has to leave the tube in her lungs to be sure that she is getting enough oxygen. At this point, the doctors ask Kevin and Joanna for permission to put Tammy on ECMO: extracorporeal membrane oxygenation. While the procedure is relatively new, the doctors assure them that it has proved to be especially effective with young children.[16] If the Shaws agree to it, Tammy's blood will be routed out of her body to a machine that will do what her lungs cannot, providing oxygen for her blood to absorb. A single tube will come out of her neck to carry her blood to the machine. Another tube will bring the oxygenated blood back into her body. She will be put in a controlled coma to keep her from moving and to allow all her body's energy to be used for repairing her lungs.

Question 6B: If Kevin and Joanna Asked You If God Wants Them to Say Yes to ECMO, What Would You Say?

Answer (a): "This sounds like exactly what Tammy needs. I can't see any reason to say no."

Answer (b): "I'm not sure what this procedure costs, but it has to be staggering. I doubt that the woman who agreed to help you pay for Tammy's surgery expected to pay for this as well. If you cannot afford to pay for it yourself, you ought to get her permission before you add this expense."

---

16. A good, brief explanation of ECMO can be found at https://www.nlm.nih.gov/medlineplus/ency/article/007234.htm. Having been at the bedside of a person on ECMO during an attempt to clear the bronchial tubes of mucus, I can report that the entire process is awe-inspiring. The size of the tubes in and out of the body and

Answer (c): "Although it is hard to admit, you have to accept that Tammy is not going to make it. ECMO may sound great, but it is a new procedure, and it is easy to see that the doctor is itching for the chance to use it. For the doctors, it is more like a toy than a tool. I think it is time to leave Tammy's body in peace rather than making her the plaything of these doctors."

Commentary on the Answers to Question 6B

The best response here is answer (a). Answer (b) makes an important observation about the financial support that the Shaws are receiving, but it makes unwarranted assumptions about what the benefactor wants. If the Shaws have not been keeping the donor updated on Tammy's condition, this would be a good time to start. If the donor explicitly said that she could not continue to help, that would lead to another important decision. Until then, the mere possibility that the donor would balk is not a reason to decline the procedure. Answer (c) includes the claim that the doctors are eager to use their new machine. This is probably true, but it is not a reason to decline their recommendation. The Shaws might ask the doctors who seem excited about the use of the machine to explain in more detail why they think it is best for their daughter. Their excitement, however, is reasonable, and not likely to be distorting their medical judgment. Answer (a) is best because it accepts that the only reasons to say no are speculative.

The Shaws agree to the doctors' recommendation. They are encouraged by the signs of brain activity before the last time Tammy's heart stopped, and they are hopeful that all Tammy needs is time for her heart and lungs to build up their strength after so much stress.

With Tammy on ECMO, the medical team is able to run tests of Tammy's brain activity. The results are deeply discouraging. The CT scan and the EEG together confirm that Tammy has suffered a

---

the dramatic change in the color of the blood going into and out of the oxygenation machine are amazing.

"global brain injury." She is not brain-dead—there is clearly some brain activity—but the times without adequate oxygen have compromised her brain functions at every level, including the brain stem. After the neurologist gives this report to Kevin and Joanna, the members of the medical team say that they need time to consult with one another about Tammy's overall prospects. They tell Kevin and Joanna that some hard choices will probably need to be made soon.

After two very long hours of praying, crying, and holding each other, Kevin and Joanna are told that the doctors are ready to explain Tammy's condition. Three doctors, two advanced-practice nurses, and Kevin and Joanna sit in a small circle next to the ECMO machine and Tammy's small, still body. The medical team says that it is not likely that Tammy will ever be strong enough to live outside a medical facility. The ECMO is doing its job, but before long they will need to take Tammy off it to see whether her heart and lungs have recovered enough to support her life. Before they take her off the machine, they need to know whether Kevin and Joanna will allow them to change her code status to "do not resuscitate." The doctors say that they don't need a decision right away, but that they will need it by the following morning.

This is not the doctors' only news. The neurologist has reviewed all the test results, and Tammy's prognosis is limited. Based on the damage revealed in the tests, it is likely that Tammy will be both deaf and blind for the rest of her life. On top of that, it is unlikely that she will ever be able to interact with the outside world. Unlike Helen Keller, who learned to give and receive ideas through touch, Tammy will never be able to make sense of what she is feeling. It is likely that she will experience pain, maybe even severe pain, but she will never be able to show or communicate her pain to others. With 24/7 professional care, Tammy can probably live at home. She will eat and sleep, and she will need to be bathed and toileted, but she will not know what is happening to her. In addition to a decision about the resuscitation order, Kevin and Joanna will need to start thinking about what they want for Tammy in the longer term.

Question 6C: What Would You Say If Kevin and Joanna Asked Whether God Would Think They Were Sinfully Giving Up on Tammy If They Agreed to the DNR Order?

Answer (a): "Of course it would be giving up! God has provided you with the means to care for her, medical personnel skilled and willing to do everything she needs, and a solemn duty to protect and nurture her life. She has survived numerous resuscitations already. Why prevent the medical team from doing more if they are needed?"

Answer (b): "It would not be giving up, but it would show that no one was willing to fight for her. The DNR order request mainly shows that the medical team wants to give up. You should resist the temptation to indulge their lack of commitment."

Answer (c): "Agreeing to the DNR order request is not giving up on Tammy, and it would not mean that you were killing her or wishing she were dead. Agreeing would only mean that if her heart stopped beating, you would acknowledge that medicine had reached the limit of what it could do to restore her to health. It would not be sinful to agree to the DNR order."

Commentary on the Answers to Question 6C

Because Tammy has pulled through so many crises, it is tempting to think that God has made it clear that he intends to spare Tammy. This temptation should be resisted. We cannot read God's intentions in this way. Decisions about medical treatment, like the request here about a future CPR attempt, should be made as they arise in light of medical evidence and not speculation about God's intentions. Answer (a) draws conclusions about the next resuscitation crisis on the basis of a guess about the meaning of God's provision to this point. Answer (b), the weakest of the three options, rests on a common but false belief about DNR order requests. When physicians ask for permission to change someone's status to DNR, they are not giving up. Someone with a DNR order is still cared for zealously by the nurses and doctors. The

DNR request only expresses what the best answer, (c), conveys: the doctors are acknowledging that medical skill has reached its limit.

After agreeing to the DNR order, Kevin and Joanna are troubled. They do not doubt their decision about another resuscitation attempt. Everyone they have talked to agrees that Tammy's tiny body has already gone through enough trauma of that kind. If she stopped breathing once she was off ECMO, it would be God's way of saying that it was time for her to be with Jesus. As they pray for guidance about the DNR decision, Joanna says, "Oh, Lord, we thank you that your promise of salvation is to us and our children. We claim the covenant promise that you made to us at Tammy's baptism, that you would be her God as you are ours. We had so hoped to see her profess her faith in you with her own voice when she was older, and we still ask that you would bring that about. But if it is not your will that she live to see that day, we rest in your promise and will look forward to seeing her when we follow her into your presence." Although they have never talked about where Tammy is headed if she dies, Kevin has been claiming the same promise to himself. They leave that time of prayer with a shared peace about her ultimate future.[17]

Although confident about God's promises, they are troubled about the decisions that are now facing them. Kevin is finding it hard to picture how he will be able to do his job as a bank vice president and still give the family the attention that they will need. Joanna is wondering whether she is sinfully selfish. The prospect of caring for a completely unresponsive child is difficult to handle. The likelihood that Tammy would experience pain that no one could detect or relieve is heartbreaking. Joanna doesn't know whether she could deal with it, and she is sure that a less selfish person would embrace the opportunity to care for someone so helpless. Both Kevin and Joanna decide to keep their

---

17. This prayer is theologically sound, claiming an important covenant promise. For more on this understanding of the future of covenant children who die, see John Calvin, *Institutes of the Christian Religion*, ed. John T. McNeill, trans. Ford Lewis Battles (Philadelphia: Westminster Press, 1960), 4.17ff., 1339ff.

individual worries to themselves. Neither wants to make things even worse for the other by sharing seemingly sinful anxieties.

As they are trying to work through these worries, the doctors remove Tammy from ECMO. The process of slowly decreasing the amount of mechanical support reaches its limit when they try to wean her from the ventilator. Her heart is stronger, so the surgery to reconstruct it has been successful, but she does not open her eyes or show signs of voluntary movement. Unless something medically surprising happens, she will stay alive only if she stays in the hospital on the ventilator. When they are sure that further improvement is unlikely, the doctors ask Kevin and Joanna what they want to do. Sad and sorry that Tammy has gone downhill so quickly, the doctors nonetheless recommend that Tammy be made as comfortable as possible and that the ventilator support be removed. It is likely that her heart and lungs will fail, but they will do all they can to make sure that Tammy is not in pain.

Question 6D: Suppose Kevin and Joanna Ask You, "What Does God's Word Say That We Should Do? Would We Be Killing Tammy If We Went Along with the Doctors' Recommendation? Are We Taking This Recommendation Seriously Only Because We Are Selfishly Putting Our Own Convenience over Her Life?"

> **Answer (a):** "Turning off the ventilator would be the same as choking her to death. You would be keeping her from breathing. Regardless of your motives, whether selfish or noble, you would be sinfully taking her life."

> **Answer (b):** "You would not be killing Tammy if you agreed to take her off the ventilator. What is killing her is an inability to get enough oxygen. It seems unlikely that you are being sinfully selfish in taking the doctors' proposal seriously. They believe that Tammy will never interact with others. If you were in her condition, it would be permissible for you to say that the medical devices are imposing a great burden on you with little benefit. Tammy can't speak for herself, and

you have the biblical authority to speak for her. You may assume that she would want what you would want if you were in her situation. If you wouldn't want the machines kept on if you were in Tammy's position, you may make that choice for her. There is nothing selfish about doing for her what you believe she would choose for herself if she could."

Answer (c): "It was brave for you to admit that your motives are so selfish. Along with repenting of these sinful motives, you should accept that you are not fit to make decisions about Tammy's care until you have put these selfish worries behind you. You should ask the doctors to keep her on the ventilator until you are sure that you can speak for her with pure hearts."

Commentary on the Answers to Question 6D

Answer (a) is simply terrible. Turning off a machine that is imposing a great burden without providing a large enough benefit is not the same as killing. Kevin and Joanna would be accepting that the treatment was imposing a greater burden than they would want to bear if they were in Tammy's situation. That is not selfish; it is what parents must do all the time in making choices for their children. Answer (c) may seem patient and helpful because it puts off making a decision, but it gets there by describing the Shaws' motives in a way that will haunt them long after this crisis is over. Answer (b) is the best response because it identifies the basis for the Shaws' authority to speak for Tammy and to say what she would choose if she could speak. They can assume that what *they* would want is what *she* would want because the Bible encourages us to believe that children who are raised in the nurture and admonition of the Lord will come to love what their parents love. The decision to turn off the ventilator will be emotionally hard, and we can help the Shaws by assuring them that their grief is righteous at the same time we assure them that they are the ones to speak for Tammy.

Kevin and Joanna's pastor has flown to Minnesota to be with them as they walk through these crucial decisions. When they pray together about this recommendation from the doctors, their pastor prays that Kevin and Joanna will see what they should do and that they will see it at the same time. The pastor says that he believes they are permitted to turn off the ventilator. But he also thinks it would be all right to keep the ventilator on while more tests are run. He suggests that they get a good night's sleep, pray on their own and together, and discuss where each thinks he or she is being led.

The next morning, Kevin and Joanna pray silently next to Tammy's bed in the ICU. They each write what they think they should do on a piece of paper and open them at the same time. Both have written, "We should let her go to be with Jesus." They tell the attending physician to schedule a time to try to wean Tammy off the ventilator. Later that day, the attempt is made. Tammy does not respond when support is withdrawn, and she dies in Joanna's arms, with Kevin and their pastor next to them.

Epilogue

One week later, a memorial service was held for Tammy, attended by 150 members of her church. Four months after that, another one of Kevin and Joanna's adopted children was diagnosed with a different heart defect. Without hesitation, they made arrangements to have the same team in Minnesota perform the necessary surgery. It was carried out in the same operating room where Tammy's had taken place. It was successful, and Tammy's brother returned home healthy.

KEY TERMS

abortion
advance directive
dialysis
ECMO
Glasgow Coma Scale
Parkinson's disease
surrogate decision

*DISCUSSION QUESTIONS

1. *We are not promised the guidance of the Holy Spirit in situations that we are not currently facing. So what is the value of thinking through what happened in real cases?
2. *Does it ever happen that no matter how we act, we will be sinning (is sin ever unavoidable)?
3. *Is Miriam keeping the fifth commandment to honor her mother if she discontinues the dialysis treatment?
4. *What approach should a pastoral counselor take when someone in the midst of a medical crisis says things that are doctrinally alarming?
5. *What role should the *possibility* of God's wondrous intervention (a *miracle* in the theologically loose sense) play in our plans and decision-making?
6. *Describe the most spiritually beautiful passing from life to death *in the hospital* that you have witnessed or heard reliably described. What made it especially beautiful?
7. *How should a pastoral counselor guide the husband and wife in the story of "Triplets in Peril" if the husband and wife disagree about what should be done?
8. *What difference does it make whether the action that results in the death of the unborn triplet is called *abortion* or not?
9. *How can someone know that his or her children are old or mature enough to discuss end-of-life scenarios involving their older family members?
10. *What should be said to someone who is afraid that his or her decisions are motivated by selfishness rather than love *if it is hard to tell what role selfishness is playing?*

FOR FURTHER READING

Frame, John M. *The Doctrine of the Christian Life*. A Theology of Lordship. Phillipsburg, NJ: P&R Publishing, 2008.
Meilaender, Gilbert. "I Want to Burden My Loved Ones." *First Things*

(March 2010). http://www.firstthings.com/article/2010/03/i
-want-to-burden-my-loved-ones.

Mottram, Kenneth P. *Caring for Those in Crisis: Facing Ethical Dilemmas with Patients and Families.* Grand Rapids: Brazos, 2007.

Orr, Robert D. *Medical Ethics and the Faith Factor: A Handbook for Clergy and Health-Care Professionals.* Grand Rapids: Eerdmans, 2009.

Quill, Timothy E., and Robert Holloway. "Time-Limited Trials near the End of Life." *Journal of the American Medical Association* 306, 13 (October 3, 2011): 1483–84.

Schenker, Yael, Megan Crowley-Matoka, Daniel Dohan, Greer A. Tiver, Robert Arnold, and Douglas B. White. "I Don't Want to Be the One Saying 'We Should Just Let Him Die': Intrapersonal Tensions Experienced by Surrogate Decision Makers in the ICU." *Journal of General Internal Medicine* 27, 12 (December 2012): 1657–65.

5

ADVANCE DIRECTIVES

Thinking about death is no fun. Imagining even a stranger's death can be distressing. Imagining our own death is worse, and completing an advance directive requires thinking through possibilities that we would prefer never happened. If Jesus returns before we die, we will never have to live through the fatal end of our mortal bodies. Although Jesus could return as soon as today, we should be living and planning as if it will not happen in our lifetimes. This means that we have the opportunity to put plans in place that can relieve our loved ones from making difficult medical decisions for us if we become unable to make them. Anyone who has walked with a loved one through the last days of life knows that many decisions have to be made. Guidance of any kind is helpful. Instructions from the one who is dying are golden. Our advance directives will give instructions to our loved ones and to medical personnel about what values we want to guide decisions about our care.

In this chapter, I will explain how to complete an advance directive in a way that conforms to what the Bible says about the sanctity of life and our obligations to God. I will use the term *advance directive* to refer to instructions about end-of-life care, but what I say here will apply to documents with other names that have the same function. A "Living Will," an "Advance Care Plan," and a "Durable Power of Attorney for Health Care Decisions" form should all accomplish the same thing, although in some states these documents may allow us only to name an *agent* or *surrogate* and not provide a way to specify treatment preferences.[1] Regardless

---

1. Concise and authoritative definitions of *living will* and other key terms are available through the Mayo Clinic. See http://www.mayoclinic.org/healthy-lifestyle

of the scope of the document, *any* written record of our preferences is a blessing to family members. Any document that specifies someone whom we want making decisions for us if we cannot—that is, any that names an agent—will make a significant difference in the lives of our loved ones. An advance directive is especially important if we have no living spouse and more than one child. In most hospitals, if we do not have an advance directive and our children are the legally empowered decision-makers, they must all agree in order to speak for us. So if it is likely that our children will have to make decisions for us, then a document naming an agent will remove the difficulty of getting all the children to agree in order for decisions to take effect.

I will be explaining a biblically permissible way of completing the Tennessee Advance Care Plan. The sections of the Tennessee form are also found in the forms developed by other states and by organizations such as Five Wishes.[2] Most states have laws specifically saying that the legally executed forms developed by other states are legally binding in their state as well. For example, if I have a completed Tennessee Advance Care Plan form and am hospitalized in Washington state while visiting my mother, the instructions on my Tennessee form will be in force in Washington state. State forms differ in mostly small ways, but hospital workers would prefer to follow instructions from forms that they are used to. Because the goal is to have a form that will easily direct our care, it is best to complete the form that our local health workers are used to seeing. It is usually not worth trying to find a state with a form that has more friendly assumptions than the local state form. Some state forms are much longer than others, but otherwise the state forms are similar in substance. We should each use our own state's form unless it is clear that it can't be used to say what we want.

The Tennessee Advance Care Plan is a state-approved form for preparing an advance directive. The form has five sections: "Naming

/consumer-health/in-depth/living-wills/art-20046303.

2. All but eight states honor the Five Wishes form, and in those that do not, the Five Wishes form may be attached to the official state form. Many people find its plain language easy to use. The Five Wishes form and instructions are at https://www .agingwithdignity.org/five-wishes/about-five-wishes.

an Agent," "Quality of Life," "Treatment," "Other Instructions," and "Signature." It is worth emphasizing that an advance directive that simply names an agent and completes the "Signature" section is still far, far more valuable than not having an advance directive at all. Naming people we have known for years as our agents and alternates is valuable even if we do not have time to discuss what kind of medical treatment we want near the end. Thinking through what we want, filling out the rest of the form, and talking with our chosen agent and alternates is best; but the most important thing to do is to name an agent. I will explain the intent and most common complications in each of these sections before making recommendations on what the Bible says about filling out each of the sections.

THE SECTIONS EXPLAINED

"Naming an Agent" Section

This is the simplest part of the form, but it needs to include more information than it explicitly asks for. After stating our full legal name, we will give the full legal name of our agent. The Tennessee form specifically says that our agent "must follow" the instructions that will appear in the other sections of the form. This "must follow" is hard to enforce, and it is best to choose an agent that we can trust to work hard to make the choices we would have made even if the agent would want to choose otherwise.

Along with the agent's full legal name, we should include as much contact information as possible. Having a form that names an agent will not do much good if the medical personnel cannot get in touch with our agent. The Tennessee form asks for one phone number and one address. Including two or even three phone numbers (home, cell, and employer) in the place for "Phone #" is best. In the space for "Address," put both a home/snail-mail address and an e-mail address. If the medical personnel need to find our agent, time is likely to be an issue. In that case, the home address will be the least useful of all the ways to contact our agent. The cell phone number is likely to be the best, so make sure that it is written in large, clear numbers.

Although most forms ask us to specify the "Relation" between the agent and ourselves, we are not required to have a family member as our agent. Our first choice in an agent should be someone who is willing to take on the task. Willingness alone, though, is not enough. Our agent should also be a person who is likely to combine a clear understanding of what we would want with the ability to act decisively in the midst of grief and anxiety. I have named my wife as my agent because I am confident that she would know and say what I would wish, and she would not make the doctors wait too long for an answer. We have discussed a wide variety of possible end-of-life scenarios, and she is still willing to take on the role if needed.

It is a comfort that my wife is willing to be listed as my agent on my advance directive, but she is not biblically obligated to speak for me. A wife or a husband typically knows best what her or his spouse would value or choose, but it is not always that way. Sometimes a close sibling with a similar health condition will know better. A child may be more comfortable deciding when time presses. An agent's job is to speak for someone who cannot. An agent is not exercising spiritual authority or sitting in judgment. So an agent can be a good friend with whom we have discussed what we want to happen if we fall ill.

Being willing to fill the role is important. Before listing anyone— even a spouse—as our agent, we should talk with him or her about it and ask for permission. If we have discussed medical matters before, the conversation may not need to be long; but if we are just starting to formulate our wishes, this conversation should be long enough for us to share our thinking. One of the virtues of the Tennessee form is that it is short. Explaining the reasoning behind the boxes we check in the sections on "Quality of Life" and "Treatment" would be a quick way to acquaint an agent with what we value in end-of-life care. Talking through the form is also a good way to review our wishes with an agent who knows us quite well.

Finally, it is important to name an agent who is committed to a biblical understanding of the value of life. If the agent is called on to fulfill the role envisioned by the document, we will be unable to make decisions. It is likely that our agent will have to decide about starting or stopping measures that would affect how long we are alive. The decisions may be confusing, and the medical personnel may put pressure on our agent despite their best efforts to wait for direction. For both our own sake and the sake of our loved ones, it is best to have an agent committed to the sanctity of life making the decisions. When under pressure, it is hard for people to resist falling back on what they would want for themselves.

Naming an Alternate Agent (or Two)

The same considerations that go into naming an agent should go into naming alternate agents. Most state forms ask for only one alternate agent, but we are not limited to only one. The alternates will be called in the order they are listed, and because the aim is to make sure that someone who knows us is available, listing a third name is a good idea. While it might be a bit unsightly, it is best to squeeze the name and contact information (two phone numbers and an e-mail address, at least) into the margin. Writing information on the back isn't safe, since some hospitals scan in advance directives with machines that capture only the front of the document.

Doctors and nurses have urged me to emphasize the value of listing three names. They are frustrated when they have a completed advance directive but cannot reach any of the agents listed. The law allows us to put more information on a sheet that is stapled to the form, but that will only complicate the task of getting our advance directive into all the places we should want it to be.

Another advantage to listing two alternate agents is the value of having talked with others about our wishes. Even though an agent is empowered to make decisions for us without consulting anyone else, knowing the names and contact information for others who are also ready provides the agent with sources of insight and prayer partners. My advance directive lists one of my brothers—an attorney—as the first alternate, and another one of my brothers—a pastor—as the second alternate. Many other members of my close family would be excellent agents. I list these two because they would be most comfortable deciding for me if required and because they would work well together if time allowed them to discuss the decisions needed.

"When Effective" Section (Empowering Your Agent Even When You Might Be Decisionally Capable)

The state of Tennessee recently added a "When Effective" section to its Advance Care Plan. It is similar to a provision on the forms of surrounding states, and aims to clarify the person whom the medical team should look to if there is a conflict between us and our agents. The original Tennessee form did not have this section because it was assumed that our agents would always defer to our judgment if we were able to direct our own care. I am glad Tennessee has added this section. While it may seem best to have our agents making decisions only when we are incapacitated, checking the "I do not give such permission" box can lead to needless delays in getting the best care. It is biblically permissible to check either of the boxes in this section. On my advance directive, I have checked the "I give my agent permission" box. I have two reasons for this choice.

First, I have great confidence in my wife to say what I would want. Since I am happy to have her making choices for me if I am incapacitated, I am also happy to have her making them even if I could be brought to understand the choices and express my wishes. Yet I can imagine circumstances in which I would recommend that someone check the "I do not give such permission" box. Someone with no close friends and only distant, minimally trustworthy relatives might name one of the relatives as his or her agent. In that case, it would be wise to say that the agent was empowered only in case of incapacitation. But for anyone confident that his or her named agent will know what to say, it is better to check the "I give my agent permission" box. This is because capacity is sometimes hard to determine, and empowering our agents only when we have been deemed decisionally incapable may complicate getting the best care.[3]

---

3. How decisional capacity is determined is described in chapter 2. A more detailed account of the process is in Andrew M. Siegel, Anna S. Barnwell, and Dominic A.

A desire to get the best care is my second reason. As long as I am clearly able to make and communicate decisions about my care, my advance directive will not be looked at. The instructions I express in my advance directive will matter only if the doctors and nurses are not sure what I want. If I suffer a serious injury in an accident, I may quickly go from decisionally capable to decisionally incapable. Otherwise, my decisional capacity is likely to wax and wane with my health. I might be decisionally capable in the morning and incapable in the evening. Getting the best care is usually a matter of moving rapidly to adjust treatment to changing medical needs. If I check the "I do not give such permission" box, then changes to my care will be delayed during the time it takes to determine—at the time a decision is needed—whether I am able to decide for myself. I'd rather have my agent make the decision than wait.

Both of these reasons for giving my wife permission to decide even if I have the capacity to do it myself rest on confidence that my wife will choose what I would want. That confidence has built up over more than thirty years of marriage, and it has been made even stronger by discussions about end-of-life likelihoods. We have talked about the choices that others have had to make, paying particular attention to what each of us would want if we were in similar circumstances. My work as an elder and an ethics consultant has given us a lot to talk about, but she has extended the conversation by bringing to my attention stories in the news about end-of-life cases. She also asks about the medical choices implicit in prayer requests or funeral services, paying especially close attention to cases involving our own health challenges. We do not always agree about what we would want if we were facing the decisions we discuss, but I'm sure she would know what I would want if she had to decide.

Purposeful conversations with our agents about the care we would

Sisti, "Assessing Decision-Making Capacity: A Primer for the Development of Hospital Practice Guidelines," *HEC Forum: HealthCare Ethics Committee Forum: An Interprofessional Journal on Healthcare Institutions' Ethical and Legal Issues* 26, 2 (2014): 159–68.

want are the foundation for the effectiveness of our advance directives. Even if it is the only section of the document filled out before it is witnessed and signed, having the section naming an agent legally completed will be an enormous benefit to our loved ones. Explaining to our agents what we value and how we would choose in a few standard cases will make it much easier for our agents to make and explain choices when the time comes. Discussing the cases in chapters 3 and 4 of this book would be a good way to get the conversation started.

"Quality of Life" Section

Everything after the section naming an agent is intended to allow us to explain what we would want done if our agent could not be reached or declines to make a decision. The boxes we check and instructions we write will be used by the medical personnel to come as close as they can to choosing what we would choose among the medically appropriate options. Everyone's goal will be to choose what we would choose rather than choosing what they would want if they were in our place. So in the unusual circumstance that an agent refused to make a choice, an advance directive and any other indications of our wishes will be taken into account in making decisions.

The purpose of the "Quality of Life" section is to say what we want in different "conditions." Checking "Yes" next to a condition means that we consider the quality of life in that condition acceptable *and thus* that we want everything medically possible done to extend our life. Checking "No" next to a condition means that we want something less than everything medically possible to be done. This is the most confusing section on all the state-approved forms. Because the language is often convoluted and asks for permission to do less than everything medically possible, it can easily seem that the form is opposed to a biblical view of human life. Having seen how the form is used over the last ten years, I am confident that the form itself is not hostile to biblical values. The form can be filled out in a way that is biblically appropriate, but it is easy to get confused by the language and to fill out the form in a way that expresses our values incorrectly. (The first version I had completed and had my friends sign got things backwards! It was embarrassing to admit that I had misunderstood the form's logic.) The instructions in the next section try to make things more clear.

The "Quality of Life" section and the "Treatment" section work together. The "Quality of Life" section says whether we want everything done or less than everything done in different conditions. The earlier chapters of this book describe many cases in which it is biblically appropriate to do less than everything. Chapter 3 works through the four "conditions" asked about on the Tennessee form. As I explain in the instructions below, my own advance directive checks "No" by "Permanent Unconscious Condition" and "Permanent Confusion." This means that if I am in either of those conditions, I want less than everything medically possible to be done. The "Treatment" section says which medical treatments I want or do not want if I am in either of those conditions.

Aside: The Vexed History of the Phrase *Quality of Life*

Before considering the "Treatment" section, it is important to explain one reason why the "Quality of Life" section is confusing and even troubling for Bible-believing Christians. Tennessee's form is like many other state forms in using the phrase. In the 1980s and '90s, that phrase was sometimes used as a way to steer decision-making *away* from what we or our family would want, instead focusing on what the medical personnel thought was an acceptable quality of life. Since I was serving on a secular ethics committee in the 1990s, I heard the phrase used this way: "No matter what her family thinks, her quality of life is horrible. No one would want to live like that. It would be a mercy to let her die." Because *quality of life* was used this way, Christians were rightly wary when the phrase was used in end-of-life discussions.

Around 2005, the phrase *quality of life* was transformed in a biblically positive way by two developments: the rise of hospice care and the emergence of palliative care as a medical subspecialty. Hospice care developed to fill the need for long-term end-of-life care outside the hospital setting. The first hospice services were set up by hospitals as a separate floor or wing, but before long it became clear that the care involved could be delivered more effectively in homes.[4] The hospice services that are formed to provide this kind of care—whether as nonprofit agencies or for-profit businesses—focus on helping people maintain as much of their ordinary manner of life as possible. *Quality of life* to hospice workers centers on what *quality* means to the person receiving the care, not on the medical personnel's idea of what kind of life is worth living. This is a dramatic improvement, making *quality of life* a term that should not alarm people committed to the value of life.

Palliative care is medical treatment that specializes in pain management and maximizing the ability to engage in the activities of daily living. All physicians are trained in pain management. Physicians and nurses with additional training in pain management, comfort care, and maintaining functionality are palliative-care *specialists*. As medical technology has enabled physicians to keep people alive longer, pain management and maintaining functionality have become increasingly complicated. Physicians have always been willing to call in a colleague who specializes in another area: a pulmonologist (who specializes in breathing and lungs) would, for example, call for a "cardiology consult" if the heart's function became an issue. In recent years, physicians are increasingly willing to call for a "palliative-care consult," bringing in the expertise of people who specialize in comfort care. As with hospice care, palliative-care specialists use the phrase *quality of life* to mean "the life that the person under their care would value." Their training manuals emphasize the importance of learning what the person that such a specialist is serving would want, and not what the specialist would want (or not want) if he or she were in need of medical care.

---

4. The care is more effective because it is more holistic. When I joined the ethics committee at Memorial in 1999, the hospital had just put together a "Comprehensive Support Service" for people whose goal of care was no longer restoring them to health. This service is no longer offered at the hospital because it is provided by outside hospice care agencies. For an overview of the rise of hospice and palliative care, see Stephen R. Connor, "Development of Hospice and Palliative Care in the United States," *Omega: Journal of Death & Dying* 56, 1 (2007): 89–99.

"Treatment" Section

The instructions given in this section are followed only if we are *irreversibly* in a condition that we have checked with a "No" in the "Quality of Life" section.[5] Biblical principles informing decisions about the four kinds of treatment listed on the Tennessee form are discussed in chapter 3 of this book. Checking "Yes" for any of these treatment possibilities means that hospital personnel will start or continue to use that kind of treatment even if we are in a condition (from the "Quality of Life" section) in which we want less than everything done. Because of this, checking all four "Yes" boxes in the "Treatment" section has the same effect as checking "Yes" in all four boxes of the "Quality of Life" section. Checking "Yes" for all four kinds of treatment will frustrate hospital personnel. Their frustration will not stem from disagreeing with our wishes. It will stem from their concern that the form does not state what we want. They are legally obligated to follow our wishes unless there is an excellent reason not to. Checking "No" for a "Quality of Life" condition and then saying "Yes" to all the kinds of treatment makes it hard to believe that we understood the form. If we want everything possible done no matter what condition we are in, we should check "Yes" for all the "Quality of Life" conditions. It is biblically permissible to ask for everything to be done regardless of our condition. But it is not biblically required. We are biblically permitted to decline treatment that is either ineffective or excessively burdensome. The "Treatment" section of an advance directive allows us to say no in advance and in a way that makes it *our* decision even if someone else has to speak for us.

"Other Instructions" Section

It is fine to leave this section blank. This section allows us to express what we want in our own words. If we are not sure that checking

5. Death is now defined in terms of irreversibility. Whether a condition is "irreversible" is difficult to define precisely, but as a practical matter doctors routinely make the determination. For a discussion of irreversibility, see John Fortunato, "'Irreversibility' and the Modern Understanding of Death," *Discussions* 9, 2 (2013), http://www.inquiriesjournal.com/a?id=795.

the "Yes" and "No" boxes in the "Quality of Life" and "Treatment" sections expresses our intentions, we can explain what we want here directly. Often, people use this section to insist that they want to be kept comfortable no matter what. That isn't necessary, since medical personnel will always work to keep us comfortable, but stating that wish may be a comfort to our loved ones. They will know that the medical staff has that wish in writing. (I do not make that request on my own advance directive because my friends who are doctors and nurses would think it showed a lack of trust in their professional integrity. My family also knows that comfort care is always provided in the hospital. Family members who do not know this may be put at ease by an express statement in the "Other Instructions" section.)

The best use I have found for this section is to express a desire to be placed in hospice care if that is appropriate and to specify that I want decisions to be based on the medical judgment of a physician that my agent trusts and the value judgments of my agent. Whether a possible medical treatment will be effective is a judgment that only a physician should make. Medical judgments about likely effectiveness are estimates. Doctors looking at the very same data may disagree about likely effectiveness. The earlier sections of the form did not allow me to specify what to do if doctors disagreed, so I use this section to say that I prefer the medical judgments of doctors whom my agent trusts. I also specify that judgments about what counts as excessively burdensome should be made by my agent. Hospital personnel would almost certainly do this anyway. I add it because I saw cases years ago in a secular hospital in which hospital administrators put pressure on the family to accept their judgment about whether treatments were "futile" or "pointless."

Organ Donation

Organ donation is a great way to bless others, so we should look for a way to help by making our organs available. In the 1990s, I declined the opportunity to use my driver's license to express my desire to be an organ donor. I was worried that having it on my license would mean that hospital workers would give up on me too quickly in order to harvest my organs. I'm now sure that safeguards are in place to prevent that from happening. Also, all the doctors and nurses I know are committed to giving the best care possible to the people who have the organs already. My driver's license now says that I want to donate my organs, but my advance directive attempts to manage how my family will be treated when organ donation becomes a possibility.[6]

In many states, the law directs hospital personnel to leave all discussions about organ donation to the local "organ procurement organization." Some states even prohibit family doctors from being part of the conversation. (The worry is that our own doctor will explain what is happening in a way that will decrease the likelihood that our organs will be used.) People from these organizations are typically sensitive, but they are also eager to have as many organs as possible available for transplantation. They can be a bit pushy. So if our family would resent having someone urging them to authorize the use of our organs, we should leave specific instructions in this section saying that we want decisions about organ donation made only with the attending physician, a physician of our agent's choice, our pastor, or all these people present.

Also, many states now allow a procedure for harvesting organs that attempts to manage the time of death so that the transplant team can be ready to go right away. This procedure is called different things in different places. It goes by "Donation on Circulatory Death," or "Donation on Cardiac Death," or "Beating Heart Donation."[7] It is used when the brain is severely damaged but brain death has not happened. If the heart and other organs are in good shape, a plan is made to assemble the transplant surgeons before discontinuing life-sustaining treatments (most commonly respirator support). If the heart stops on its own within an hour (or so, depending on the state), the person is

6. An especially compelling argument in favor of organ donation is given by Gilbert Meilaender's *Bioethics: A Primer for Christians*, 2nd ed. (Grand Rapids: Eerdmans, 2005), 88ff.

7. For a thoughtful discussion of this practice, see James F. Childress, "Organ Donation after Circulatory Determination of Death: Lessons and Unresolved Controversies," *Journal of Law, Medicine & Ethics* 36, 4 (Winter 2008): 766–71.

declared dead and the organs are taken. I am not yet comfortable that life-honoring safeguards are in place for this procedure, so I recommend stipulating "Only after brain death."

"Signature" Section

The importance of this section is obvious. The legal force of the document depends on completing this section appropriately. Finding witnesses willing to attest that we signed the form in their presence can be a hassle. A church Sunday school class or a small-group Bible study is a good place to get the signatures, both because many people are present and because they should be willing to hear us explain what we are asking for. The witnesses are not in any way promising to make decisions, visit us in the hospital, or pay anything. They are only saying that the signature on the form is *our* signature. Completing the form correctly means that the doctors and nurses will know that they should follow the instructions on the form as carefully as they would follow our own words if we were able to make decisions.

The last part of the form says, "What to Do with This Advance Directive." Following those instructions makes it likely that the people who need the form will have it when the time comes. Far too often, people complete an advance directive and neglect to put the form where it can be found. The form isn't needed until we have lost the ability to speak for ourselves, so if it isn't on file or in the possession of our agent, no one will know where it is. Do everything that the form suggests you do with it after it is signed.

SECTION-BY-SECTION RECOMMENDATIONS FOR COMPLETING AN ADVANCE DIRECTIVE

The instructions below are addressed to the person ("you") filling out the form. In some places, the explanations repeat background information found in other parts of this book. It should be possible to use only these instructions to work through the form.

ADVANCE CARE PLAN

I,_____, hereby give these advance instructions on how I want to be treated by my doctors and other health care providers when I can no longer make those treatment decisions myself.

The phrase "when I can no longer make those treatment decisions myself" means "*in case a decision is needed and I cannot make it.*" Doctors and nurses prefer to have you making the decisions. If there is a time when you cannot, they will use this form to find out what you would wish. If you regain the ability to make decisions, they will stop using this form and try to have you tell them what you want.

You will be the one to make decisions as long as you are *decisionally capable.* (This is the term that the doctors and nurses will use when deciding who should make decisions about your care.) You are decisionally capable if you meet three criteria:

- You can show that you have a system of values.
- You can "adapt means to ends," meaning that you can see how to connect your actions to your desires/values.
- You can communicate your choices to others.

Adapting means to ends is something that you do all the time. If your *end* is leaving the room, a *means* adapted to that end is walking toward an open door. If you tried to get out by flapping your arms, it would show that you were not able to choose means that would accomplish your desired end.

It may happen that the doctors or nurses will think you are not decisionally capable when, in fact, you are. This is most likely to happen when you are medicated or very tired. This is not something to worry about if you have completed this form. In that case, the doctors or nurses will ask the *agent* you name in this section to make decisions the way you would make them.

Agent: I want the following person to make health care decisions for me. This includes any health care decision I could have made for myself if able, except that my agent must follow my instructions below:

Name: _____ Phone #: (__) _____
Relation: _____
Address: _____

The *agent* you name here is the *one* person whom the doctors and nurses will look to when medical decisions need to be made *and* you cannot make them. Your agent's task is to speak *for you*. Your agent may seek advice from other people about what you would want. If you would want your choices to be biblically sound, your agent might ask others you would trust to say what guidance the Bible gives.

It is important to give as much information as you can about how to contact your agent. The form asks for an address and phone number, but most state forms were designed before cell phones and e-mail addresses became the best ways to reach people. List every way to find your agent: cell phone number, e-mail address, home phone, work phone, and home address.

Name an agent whom you trust to speak for you. This should be someone who is able to listen to advice but will say what you would say even when others disagree. Your agent is not legally obligated to ask for anyone's opinion. Your agent is not required to put decisions to a family vote or wait until the family reaches a consensus before making a decision for you. Asking for the advice of others you would trust is a good idea, but one great advantage of having a clear agent is that the doctors and nurses can get decisions made as quickly as good medical care demands.

If you are married and your spouse is able to do and wants the job, that is the best choice. (By law, your spouse is your agent if you do not name one. And choosing someone other than your spouse will make the doctors and nurses a bit uneasy unless there is an obvious reason for the choice and your spouse agrees. The doctors and nurses will understand if your spouse is ill, emotionally fragile, or ready to explain why someone else is named as your agent.)

Alternate Agent: If the person named above is unable or unwilling to make health care decisions for me, I appoint as alternate the following person to make health care decisions for me. This includes any health care decision I could have made for myself if able, except that my agent must follow my instructions below:

Name: _____ Phone #: (__) _____
Relation: _____
Address: _____

Naming an alternate agent is important, and you should list as much contact information as you can here as well. Your agent may not be available, or the hospital may not be able to reach him or her in any of the ways you listed.

Some state forms leave space for you to name a third agent (an alternate to the alternate). That is a good idea even if the form doesn't ask for it. You, your family, the doctors, and the nurses are all much better off if a clear agent is ready to speak for you.

My agent is also my personal representative for purposes of federal and state privacy laws, including HIPAA.

This means that your agent will speak for you about who can know what is happening to you in the hospital. *HIPAA* is the abbreviation for the Health Insurance Portability and Accountability Act. Among other things, it includes the federal laws that aim to protect the privacy of your medical information. If you are not able to make decisions, your agent will determine what others can know about your condition in the hospital. No one should find out about your medical condition without your agent's approval. This means that your agent will speak for you about what the church should know about your situation. The church should not announce or publish that you need prayer for your medical condition without your agent's permission.

It is best to tell the people whom you are listing as your agent and alternate agents that you are naming them in your advance directive. Talking with them about what you want if you are too sick to speak for yourself will help them represent you faithfully. A gentle way to start the conversation is to talk about what you would want the church to know and how you'd want your condition to be communicated to the church.

<u>When Effective</u> (mark one):

☐ I give my agent permission to make health care decisions for me at any time, even if I have capacity to make decisions for myself.

☐ I do not give such permission (this form applies only when I no longer have capacity).

If you trust your agent to make decisions, it is best to check the first box here ("I give my agent permission . . ."). Checking the other box means that the doctors and nurses might delay giving you treatment you need while they figure out whether you are able to make decisions yourself. You would not want to wait if you were temporarily confused, exhausted, or foggy from medicine.

Some state forms do not have this "When Effective" section. (The state of Tennessee only recently added it.) In that case, your agent will be asked to speak for you only when the doctors and nurses are sure that you can't speak for yourself.

<u>Quality of Life:</u> By marking "yes" below, I have indicated conditions I would be willing to live with if given adequate comfort care and pain management. By marking "no" below, I have indicated conditions I would not be willing to live with (that to me would create an unacceptable quality of life).

This section ("Quality of Life") and the next section ("Treatment") work together. If you are in a condition described by one of the four

"Quality of Life" types *and* you have checked "No" next to it, then the doctor will look at the "Treatment" section to see what (if anything) you want done about your treatment. If you check "Yes," the doctors and nurses will do everything medically indicated to keep you alive if you are in that condition (that *quality of life*).

No matter what you check in either of these sections, the doctors and nurses will work hard to keep you comfortable. Asking for a "palliative-care consult" or a pain-management specialist is the best way to make sure that everything is being done to keep you comfortable. Palliative-care specialists are up to date on the best methods; they are usually not as pressed for time as the attending physician; and they are especially good at helping your agent see the big medical picture.

☐	☐	**Permanent Unconscious Condition:** I become totally
Yes	No	unaware of people or surroundings with little chance of ever waking up from the coma.

I recommend checking the "No" box for this condition. If you will never wake up, the physical, psychological, social, financial, and spiritual burdens that come with aggressive treatment greatly outweigh the benefit of being kept alive. Checking "No" here means that you do not want *everything* medically possible done to keep you alive if you are permanently unable to respond or interact with other people. (You may be able to interact with God, but we don't know, and no one else will be able to tell. You will not enjoy any spiritual goods in the ordinary way.)

If the doctors determine that you are in this condition and you have checked "No" here, they will look at the "Treatment" section below to see what kinds of treatment you want in addition to being kept comfortable.

The determination that you are IN one of these conditions is crucial. It is worth asking your agent to request a second opinion if you are in a condition that you have checked with "No" in this section.

☐   ☐   <u>Permanent Confusion:</u> I become unable to remem-
Yes   No   ber, understand, or make decisions. I do not recog-
              nize loved ones or cannot have a clear conversation
              with them.

I also recommend checking the "No" box for this condition. If I am permanently confused, then I am not able to read or hear God's Word, worship with other believers, or enjoy other spiritual goods in the ordinary way. That would be a much greater burden than the benefit of having my body kept alive by aggressive medical treatment.

So if I am in this condition, I would want my treatment limited as described in the "Treatment" section below.

Note: Wanting my treatment limited is not at all the same thing as wanting to be killed, however gently. Declining CPR or even artificially delivered food and water does not mean that I want people to stop caring for me. I will still want to be shown love and affection, be read to from time to time, have my family around me enjoying each other's company, and be offered food in a safe way.

☐   ☐   <u>Dependent in all Activities of Daily Living:</u> I am no
Yes   No   longer able to talk or communicate clearly or move by
              myself. I depend on others for feeding, bathing, dress-
              ing, and walking. Rehabilitation or any other restorative
              treatment will not help.

I recommend checking "Yes" for this condition, although it is a close call. By checking "Yes," you would be saying that you want medical treatment to be aggressive. The "Treatment" section below would *not* be looked at.

I recommend "Yes" for this condition because although I would be depending on others and would have trouble communicating, I would not be confused. I would still be able to enjoy spiritual goods such as reading the Bible and participating in worship in the ordinary way. I suspect that I would not enjoy depending on others. But that is not a sufficient reason to limit life-sustaining medical treatment.

Note: I know biblically serious Christians who check "No" here. Among other factors, financial considerations can play a role.

☐ ☐ **End-Stage Illnesses:** I have an illness that has reached
Yes No its final stages in spite of full treatment. Examples: Widespread cancer that no longer responds to treatment; chronic and/or damaged heart and lungs, where oxygen is needed most of the time and activities are limited due to the feeling of suffocation.

I recommend checking "Yes" for this condition.

End-stage illnesses can last a long time, and some illnesses allow you to live a rich, full life even as they get worse. The "Examples" given here on the Tennessee form are quite different. Cancer that isn't responding to treatment might still allow you to continue to work and to attend worship, or it might leave you bedridden and confused. Chronic heart or lung disease might require you to carry oxygen with you when you leave the house, or it could have you feeling as though you are suffocating most of the time. So being in the final stage of an illness isn't by itself a reason to limit treatment.

If my condition deteriorates to the point that I am permanently unconscious or permanently confused, then the "No" that I checked for those conditions would apply and my "Treatment" limitations would be followed.

Treatment: If my quality of life becomes unacceptable to me (as indicated by one or more of the conditions marked "no" above) and my condition is irreversible (that is, it will not improve), I direct that medically appropriate treatment be provided as follows. By marking "yes" below, I have indicated treatment I want. By marking "no" below, I have indicated treatment I do not want.

☐ ☐ **CPR (Cardiopulmonary Resuscitation):** To make the
Yes No heart beat again and restore breathing after it has stopped. Usually this involves electric shock, chest compressions, and breathing assistance.

I recommend checking "No" here, declining CPR for the "No" conditions.

CPR is amazing, but it is physically aggressive to the point of possibly breaking ribs. It involves flooding the body with drugs, and less than 10 percent of people who receive CPR in the hospital ever leave the hospital at all.

If I am in a condition in which I would not want my life maintained by aggressive medical means (the "No" boxes above), then I do not want people to try to restart my heart with CPR. I would rather go to be with Jesus.

☐	☐	**Life Support / Other Artificial Support:** Continuous
Yes	No	use of breathing machine, IV fluids, medications, and other equipment that helps the lungs, heart, kidneys, and other organs to continue to work.

I recommend checking "No" here, declining these kinds of treatments for the "No" conditions.

The treatments mentioned here (tubes down the throat to breathe for you, tubes into your veins to do what your kidneys or liver are no longer doing well enough) are extremely useful when there is a medical reason to believe that you will be healed/restored and able to leave the hospital. If I am in a "No" condition (from the section above), I do not want the burdens that come with these treatments imposed just to keep me alive in the hospital.

☐	☐	**Treatment of New Conditions:** Use of surgery, blood
Yes	No	transfusions, or antibiotics that will deal with a new condition but will not help the main illness.

I recommend checking "No" here, declining treatment for new problems if one of the "No" conditions applies.

Because the doctors and nurses will always be working to keep me comfortable, they will treat the pain caused by new conditions no matter what is checked here.

If I cannot be restored to the ability to choose for myself (and thus to engage in worship and other spiritual goods), then I want new conditions treated only if they are increasing my pain. Treating something that is not increasing my pain would be unnecessary.

☐   ☐   **Tube feeding/IV fluids:** Use of tubes to deliver food
Yes   No   and water to a patient's stomach or use of IV fluids into a vein, which would include artificially delivered nutrition and hydration.

I recommend checking "No" here also, declining *artificially* delivered food and water.

This is the most difficult choice on the Tennessee form (and most other forms as well). Many biblically serious Christians oppose saying "No" here, however.

I have been convinced by pro-life Christian physicians and swallow specialists that for someone in a "No" condition, the burdens (mostly of discomfort) from the tubes used are significant. The tubes are in the veins (for liquids), through the nose and down the throat, or surgically inserted into the stomach (for food). I always want food and water offered in a safe, ordinary way, but not if I am in a "No" condition. If my mouth is kept moist, I will not feel thirsty; and when I stop reaching for food, I am not likely to feel hungry. I will not die of hunger or thirst.

Other instructions, such as burial arrangements, hospice care, etc.:

_____

_____

_____

(Attach additional pages if necessary)

On my form as "Other instructions" I say:

"I would like to be enrolled with a hospice service if one is available"; and

"I do not want medical treatment used to extend my life if it is ineffective for restoring to me the ability to make decisions for myself (in the opinion of a physician trusted by my agent) or it is excessively burdensome physically, spiritually, or financially (in the opinion of my agent)."

I have been assured by attorneys that the parenthetical "in the opinion of" clauses will lead the doctors to have my agent interpret these instructions. If no agent is available, hospital personnel will likely be confident only in estimating the physical burdens.

<u>Organ donation:</u> Upon my death, I wish to make the following anatomical gift (mark one):

☐ Any organ/tissue   ☐ My entire body
☐ Only the following organs/tissues: _____
☐ No organ/tissue donation

Here I recommend checking "Only the following organs/tissues" and listing "Heart, lungs, kidneys, liver, corneas." I also add the stipulation "Only after brain death."

SIGNATURE

Your signature must either be witnessed by two competent adults or notarized. If witnessed, neither witness may be the person you appointed as your agent or alternate, and at least one of the witnesses must be someone who is not related to you or entitled to any part of your estate.

Signature: _____   Date: _____
                    (Patient)
Witnesses:

1. I am a competent adult who is not named as the agent. I witnessed the patient's signature on this form.

2. I am a competent adult who is not named as the agent. I am not related to the patient by blood, marriage, or adoption and I would not be entitled to any portion of the patient's estate upon his or her death under any existing will or codicil or by operation of law. I witnessed the patient's signature on this form.

_____

Signature of witness number 1

_____

Signature of witness number 2

Having two (financially) disinterested witnesses for your signing the document is the hardest practical part of completing this form. (But you can use a notary public if that is easier. See below.)

This document may be notarized instead of witnessed:

STATE OF TENNESSEE

County of _____

I am a Notary Public in and for the State and County named above. The person who signed this instrument is personally known to me (or proved to me on the basis of satisfactory evidence) to be the person who signed as the "patient." The patient personally appeared before me and signed above or acknowledged the signature above as his or her own. I declare under penalty of perjury that the patient appears to be of sound mind and under no duress, fraud, or undue influence.

Notary Public: _____
                          Signature

My commission expires: _____

WHAT TO DO WITH THIS ADVANCE DIRECTIVE

- Provide a copy to your physician(s)
- Keep a copy in your personal files where it is accessible to others
- Tell your closest relatives and friends what is in the document
- Provide a copy to the person(s) you named as your health care agent

Do not skip these steps. The staff at your personal physician's office should know what to do with a copy of this form. They may want you to add your Social Security number and birth date to it, since they catalogue their records with those numbers. Copies should be given to the people whom you named as your agent and alternate agents. You should put a copy wherever your family will look for your health and financial records, and with your will.

KEY TERMS

agent
decisional capacity
organ donation
palliative care
quality of life

STUDY AND *DISCUSSION QUESTIONS

1. How are forms entitled "Living Will," "Advance Care Plan," "Durable Power of Attorney for Health Care Decisions," and "Advance Directive" related?
2. What is the role of the agent designated by an advance directive?
3. Why is it important to include multiple ways to contact the agent designated on an advance directive?

4. *Are we obligated to name our closest family member as our agent? Why or why not?

5. Under what conditions should the agent be empowered to make decisions even if the principal (the person completing the advance directive) is decisionally capable?

6. What does *quality of life* now mean in the context of end-of-life health care decisions?

7. What use of *quality of life* in the past led to Christians' distrusting people who wanted to use the term?

8. *What should a pastoral counselor do if a decision-maker (principal or surrogate agent) is unwilling to proceed because the term *quality of life* was used?

9. What is *palliative care*?

10. Why are some physicians reluctant to call for a palliative-care consult?

11. What will the medical personnel do if a person's heart stops beating while the person is admitted to the hospital if he or she has an advance directive that checks *only* the "I do not want CPR" box (and nothing in the "Quality of Life" section)?

12. *What should a pastoral counselor do if someone insists on checking boxes on an advance directive that are likely to result in greater confusion for the medical personnel?

13. *What should a pastoral counselor do if an agent for a decisionally incapable principal makes choices that the counselor is confident the principal would not make if able?

14. *Is it wise for the author to leave the "other instruction" that asks his wife to discontinue treatment that is not humanly likely to maintain or restore his ability to enjoy the ordinary means of grace?

15. What are the pros and cons of checking the boxes expressing a desire to be an organ donor?

16. What should someone do with his or her advance directive form when it is completed (with signatures, etc.)?

17. *At what age should Christians be urged to complete an advance directive for the first time? What difference might it make?

FOR FURTHER READING

Balaban, Richard B. "A Physician's Guide to Talking about End-of-Life Care." *Journal of General Internal Medicine* 15, 3 (March 2000): 195–200.

Caring Connections. "Talking with Others about Their End-of-Life Wishes." Subsection of "Planning Ahead: Have You Made a Plan?" http://www.caringinfo.org/i4a/pages/index.cfm?pageid=3282.

Childress, James F. "Organ Donation after Circulatory Determination of Death: Lessons and Unresolved Controversies." *Journal of Law, Medicine & Ethics* 36, 4 (Winter 2008): 766–71.

The Conversation Project. http://theconversationproject.org.

Sabatino, Charles P. "The Evolution of Health Care Advance Planning Law and Policy." *Milbank Quarterly* 88, 2 (2010): 211–39. http://www.jstor.org.ezproxy.covenant.edu/stable/25698387.

Schlissel, Elliot. "History of Living Wills." http://www.schlissellaw firm/com/history-of-living-wills/.

Society of Critical Care Medicine. "Resolving End-of-Life Conflicts in the ICU" (August 5, 2010) (podcast).

6

MONEY AND
END-OF-LIFE DECISIONS

Money makes it hard to think clearly. God's Word tells us that money has always been a source of trouble, and in our material-loving culture, its power to set the agenda in our thinking calls for close attention and prayer. The impact of financial considerations on medical decision-making is enormous. Medical care is typically quite expensive. It is usually very difficult to find out what medical attention will cost before deciding whether to accept or reject it. And the surrounding Western culture increasingly expects that surely *someone* will pay for medical care even if we (as individuals or families) cannot. Most people facing end-of-life decisions are beginning the process of grieving the loss of a loved one. Asking them to think about financial loss as well can seem cruel, and yet shying away from the topic only makes things worse. As awkward and harsh as it may seem, bringing the issue into the light of candid, biblically informed conversation can be a blessing. This chapter aims to provide biblical principles to inform efforts to take money into account in medical decision-making.

Chapters 1 and 2 explained the biblical basis for two principles that affect money matters:

Permission to Decline Treatment: God's Word permits us to decline life-sustaining medical treatment that is ineffective or that we, as servants of Christ, judge to be excessively burdensome.

Against Planning on a Miracle: God's Word calls us to pray when we are sick or in distress, asking God to work a wonder according to his will; but we are called to submit to God's will, making plans that do not depend on God's working a miracle.

These principles are important, but they will sometimes lead to decisions that don't make sense to non-Christian health care workers.

LIMITING TREATMENT BECAUSE OF LACK OF RESOURCES

A third principle from Scripture is especially likely to puzzle people today:

Prohibition against Unpayable Debts: God's Word forbids accepting medical services for which we cannot reasonably expect to pay out of resources that we possess, that we can expect to earn, or that we have been explicitly promised by reliable people.

This biblical prohibition is uncontroversial when the promise to repay is about luxury items. We are obligated *not* to make promises that we have no earthly reason to believe we can keep. Medical care, however, is usually not a luxury item. When I have discussed this prohibition with practicing physicians, even godly Christian physicians are troubled by the implications. They do not doubt that we are biblically obligated to pay all our debts. They are also sure that we are biblically obligated to be careful to make promises that we can keep. What troubles honest physicians is the way that the current American health care system works *against* making informed promises about paying for treatment. Many of them have concluded that the best medical outcomes are realized when everyone involved—physicians, nurses, hospital administrators, sick people, and their families—sets aside concerns about money and pursues the best medical care available. The money part can wait and will be sorted out afterward. In their experience, it usually works out.

Because I know very little about what it takes to practice medicine, I find it hard to dismiss this line of reasoning from so many Christian physicians whose wisdom and spiritual maturity I respect. And yet it seems important here to explain the biblical grounds for expecting everyone to treat the promises they make to pay for medical services when they give consent for medical treatment as genuine *promises*. I readily concede that the way in which money works in the American health care system makes it very hard to make informed promises about payment, and I lament the ways in which the system pushes both physicians and sick people to make decisions in a fantasy world, making financial responsibility extremely difficult. Thoughtful attention to this prohibition may lead Christians to make treatment decisions that surprise the people around them. A case study should help make the complexity and the implications of the prohibition clear:

> A 79-year-old man, Ben, has been rushed to the hospital with shortness of breath and heart pain. While his heart is sound, Ben is found to have acute pneumonia on top of chronic emphysema from a lifetime of smoking. With BiPap support when sleeping and a high-flow nasal cannula the rest of the time, he is able to carry on short conversations, understand things read to him, and watch television. When he was admitted to the hospital, Ben read and signed the standard forms consenting to medical treatment and agreeing to pay for the services he received. It is evident that he is in some pain most of the time, but he is tough and never complains. Sadly, Ben's financial assets are nearly gone: he has sold all his property; his bank accounts are nearly empty; he has exceeded the lifetime maximum for his insurance policy; and he has used up all his government benefits. Ben embraces Christ's work on his behalf and loves God's Word; his wife died three years ago; his five children and sixteen grandchildren all love Christ and live independently of him; and he was recently reconciled to the one person against whom he had nurtured a grudge. The attending physician—an intensivist—says that Ben has three options:

Money and End-of-Life Decisions   201

1. Be intubated and placed on a respirator. With this treatment, he could live in the ICU for as long as six months.

2. Increase the use of BiPap and attack his respiratory difficulties. With this treatment, he may live in the ICU for as long as six weeks.

3. Discontinue the use of BiPap and be transferred to a comfort-only bed. With this treatment, he may live as long as six days.

When Ben asks about the cost of each of these options, the physician responds that she has no idea, but a case manager at the hospital estimates that Ben's government assistance will pay for only option 3.[1]

The "Prohibition against Unpayable Debts" principle means that Ben may choose only option 3. To most people in America today, this will seem like an unfair, unnecessary, and possibly cruel restriction on Ben. Yet the Bible is our final standard for fairness, necessity, and blessing. While it is a sad reality, only option 3 is biblically permissible because of Ben's financial situation.

When Ben was admitted to the hospital, he or his legal representatives signed forms consenting to the treatment he would receive and agreeing to pay for all the medical services he would accept. His signatures on these forms were promises. Even though Ben needs medical help badly, the treatment he is receiving in the ICU is in exchange for his promise of payment. When he first came to the hospital, the law required the emergency department to stabilize his condition regardless of his ability to pay, but if Ben were to insist that he never intends to pay for any of his treatment, the hospital would have the right—and possibly

---

1. The facts in this case follow the death of my own father in June 2014, but with three crucial differences. My father's pain was much greater because of a softball-sized malignant mass in his right lung; he had executed an advance directive calling for DNR/DNI; and he had the financial resources to pay for all three options. See chapter 1 for my father's outcome.

the obligation—to discharge him.[2] American hospitals today (2017) will continue to treat Ben even if he says that he won't pay, but that does not change Ben's legal and biblical obligation to keep his promises.

The standard form that people sign when they are admitted to an American hospital includes a paragraph something like this:

> Payment Guarantee: *The undersigned agrees*, whether he or she signs as a patient, as patient's guardian, as patient's agent, or representative, or as guarantor on behalf of patient, *that in consideration of the services rendered* to the patient, *he or she and/or guarantor hereby individually obligate themselves to pay the account owed* by the patient to Memorial Hospital. Should the account be referred to a collection agency or an attorney for collection, the undersigned shall pay reasonable attorney's fees and/or collection agency fees, and all other costs of collection, including court costs. *The undersigned further agrees to pay interest at the maximum rate allowed by law on any balance remaining more than 30 days from discharge or treatment date.* The undersigned further authorize the transfer or any overpayment on this account to be applied to any accounts on which the undersigned is a patient, guarantor, or otherwise legally responsible.
>
> I, the undersigned, declare and represent that I have read this document, understand it, and that any questions have been answered to my satisfaction. The undersigned further certifies that he is the patient or is duly authorized by the patient as the patient's general agent or representative to execute the foregoing and accept its terms.[3]

People who refuse to sign the admission form do not receive treatment, so anyone who is in a hospital room for treatment outside the emergency

2. The official statement of these federal requirements is found at https://www.cms.gov/Regulations-and-Guidance/Legislation/EMTALA/.

3. Emphasis added. This wording is from the "General Consent" form at Memorial Hospital, Chattanooga, Tennessee. Similar wording can be found in the admissions form for many other hospitals. See, for example, the University of Virginia Culpeper Medical Center form: https://www.uvaculpeperhospital.com/media/1542/2015-10-uva-culpeper-hospital-consent-for-treatment-form-english.pdf.

department either has signed the form or has had it signed by a legal representative. Ben must have signed a form that included promises like these. So Ben has made a solemn promise to pay for any treatment he agrees to. If he were to choose option 1 or 2, he would be promising to pay for the services involved. Because he has no reasonable expectation of raising the money needed to pay for the services, he would be making a false promise if he were to choose either option 1 or 2.

The Biblical Case against Promising to Pay without Adequate Grounds

The biblical case against false promises to repay is clear. A promise is a vow. Ecclesiastes 5:4–5 says that it is better not to vow at all than to vow and not repay. Psalm 37:21 observes that the wicked (as opposed to the righteous) borrow and do not repay. Romans 13:8 exhorts us to be indebted to no one. For Christians—those who bear the name of Christ—a promise is a vow that implicates the honor of God's name. So a knowingly false promise violates the third commandment not to take the Lord's name in vain (Ex. 20:7) and Jesus' explication of this commandment in Matthew 5:33–37 (let your "Yes" be "Yes" . . .). Even though the economic circumstances in Old Testament times and the first-century world were somewhat different from ours today, Scripture commands us to make only promises that we intend to keep and have a sound reason to believe we can fulfill.[4] In addition, other passages of Scripture treat borrowing as enslavement (Prov. 22:7) and take for granted the folly of making choices without counting the costs (Luke 14:28–33). Counting the costs of treatment options in the hospital today is maddeningly difficult, but that difficulty does not remove our obligation to make promises only when we have good reasons for thinking we can keep them. God's Word forbids accepting medical treatment in exchange for a promise to pay when we cannot expect to keep the promise to pay out of our own resources or out of gifts already explicitly pledged for that purpose.

4. See, for example, Gene A. Getz, *A Biblical Theology of Material Possessions* (Chicago: Moody Press, 1990), 263ff.

The dire state of Ben's health is a key part of this problem. He can afford only option 3 because *none* of his options includes the ability to earn more money. His age is also a factor, since even if he could return to work, it would be for only a short time. Because his children are adults, he can plan to use their resources only if they approve and commit to helping him. If Ben were a young man, he could use his likely future earnings and even legally commit his minor children to using their earnings to pay for medical treatment now. Ben has none of these kinds of resources to include in a reasonable plan to repay.

Answering Objections to the Prohibition against Promising to Pay without Grounds

Even though the Scriptures are clear about not making promises that we cannot keep, it is tempting today to think that medical debts are somehow different. We might think that no one—including the hospital—expects anyone to read the admission form carefully. The form says that the person signing it understands what it contains and has had all questions about it answered; but we might think that these conditions cannot be met by anxious, distracted people going through the hospital admissions process. We might also think that because the prices for medical services are sometimes disconnected from ordinary market forces, it is unreasonable to expect anyone to pay the full "sticker" price. We might even think that human life is so valuable that bringing money into the discussion about end-of-life medicine shows a callous disregard for the sanctity of life.

As plausible as these misgivings may seem, they should not be decisive for Christians concerned to honor God's law. The temptation to imagine that no one expects a signed admissions form to mean anything rests on wishful thinking. The hospital certainly intends to be paid. The courts hold the hospitals and doctors responsible for fulfilling the promises that they make; the hospitals and physicians reasonably expect those receiving their services to pay for them.[5] The

___

5. Most health care providers realize that insurance companies have made deals to pay only a percentage of the sticker price. The person receiving care promises to pay

promises included in the forms use complicated language because simpler language might leave loopholes that unscrupulous people would to use to claim that they are not obligated to pay. However the promise is worded, our word is to be our pledge. If the form simply said, "By signing this form, I promise to pay for all the services I receive," it would be easier to follow. The substance of the promise, however, would be the same.

The objection that the hospital admissions process is asking for a promise at a terrible time is compelling, but not sufficient to remove the obligation to pay. The admissions process in the hospital is rarely a place for careful, stress-free, detached deliberation. Shock, anxiety, medical ignorance, and massive uncertainties about the future all work against thinking all the way through what is happening and (maybe especially) against paying close attention to the tiny print on all the forms. Given all these obstacles, we should have compassion for people who sign the forms and only later discover that the collection agency is serious. None of this changes the situation for Ben. He has been asked to choose among treatment options. He has already signed the forms that commit him to paying for the services he receives. It is not standard hospital practice for the physician to ask Ben to remember his promise to pay or to think through his financial resources when choosing among the options. A pastor, elder, or believing friend, however, should gently help Ben add the money question to his deliberations. No one, including Ben, is helped by pretending that the money part of the decision is irrelevant.

Highlighting the great value that God's Word places on human life is consistent with including the financial implications in Ben's decision-making process. Just as Ben's life is precious, so is his integrity and the honor of God's name. One clear mark of an honest person is the determination to keep a promise even when it involves sacrifice. By rejecting treatment options that he cannot afford, Ben would not

---

what is charged until a lower amount is demanded. Some insurance companies will assist in estimating out-of-pocket (real) costs in advance. A more general resource is http://fairhealthconsumer.org/medicalcostlookup.php.

be valuing money over his life. He would be valuing keeping his word over securing what could be a slightly longer life in the hospital.

If Ben is resolved to accept only medical treatment that he can afford, he is likely to discover that it is very difficult to find out exactly what each of the options will cost. Agreeing to medical treatment in America today is not like agreeing to have a plumber fix a backed-up sewer line. The plumber would estimate the cost of the job up front. If the job turned out to be more complex than the plumber estimated, the work would stop until a new agreement was reached about the cost of finishing the job. In the hospital, no one offers an estimate of the total costs involved. For someone who has health insurance, it is sometimes possible to get a very general estimate of likely out-of-pocket costs. United Health, for example, maintains a website that gives its clients an expected total cost for a specific procedure performed at a specific facility. Using this service, someone covered by a United Health plan could find out ahead of time that a total knee replacement with follow-up therapy at a local hospital would cost "only" $10,000 after meeting the deductible.

The $10,000 in this case is an estimate, but it is not an estimate like the plumber's. With the plumber, if the job cannot be done for the estimate agreed on, the person with the backed-up sewer line can choose to discontinue the work. After agreeing to the estimate, the plumber cannot keep working, assuming that whatever the cost, it will be paid for by someone. The promise to pay the plumber the estimated costs might need to be revisited, but it is not open-ended. Accepting medical treatment in America today (and signing forms promising to pay whatever it costs) is effectively writing a blank check, leaving it to the hospital, every physician or therapist who contributes to the case, and the insurance provider to fill in the final amount.

It is a mercy that the medical bills that eventually arrive usually make sense even when they are staggeringly high. Conscientious people rearrange their lives and work to repay what they owe. Ben, however, cannot honestly plan to wait for the bill to arrive and then try to figure out a way to pay it. No matter which options he chooses, he will never be able to make more money. While it is a frustrating aspect of a fallen world, because he knows he lacks the resources to pay for option 1 or 2, Ben should decline those options.

Against Planning on the Generosity of Others

Ben's financial assets are not the only way in which his bills might be paid. Others may step forward to pay them for him. Another biblical principle guiding Ben's decision addresses the possibility of help from others. Jesus' parable of the laborers in the vineyard (Matt. 20:1–15) assumes that the workers should expect only what they had been promised.

Against Presuming on Charity: God's Word counsels against making promises that depend on the generosity of others.

While Ben may accept financial help from others, he may not presume upon others' helping without explicit promises from them.

Setting aside questions whether the government should be paying for any of Ben's three options,[6] two other possible sources of payment deserve careful attention: the church (as a diaconal responsibility) and businesses that turn a profit in the medical services industry. With both the church and the businesses, a clear promise to pay Ben's costs would be a marvelous instance of generosity. Even so, neither the church nor the businesses have a biblical obligation to make the promise to Ben.

The diaconal ministry of the church was established to meet the needs of widows (in Acts 6) and others in distress.[7] The church receives

6. The responsibility of government entities to pay for medical care is both complicated and a matter of political debate. Whatever the government's role *ought* to be, for Ben and others making end-of-life medical decisions, what matters is only what the current government has *promised* to pay *for their care*. Ben's government-promised assistance has been depleted. For an overview of the ethical issues surrounding government funding and control of medical care, see "Social Justice and Access to Health Care," in *Biomedical Ethics*, ed. David DeGrazia, Thomas Mappes, and Jeffrey Brand-Ballard, 7th ed. (New York: McGraw-Hill, 2011), 623–706.

7. For a brief account of the role of deacons, see Sean Michael Lucas, *On Being Presbyterian: Our Beliefs, Practices, and Stories* (Phillipsburg, NJ: P&R Publishing, 2006), 109, 142–43; *The Book of Church Order of the Presbyterian Church in America,*

money and other gifts from its members in order to meet these needs. A strong case can be made that church members have a biblical obligation to give at least 10 percent of their income to the church for it to use to carry out its ministry, but even if every member is tithing, church funds are limited. The health care costs of church members are certainly a legitimate object of diaconal support. Health care costs are not, however, the only or even the most important needs that church members and other neighbors face. The church as a body has a clear biblical obligation to use its resources to assist those in need. It does not have a biblical obligation to provide all the funds that every church member has for every need.

Even if Ben's church had enough in its diaconal fund to pay for either option 1 or 2, the church would still not be obligated to offer money to Ben to expand his treatment options. The church *could* decide to offer the funds, but God's law does not require the church to offer them. The officers of the church have a biblical obligation to use the church's resources prudently. Responsible stewardship of these resources means taking likely future needs into account. Ben is probably not the only church member with financial needs, and it would be appropriate to decline offering the money to Ben in order to have funds available to help others. The church could make a special appeal for gifts from members to make it possible to make a prudent offer to Ben. The church may, on the other hand, study the history of its diaconal support and determine that using church funds to expand end-of-life treatment options would be an unsustainable practice.

Regardless of the church's decisions and policies, any funds that the church chose to make available to Ben would be generous gifts, not support owed to him. Ben cannot righteously promise to pay for option 1 or 2 based only on the possibility that the church will help. The same line of reasoning rules out making promises that depend

---

6th ed. (Lawrenceville, GA: Office of the Stated Clerk of the General Assembly of the Presbyterian Church in America, 2016), 7-2, 9, http://www.pcaac.org/wp-content/uploads/2012/12/2016-BCO-Reprint-for-web-bookmarks-links-rev.-10-5-16.pdf.

on acts of generosity by others involved in his care. The hospital caring for Ben, like nearly all other American hospitals, ends up giving away large sums of money to its customers by deciding not to pursue payment. A nurse might tell Ben, "Last year this hospital gave away $4.2 million worth of medical services, and the doctor who gave you the options decided not to collect on over $100,000 in fees." On the basis of this information, Ben could ask whether the hospital and the doctors would be willing to provide their services for free. If they explicitly agreed that they would, options 1 and 2 would become biblically available to Ben. If they did not clearly release Ben from his promise to pay, however, he would not be permitted to plan on their charitable support.

Ben's insurance carrier, current or former employers, and various governmental agencies might also step forward and offer to cover the costs of options that Ben cannot afford. Any or all of these could expand Ben's legitimate options. But the mere possibility of their generosity is not enough for Ben to include their support in his decision about his options.

The limitations that Ben's financial situation put on his treatment options are real sources of grief. Medical care in the United States today is amazing in what it makes possible. For most of human history and in many parts of the world even today, Ben would be looking at only an option 4: stay as comfortable as possible at home while dying in pain. Whether rich or poor, that is the only option that most people have ever had. Ben lives at a time when and in a place where the medical options are abundant, and he is given the power to choose among them. A person like Ben living in a country with socialized medicine would probably not be offered option 1 or 2 even if the hospital he was in had the equipment and the expertise to make them possible. In those countries, decisions about end-of-life care are made by government agencies working to use the overall health care budget for the good of all. Anyone grieved by the way Ben's poverty limits his biblically appropriate options should acknowledge that it is a grief that depends on Ben's being blessed with available technology and the freedom to make the choice at all.

LIMITING TREATMENT EVEN WHEN MONEY IS AVAILABLE

Not having the money to pay is a strong reason to decline a medical treatment option. Yet it is not the only way in which financial considerations should inform end-of-life decisions. God supplies us with financial resources so that we might do good to our family, our neighbors, and ourselves. Living as long as possible is a great good on which we might spend our resources, but it is not the only good that money can buy. Another principle explained in chapter 2 applies here:

The Duty to Steward Our Resources: God's Word requires us to make faithful use of all our talents, opportunities, and resources: time, energy, attention, and money.

To see how this principle might matter, consider Bob. His situation is just like Ben's (a believer, 79 years old, widowed, and in the hospital facing a choice among three options), but Bob has just enough money put away to afford all three of the options that the physician is presenting. Because he can sincerely promise to pay for the medical services involved, Bob is biblically permitted to choose any of the options. Living longer is a biblically approved good even if it is all spent in an ICU.

Other Biblical Goods That We May Pursue Instead

Having biblical *permission* to choose any of the options does not mean that Bob is biblically *obligated* to choose the one that keeps him alive the longest. Bob can still righteously decide that spending months on a ventilator imposes burdens on him that greatly exceed the benefits involved. He may judge that the physical burden is excessive. He may judge that the psychological, social, or spiritual burden is excessive. And he may judge that the financial burden is excessive even if all the other burdens seem manageable. Bob may have intended to have a portion of his estate used to support the spread of the gospel in central Asia. This is a biblically appropriate good, and so it is a legitimate use of Bob's resources. Bob would be biblically permitted to use his resources to spread the gospel rather than live longer in an ICU bed. In that case, he would be deciding that the burden of *not* being able to support the evangelism effort greatly exceeded the benefit of living longer in the hospital.

Supporting the spread of the gospel is not the only good that Bob might deem more important than living longer in the hospital. His failing health is drastically limiting his resources of time, energy, and opportunity. Bob does not have long to live. He is likely to tire very quickly for the rest of his life no matter what the doctors do. The chief resources that Bob can steward while on a ventilator would be his ability to pray and his money. First Thessalonians 5:17 and 1 Timothy 2:1 call on Bob to be zealous in prayer as long as he is able. The Scriptures do not require him to keep himself alive for the purpose of laboring in prayer. All of Bob's money is ultimately a gift from the Lord, and Bob is responsible to use it in a way that pleases his Master. Bob must use his resources to get food, clothing, and shelter for himself. Neglecting those basic requirements would be irresponsibly compromising his resources of time, energy, and attention. As sick as Bob is, none of the medical options will restore his energy and attention. Bob is permitted to spend his money on other goods.

One good that Bob might choose over the expensive medical options is leaving an inheritance for his children. Almost all the references in Scripture to "inheritance" are about the *spiritual* inheritance that we have in Christ. Bob cannot purchase that for his children. What he can provide is infinitely less valuable than Christ's atoning work, and yet the money it would take to keep Bob alive on a ventilator could be a great help to his children. The Bible does not command us to leave an inheritance. But Proverbs 13:22a says, "A good man leaves an inheritance to his children's children." Proverbs 19:14 notes that wealth is inherited from fathers; and in Proverbs 8:18, Lady Wisdom herself says that enduring wealth is with her. Leaving an inheritance is clearly a good thing to do:

The Goodness of Leaving an Inheritance: God's Word encourages us to leave an inheritance to our children.

All sorts of other biblically appropriate goods might be chosen over more days in the hospital. Bob could forgive debts that others owed him. He could remove a cause of division among brothers by paying off a loan between them. He could give his money to the deacons to meet church needs as they thought best. As part of his effort to be a faithful steward of his resources, Bob may choose option 1 or 2, or he may choose option 3 and use his money to pursue other biblically appropriate goods.

The cases of Ben and Bob are medically dire, but they are relatively easy because both men are able to make the decisions involved. They are able to decide for themselves what burdens are excessive, and can act as the stewards of their own resources. If Bob chooses to spend his money on leaving an inheritance or supporting evangelism, he will reap the benefits of accomplishing those good ends and bear the burden of living a somewhat shorter life. If he chooses to spend his money on medical treatment, he will enjoy the benefit of a longer life and bear the burdens that come with that treatment. Each has the authority to steward his resources within the wise limits of God's law. Financial considerations in medical choices become more complicated if the decisions must be made by others.

Finances and Speaking for Loved Ones

Both civil law and the Scriptures give other people the authority to make choices for men like Bob if he cannot make them for himself. Spouses, for example, have the power to make decisions for each other. Having been made one flesh by God (Matt. 19:4–6), husband and wife are one. They do not merely guess about what is good for each other. If either is unable to speak or decide, the other speaks for the one who is not able. As explained in chapter 2, this makes a crucial difference when medical decisions are needed. What the Scriptures teach about the one-flesh union of biblical marriages warrants this biblical principle:

Covenant Decision-Making Authority: God's Word authorizes spouses to speak (give a substituted judgment) for each other.

While the authority rests on a covenant connection, confidence about the decision being made on behalf of a spouse should rest on knowledge of what that spouse would choose.

To see how this principle applies, consider the case of Carl. His situation is similar to Bob's (79 years old, weak heart, needing oxygen support, adequate financial resources, and offered the three options 1, 2, and 3), but Carl is unconscious and his wife, Anne, is still alive and able to speak for him. Carl cannot choose between the three options because he is unconscious. Instead, the physician will ask Anne which of the three Carl would want. The choice will not be easy for Anne. The gravity of the situation, the enormity of the consequences, and the pain of knowing that the end is likely near will all weigh heavily on Anne. The choice is Carl's to make; she has the authority to make it on his behalf.

Anne and Carl may have discussed what he would choose in a situation similar to this one. That would help a lot, but it wouldn't make the choice emotionally easy. Carl may have left an advance directive or other clear instructions where Anne could easily find them (with his personal physician, or with the hospital when he was admitted). Those instructions would help Anne confirm what she believes Carl would want, and the documents would convince the medical staff to accept Anne's decision without hesitation. Prior conversations and written instructions would increase Anne's confidence that she was speaking for Carl. Nothing, though, will make the choice obvious, and this is especially true if Anne knows that Carl would want the financial consequences to be taken into consideration.

Carl and Anne have the biblical authority to steward all their resources. Carl's time, energy, and opportunities for service and enjoyment are now greatly limited by his physical condition. Carl and Anne's financial assets, on the other hand, are still available. It may seem clear to Anne that the money ought to be spent in keeping Carl alive as long as possible. If she is sure that Carl would want it spent that way, she should say, "Carl would want option 1." Saying it that way will help her focus on the specific choice she is making. She is not being asked to say what *she* would want. Anne's task is to say what *Carl* would want. Has Carl ever talked about how he wants to die? Has he expressed his feelings about people who spend their money fighting to live a bit longer in a hospital bed? Does his advance directive indicate his priorities in this situation?

Carl may never have talked about his own death or left written instructions, but Anne can probably remember things he said about providing for her if she lived longer, about leaving an inheritance for their children, or about using their wealth to support spiritually worthy causes. Before Anne chooses option 1 because she is not ready to lose Carl, she ought to consider what Carl would choose if he could. "What Carl would choose" is complicated. Because they are one in God's eyes, Carl would not be choosing only to please himself. If Carl were able to choose for himself in this situation, he should be eager for Anne's input, taking Anne's desires into account in choosing among the options. Anne may have a strong preference for option 2, willing to spend some of their time and money to make doubly sure that the medical remedies are exhausted and to give her time to adjust to her loss. Carl should see serving Anne's needs as a great good that their resources can accomplish now.

Ultimately, Anne is choosing for *them*. The hospital staff will urge her to speak for Carl, choosing as he would. Her decision will be followed most readily if it is in the form "Carl would want . . ." Anne, though, will know that she is choosing for *them*. If she and Carl have not discussed what he would want in a situation like this, she will have to imagine both sides of a conversation between Carl and herself about it. He would listen to her desires for him and for the use of their resources. She would listen to his desires. Together they would agree on a way forward, taking into account his needs, her needs, and the use of their resources. Thinking through all this on her own will be hard for Anne. Friends and family can help her, and she would be wise to ask for their sense of what Carl would want. In the end, the decision will be like many other decisions that Anne and Carl have made together in the past: informed by the advice of loved ones, but finally theirs.

Making the decision with Carl close by but not participating will be disorienting for Anne. His inability to contribute will tempt Anne to think that she is selfish or unspiritual if she allows money to play a big role in the choice. If Carl would want the money spent on other biblically approved goods, Anne should try to honor his desire. Christians in America avoid talking about their own money in church or among church friends. This can lead us to think that money should be excluded from all spiritually serious conversations, and give us the vague sense that allowing financial implications to affect medical choices is shallow—or even worldly. Anne (and all of us) should give money matters their appropriate place. Faithful stewardship of our resources is spiritually serious. Friends and fellow church members can help Anne by gently asking her to talk about what Carl wanted from the future. What did he want for himself? What did he want for Anne? For their children? How were they hoping to use their wealth? Money should not be the first concern; yet it should not be left out. Speaking for Carl means considering what he would have considered, including the costs of treatment and the other things that they might have done with the money.

The task of taking all these things into account when speaking for Carl would be even more difficult if Anne cannot or will not do it. In that case, the task would fall to Carl's children, both by law and according to God's Word. States differ on what it takes for children to speak for their parents. Most hospitals interpret state law as requiring that the children reach a consensus before their decision can count as a substituted judgment for someone like Carl. A few states count a majority of the children as speaking for the parent, pushing siblings to lobby for their positions before having a family vote. Every state accepts the decision of a legally appointed agent over even the wishes of a majority of the children.

Even though it is probably obvious, here is another place to highlight the great blessing that Carl can give his loved ones by completing a legally enacted advance directive and leaving it where it will be found when decisions are needed. If Anne is able to make decisions for him, Carl's words and preferences in the advance directive will help her imagine his side of the conversation about what to do. If Anne is not able to make choices, the advance directive will name a list of alternate agents, in order. If the document gives decision-making power to one of Carl's children, that child will have the authority to speak for Carl even if the rest of the family is impossibly deadlocked about what to do. A wise child will surely ask the siblings (and grandparents, uncles, and aunts) for input, but the named agent will have the legal and biblical authority to make the decision for Carl.

Because Carl would have the biblical authority to decline or accept option 1 or 2, any of Carl's legal surrogates will have the authority to choose as they believe Carl would choose. Anne, for example, has the authority to say that Carl would not want option 1 because *they* valued saving some of the money to meet her needs over Carl's living a bit longer on machines in the hospital. (When she explains the choice to the physician, Anne should say that *Carl* would consider the burdens of option 1 to greatly exceed the benefits. The hospital wishes to do what Carl would want. Asking the hospital to acknowledge that Carl and Anne are one person in God's eyes is not worth the confusion that it would cause.)

Anyone else speaking for Carl will need to remember that the money is not theirs. Often, children are willing to spend their parents' money on good things (such as more days of life) that the parents themselves would not choose. Sometimes the children's reasons are noble. Yet if their parents' wishes are biblically appropriate, the children should make the choices that their parents would make. If Carl would not choose to live his last days on a ventilator, his children should not choose option 1 for him. Carl may have said that he does not want to endure the discomfort, isolation, and spiritual limitations that would come with option 1. He may have said that he wants his money spent on caring for their mother rather than on exotic medical treatment. He may even have said that he wants his money spent on his grandchildren rather than on this kind of medical treatment. The children or another agent should honor Carl's efforts to steward his resources faithfully.

Before leaving Carl's case, it is worth noting that hospital workers today will be surprised if Carl's family openly talks about doing what

Carl would want, including what Carl would want to happen to Anne and the money. The hospital staff's reluctance (or simple inability) to talk about the money side of things reinforces an American cultural inclination to pretend that money should not matter in medical decisions. Away from the hospital, everyone knows that medical treatment is expensive. Inside the hospital, talk of money is somehow vulgar. End-of-life choices are an opportunity for Christians to show that we do not live according to our culture's values. Christians live to serve Jesus. Our lives, our talents, our opportunities, and even our material possessions ultimately belong to him. By talking openly about everything that goes into our medical decisions, we have the opportunity to show what it means to live to serve Jesus. Our honesty about money and readiness to value things other than slightly longer life might not prompt others to ask us about Jesus or our hope in him. The oddness of it will nonetheless lead them to wonder. We can pray and trust that they will find answers from other believers.

MONEY AND MEDICAL TREATMENT FOR CHILDREN

Thinking through medical decisions for a very sick 79-year-old is difficult—and it should be. Disease and death are persistent reminders that the world is broken because of sin. When death is imminent because medical options are limited for any reason, whether financial or not, we are rightly grieved. Choices about medical treatment for gravely sick children are typically more heart-wrenching than choices for people who have "seen their children's children." These choices often also involve considerations that usually do not apply to choices for the elderly. Parents have a biblical duty to provide for their children (Prov. 31:10–31; Matt. 7:7–11), but that duty does not take precedence over all other demands (1 Tim. 5:8; 1 Peter 4:7–11):

Obligation to Provide and Serve: God's Word requires us to care for those who depend on us and to use our time and talents to serve others as we are able.

In order to see some of the additional complexity that can arise, consider the case of Joel:

Estimating Future Earning Potential: The Case of Joel

Joel is the 5-year-old son of Megan and Bryan Miller. Concerned about dizziness and then mild seizures, the Millers agree to have Joel tested. The scans reveal that Joel has a brain tumor. A biopsy determines that the tumor is malignant. The Millers are heartbroken and scared. The doctors involved believe that with aggressive treatment and strict attention to the treatment plan, Joel has an 80 percent chance of complete remission. Humanly speaking, the odds favor Joel's living a productive life once the fight with cancer is over. As a medical matter, it is easy to see that the Millers should agree to follow the doctors' instructions. As a financial matter, the picture is less clear.

Megan and Bryan are both between jobs. One of the reasons they were reluctant to have Joel tested was financial. They weren't sure they could even afford the *tests* that were recommended. If the tests were out of reach, they were sure that any treatment would be also. Bryan is an auto mechanic and has never had health insurance. Megan's work as a software developer had benefits, and when she quit work to focus on Joel, Bryan had steady work. They planned to purchase a government insurance plan, and so Megan did not pay to continue her company health insurance policy. The process of finding a government plan was difficult. Between the hassle and the high cost, they had not finished the process when Joel was diagnosed. Although they can still get basic coverage, the deductibles are high and the maximum benefit is low. Even with help from a consultant recommended by the cancer clinic, they do not honestly see how they could ever pay for the cost of Joel's treatment.

The decision that the Millers must make in this case is terrible. On top of the anxieties surrounding the prospect of some combination of radiation therapy, chemotherapy, and brain surgery, they do not have the money to pay for the treatment that Joel needs. Together they have been crying to the Lord in prayer for Joel's supernatural healing and for God somehow to provide them with the money. The Lord's answer so far has been to show his love in other ways. Their friends have drawn close to them. They have grown in their prayer lives. They are more at peace with each other than they have ever been. Yet Joel's seizures are growing more frequent, and no one has stepped forward to offer to help them pay for the treatment.

Megan and Bryan talk about organizing a fund-raising drive. They talk about bake sales, car washes, and putting pictures of Joel on donation cans in local stores. In the end, they decide against this approach. Megan decides against it because she has done research on how much they could hope to raise this way. Once the costs of the efforts are subtracted, the gain will not be nearly enough to make the treatment affordable.

Bryan decides against the fund-raising approach because he isn't comfortable with squeezing his friends and neighbors for money. He has seen others take the fund-raising approach before Joel's diagnosis, and it has made him uncomfortable. Sometimes he bought some brownies or put a couple of dollars into the donation can, but it never seemed quite right. After studying the problem of his attitude, he has determined that God's Word calls him to be both generous and prudent. Before Joel was diagnosed, Bryan had decided that it wasn't prudent to give haphazardly to these requests, giving a little bit when the appeal hit him emotionally but always resenting being asked. Confident that the deacons at his church would know far better where the most pressing needs are, he stopped giving to these private appeals and instead started giving beyond his tithe to the deacons' mercy fund. His income has been meager recently, so his contributions have been small, but they have been steady. He recommends to Megan that they ask the church for help rather than having a public fund-raising campaign.

Megan agrees with Bryan's approach. The deacons carefully consider their request and the church's resources, and make a little over $3,000 available to them. Bryan and Megan are moved by the offer, since they know it is a sizable portion of all that their church has. It is more than they are likely to raise by a public campaign, and yet it isn't nearly enough to ensure their ability to pay for the treatment.

It may seem that there is no choice for the Millers to make. Their situation may seem identical to the situation that Ben faced earlier in this chapter. For lack of resources, it may seem that the Millers cannot honestly promise to repay the cost of cancer treatment for Joel. In the Millers' case, however, there is a crucial difference between Ben's situation and theirs. Joel is young and is likely to recover and earn money on his own. Megan and Bryan also have years of earning potential ahead of them. The reasonable prospect of these future earnings makes it possible for the Millers to make an honest promise to pay for the treatment.

The Bible commends God's people for making careful, responsible plans for future needs and to include future opportunities in their plans. Proverbs 6:6–11 and 30:25 tell us to consider the foresight and industry of ants, creatures that store up resources against future needs. Psalm 20:4 and Proverbs 15:22 and 20:18 note that God blesses plans based on wise counsel. Jesus' warning about counting the cost of discipleship in Luke 14:28–33 implies a commendation of those who *do* count the cost. A promise to repay a debt on the reasonable expectation of future earnings is not a false promise. It can be a solemn undertaking to devote future earnings to present needs. The following biblical principle applies to the choice that the Millers must make:

Making Prudent Plans: God's Word encourages us to make reasonable plans about future resources and needs.

The Millers may not have the money now to repay the costs for the cancer treatment. Humanly speaking, it would be reasonable for them to think that they and Joel will earn enough money to pay off the costs involved. The reasonableness of this expectation will depend on many things. The likely total cost of the medical treatment will matter. The likely future earning potential of Megan and Bryan and then of Joel when he is older will matter. Even though the time for deliberation is short, the Millers should be encouraged by their godly friends to get estimates on the expenses involved and to think through likely future earnings.

As was true for Ben, the Millers should not make promises to repay that depend on gifts that have not been promised (from their extended family, their friends, the hospital, the insurance company, or the government). They are biblically permitted to make public appeals or to ask their family for help. Their request to the church's mercy fund is certainly appropriate. But they should not count on what others *might* give without explicit promises. None of these other sources of funding has a biblical obligation to devote resources to Joel's treatment. It is right to lament over the brokenness of the world and our limited ability to push back against it. Brokenness and limitations do not obligate anyone to commit the resources necessary to pay for Joel's treatment. If careful estimations of future earning potential and the funds promised by others still cannot be expected to cover the costs of treatment, the Millers will need to say no to it.

In the case as described, it is likely that the Millers will determine that by combining their own earnings with Joel's, they will be able to repay the costs of the treatment. On the basis of that sober estimate, they are biblically permitted to start the treatment regimen. They will be making promises both for themselves and also for Joel. Their decision to start the treatment is technically made on Joel's behalf, saying what he would want (rather than what they desire for him). God's Word gives the Millers the authority to speak for Joel as their child. They can accept the treatment for him, and they can make the promise on his behalf to pay for it with his future earnings.

Most parents in the Millers' situation would make all these promises, praying that God would give them the strength or help to repay the debts by means natural or supernatural. Their promises would be faithful because they would have good reasons for thinking that the natural means will be sufficient. Even so, having the biblical authority to make these promises to secure the cancer treatment does not mean that they have a biblical *obligation* to start the treatment. The doctors' estimate of what is likely is not a guarantee, and the Millers' expectations about future earning power are also estimates. The Millers may instead decide not to rely on these estimates. They are not biblically obligated to keep Joel alive as long as medical means allow. They are obligated to make the choices that Joel himself would make.

Because Joel is a child, they cannot use what he has said or chosen in the past to inform their sense of what he would choose. Instead, they must imagine what he would choose after growing up in their care. God's Word permits them to imagine that Joel, raised under their loving, prayerful care, would come to value what they value. Proverbs 22:6 teaches that a child who is taught faithfully will not depart from that way. Deuteronomy 6:7–9, 20–25 calls God's people to model faithfulness to their children in deed and word. Here and elsewhere in Scripture, the faithfulness of parents contributes to the faithfulness of their children (2 Tim. 1:5). Speaking for this mature Joel, they can ask themselves what *they* would want if they were in his place. The biblical promises to parents about loving parenting warrant a further principle:

Expectation of Children's Growing to Have Similar Values: God's Word gives diligent parents confidence that their children will grow up to share their loves and commitments. While the children are young, parents may assume their own biblical priorities when speaking for their children.

In Joel's case, the likelihood of recovery and eventual repayment of the costs makes it likely that the Millers will agree that if they were in his condition, they would choose the cancer treatment for themselves. A different case will show that in different circumstances, the way forward may not be so easy. Consider the cases of Kyle Little and Ian Murphy:

Estimating Other Family Demands: The Cases of Kyle and Ian

Kyle and Ian also need cancer treatment similar to Joel's. Like Joel, Kyle is an only child; but unlike Joel, the diagnostic tests have determined that Kyle's cancer has metastasized to other organs, including his pancreas and lungs. Kyle's chances of driving the cancer into remission are under 15 percent. Ian, on the other hand, has Joel's favorable prognosis, but Ian has five siblings all under the age of 11.

Like Joel's parents, Kyle's parents (the Littles) and Ian's parents (the Murphys) have very limited financial resources. The Littles and the Murphys must each think through their financial situation before starting cancer treatment. Both of these families face complications that Joel's parents did not.

The Littles cannot confidently include Kyle's future earnings when estimating their ability to repay the costs. They may see a way to make a good-faith promise to pay for the treatment, but even then they need to consider what Kyle would choose if he could speak for himself. The Littles have the authority to speak for Kyle, and to consider what they (the parents) would want *for themselves* if they were in Kyle's situation. If they agree together that they would rather go to be with Jesus than struggle to endure all the pain and difficulty of a battle with cancer that is likely to fail, then they have the authority to speak for Kyle, declining the treatment and focusing on maximizing the days he has left. Here, money is not the crucial factor. If the Littles could see a way to pay for the treatment eventually and believed that a mature Kyle would want the money used that way, they would also have the authority to choose treatment for him.

The Murphys' financial situation raises a different set of questions. They have the authority to speak for Ian, accepting the treatment and the promise to help in repaying the costs. They also have the responsibility to care for their other five children. If they choose the cancer treatment for Ian, the commitment to pay the expenses will limit what they will be able to spend on their other children. They have the authority to speak for their other children, to commit each of them to giving up all that they might have received in order to pay for Ian's medical treatment now. No one could blame them if they chose to use the family's resources this way. But they are not obligated to choose the cancer treatment. The Murphys may, instead, decide that a grown, mature Ian with their values would not want all the family's present and future resources spent on his treatment.

Whatever choice the Murphys make in this case will be hard. Much will depend on the details of Ian's prognosis, and the needs of Ian's siblings (both physical and otherwise). Although Ian's medical need is urgent, his parents are obligated only to say what Ian would choose if he were mature and able to understand all the considerations that they (the parents) understand. God's Word provides principles that inform their decision, but in this case it does not make the decision for them.

THE ULTIMATE PLACE OF MONEY IN TREATMENT DECISIONS

Friends and counselors who are eager to pray with and assist people like those in this chapter's scenarios need to be careful when offering advice. The stress involved in these decisions is intense. The medical facts alone can be overwhelming. Shock, grief, and sometimes guilt about past mistakes can be complicating factors even when the financial impact is small. In most cases, though, money is a factor. Selfishness, fear, and even greed only add to the distress and confusion. As time allows, godly friends should encourage those facing decisions to move through the many considerations in an orderly manner, stopping frequently to pray that the Holy Spirit will heal, provide, comfort, and guide. What we should most earnestly desire is comfort and guidance. Both are promised to us in abundance, and we know that it is God's will to supply them.

Sometimes it is not God's will to heal our bodies. Sometimes it is not God's will to provide the money that we believe is absolutely necessary. No matter what happens, we know that God is providing all that we need according to his riches in Christ Jesus (Phil. 4:19). God does not wait to see whether we will generate enough faith on our own and then provide for us only if we have earned it. Every tiny bit of faith that we have is the work of the Holy Spirit in us. All that we have is according to God's grace. He provides both the faith and the other things we need.

Along with the obligation to make momentous choices comes the opportunity to show all those around us what it means to walk confidently as God's children. When healing does not come or the money falls short, we do not despair. Rather than clinging to life at the expense of false promises or abandoning our plans to accomplish other biblically approved goods, we are empowered to decline expensive medical treatment in order to accomplish those goods. We can treat the stewardship of our financial assets as one part of a much larger task of faithfully stewarding all that we have.

KEY TERMS

diaconal ministry
false promise
future earning potential
stewardship
"sticker price" for medical care
substituted judgment
unpayable debt

STUDY AND *DISCUSSION QUESTIONS

1. What is the biblical basis for the obligation to pay our debts?
2. What is biblically wrong with taking on debt that we have no earthly reason to think we can repay?
3. *How are rights and obligations related?
4. *How would conversations about what we ought to do change if all claims about rights (to receive) were expressed as claims about obligations (to provide)?
5. What biblical obligation does the church have to pay for medical care that one of its members needs but cannot afford?
6. What legal obligation does the hospital have to provide emergency medical treatment to people who ask for it?
7. What biblical obligation does the hospital have to provide non-emergency medical treatment to people who cannot afford it?
8. *What would happen if Christian medical providers charged less than non-Christians for their services?
9. Are Christians biblically obligated to pay an inflated price for medical treatment if they sign a "consent" form that includes a promise to pay for services received?
10. Under what conditions is it biblically permissible to decline life-sustaining medical treatment *in order to* spend the money it

would cost on something else (which means dying sooner than otherwise)?

11. *What steps should be taken to prevent financial considerations from overwhelming all other factors in end-of-life medical decisions?

12. How does a biblical understanding of marital union affect end-of-life money decisions between biblically married husbands and wives?

13. How might prudent estimates of future earning potential affect decisions about expensive life-sustaining medical treatment?

14. Are Christians biblically obligated to make charitable contributions to help others pay for life-sustaining medical treatment?

15. *What steps should Christian parents take to maximize the financial resources available to secure the medical services that their children need to survive and thrive? What steps should they *not* take?

16. How does Jesus' parable of the talents (Matt. 25) inform the role that finances play in end-of-life medical decisions?

FOR FURTHER READING

Crouch, Andy. *Playing God: Redeeming the Gift of Power*. Downers Grove, IL: InterVarsity Press, 2013.

Curtis, J. Randall, Ruth A. Engelberg, Mark E. Bensink, and Scott D. Ramsey. "End-of-Life Care in the Intensive Care Unit: Can We Simultaneously Increase Quality and Reduce Costs?" *American Journal of Respiratory and Critical Care Medicine* 186, 7 (October 1, 2012): 587–92.

Delehanty, Hugh, and Elinor Ginzler. *Caring for Your Parents: The Complete Family Guide: Practical Advice You Can Trust from the Experts at AARP*. 2nd ed. New York: Sterling, 2008.

Getz, Gene A. *A Biblical Theology of Material Possessions*. Chicago: Moody Press, 1990.

7

HOSPITAL REALITIES: MAKING THE MOST OF THEM

THE DISTORTED PICTURE FROM HOSPITAL DRAMAS

For most people, expectations about the way things work in the hospital come from television or movie portrayals. Fictional hospital dramas are usually compelling. They show realistic medical personnel dealing with realistic (but exotic) medical problems. Sadly, the fictional portrayals are usually poor preparation for the reality of most end-of-life challenges. Fiction distorts reality in important ways.

First, hospital dramas typically place two-dimensional characters in dramatically simple situations. The characters understand what they want. They are motivated by desires that are simple and unmixed: greed, compassion, love, ambition, and so on. Often, characters represent *types* rather than the complicated, conflicted, and confused *individuals* who face real-life challenges. Real people facing choices can be tempted by fictional dramas to think that they must decide which one desire or motive is the main one in their real story. That kind of thinking only makes things worse.

A second way that fictional hospital dramas distort reality concerns the flow of time. Fictional portrayals must hold the audience's attention. As a result, a lot happens, and most things happen fast. Reality is usually more tedious. Brief periods of intense activity are islands in a sea of waiting. Time to think turns into time to worry, and time to reflect brings fears and second thoughts. It is important to recognize the ways in which long waits can lead to frustration and doubt and to pray for comfort and faith.

Fictional hospital dramas also present moral deliberation in a distorted way. Often, fictional hospital stories are about people facing choices that are painful. Sometimes it is the pain of making great sacrifices. Recently, dramas have highlighted people who make choices that go against principles they have held for most of their lives. The people who abandon their principles find it painful, but in these stories they are driven to it by a new "insight," usually against biblical principles. The distortion in all these cases is the suggestion that making sound end-of-life choices must involve moral anguish. That is simply not true, and the dramas can lead people to believe that if a choice isn't morally difficult, it must be selfish or shallow. As God's children, we know better. Choices near the end of life are difficult because we are facing the loss of a loved one's company. But they do not have to be anguished. As in other areas of life, biblically faithful choices can be clear and made in peace.

Finally, fictional hospital dramas are spiritually flat. Stories unfold without reference to the vital, living presence of the Holy Spirit and the light given by God's Word. When Christian convictions play a role in current dramas, they are portrayed as antiscientific, fearful, and irrational. At best, these dramas teach Christians to keep their biblical beliefs entirely to themselves, depriving them of the comfort that comes with sharing all our thinking with those providing care. At worst, the spiritual emptiness of fictional dramas convinces Christians that they should not even *think* about gospel realities in the hospital.

This brief chapter aims to push past the distortions in fictional portrayals and prepare people to navigate two challenges that often arise in American hospitals today: the absence of the physician whom you see for most other health issues, and the difficulty of finding someone who can give the big picture of what is happening. These challenges are especially serious for the loved ones of someone who is unconscious or otherwise unable to make decisions.

EXPECT TO DEAL WITH STRANGERS

Most people know that when they get to the hospital, they will not know any of the nurses, technicians, or therapists who will be caring for them. But a sick person expects to see his or her doctor there. Before the year 2000, the doctor who had been giving the person physicals and advice about the need for lifestyle changes would have visited the person in the hospital. This visit would have been a source of comfort. Even more importantly, this visit would give the sick person and the family a trusted source of information. The family doctor would be someone they could rely on to be their advocate with all the new doctors and nurses. She or he could ask questions, fiddle with medical equipment, and order diagnostic tests.

Since about 2000, it has become rare for private physicians to visit people in the hospital. Even if we *want* our private doctor to visit us in the hospital, most private doctors will (correctly) insist that the hospital has physicians on staff who can give us the very best medical attention. The addition of experienced physicians who are full-time hospital employees is probably the biggest way in which hospital care in 2017 differs from hospital care in 2000. We should not lament this change. End-of-life medical care is complicated and changing rapidly. On top of this, every hospital has its own specialized equipment, protocols for handling medical records, communications channels, and management hierarchies. Even the most knowledgeable specialist from the outside will struggle to be effective. Asking private physicians to second-guess staff physicians is neither wise nor helpful.

Before 2000, most physicians who were on site around the clock in a hospital were medical residents. They were doctors-in-training: medical students who had finished their coursework. The medical care they gave was often competent, but it was still care given by relatively inexperienced practitioners who were supervised from a distance by experienced physicians.

In "teaching" hospitals, medical care still makes routine use of residents. But in both teaching and other hospitals in 2017, a doctor who walks into a sick person's room is increasingly likely to be either a *hospitalist* or an *intensivist*. These are experienced, licensed physicians—full medical doctors (MDs)—who are employees of the hospital. A hospitalist sees, diagnoses, and writes orders for all the sick people on a hospital "unit" (floor, wing, or specialized area). An intensivist sees, diagnoses, and writes orders for all the sick people in an intensive care unit. Intensivists are typically specialists in intensive medicine.[1] Hospitalists are most often specialists in internal medicine or family-practice medicine. As an ordinary part of overseeing the care of everyone on a unit, they will call in other specialists who are experts in other bodily systems as they are needed. We should want those experts called in, since the generalists will know when they need help. An intensivist may, for example, call for a cardiology consult to advise about the best way to deal with a heart problem. A hospitalist may call for a palliative-care consult to assist with prescribing the least disorienting course of pain medications.

Both hospitalists and intensivists are staff physicians. They are employees of the hospital and typically are "on" for a week and then "off" for a week, but the pattern may be somewhat different from hospital to hospital. A staff physician who is "on" will be physically at the hospital, typically for a twelve-hour shift from 7:00 A.M. to 7:00 P.M. or 7:00 P.M. to 7:00 A.M., and sometimes overlapping with groups who change shifts at 2:00 A.M. and 2:00 P.M. Usually, many more staff physicians are "on" during the day shift, but in a hospital with staff physicians, there will always be one at the facility. The medical care is continuous throughout a hospital stay because the staff physicians explain to one another what is happening with each person under their care in a "handoff." The handoff can be face to face, through written progress notes, or by other communication means, but every person in the hospital should expect that a physician is specifically overseeing the person's care all the time.

1. Descriptions of these kinds of staff physicians can be found at https://www.acponline.org/about-acp/about-internal-medicine/general-internal-medicine/hospital-medicine (for hospitalists) and https://www.umassmemorialhealthcare.org/umass-memorial-medical-center/services-treatments/critical-care/what-intensivist (for intensivists).

Common titles for the physician responsible for a person's care are *attending physician, physician of record,* and *licensed independent practitioner.* Medically, legally, and morally, this physician is responsible for what happens to someone in the hospital. In keeping with this responsibility, the attending physician is also the person best able to explain the overall medical situation. When the attending physician is in the room, getting that overall picture should be a top priority; but it may not be easy. Hospitalists and intensivists find it difficult to be in one place for long. Other people on the unit are likely to need urgent attention before the overall picture can be explained. Since the attending physician may not have time to explain the big picture, it is worth knowing other ways to get it.

GETTING THE BIG PICTURE

Making treatment decisions in the hospital can be difficult even when the medical situation is crystal clear. This rarely happens. The most knowledgeable and careful medical professionals talk about probabilities rather than certainties. The consequences of the options they offer often depend on factors either out of their control or simply unknowable. Medical expertise is rapidly advancing, and it is able to handle more and more problems. But with this increase in ability have come increased complexity, more diagnostic tests, and more specialists' adding their voices to conversations about care. Forty years ago, a stay in the hospital might involve talking to the family physician and one other doctor, probably a surgeon. Only a few tests would be ordered. The family doctor would clearly be the quarterback directing the medical care. People making decisions would almost always follow the family doctor's advice, and if the family had questions, the family doctor would answer them.

A hospital stay today is very different. The physician whom the person in the bed has been seeing for years is unlikely to visit the hospital in an official capacity. (Older family doctors still make hospital visits, but they visit as friends. If they have opinions about the medical care that is happening, they are likely to express them only in guarded terms.) Care in the hospital is now dominated by specialists and physicians employed by the hospital. The specialists are most often either hospital employees or physicians officially affiliated with the hospital. They know the hospital's policies, records systems, and culture. The most important practical implication of the move away from family doctors' visiting their people in the hospital is the loss of a clear quarterback managing the care of the person in the bed. Although every hospital has a specific way of determining who the doctor of record is for each person at any given time, in practice sick people and their families can find it hard to get the big picture even when everyone involved is being responsible. It is always okay to ask who the attending physician is.

Problem: Transitions between Physicians

Although the family doctor in the past might not visit the hospital every day, he or she would continue to visit even if the hospital stay lasted longer than a week. Today, the standard rotation for staff physicians is seven days on followed by seven days off. Tuesday morning is a fairly common time for one physician to end a week and for another physician to take over. In this transition, the attending physician changes for all the people in beds on a ward, floor, or unit. The heart of this transition is a written summary of the medical situation for each person for whom the attending physician has been caring. The physician who is rotating off writes these summaries; the physician who is coming on reads the summaries. In some hospitals, this written record is called an *interim discharge summary*. The person being cared for is not being discharged from the hospital. He or she is being discharged from one doctor's care to another's.

For those not familiar with this transition, the arrival of a strange new doctor can be confusing. Early on Tuesday, the physician coming on will visit each room to meet the people described in the summaries. The new staff doctor probably knows only what the previous week's attending physician wrote in the summary. When other duties make it impractical to read more than the summary, it is likely that the new doctor will ask questions that the sick person and the family have already answered. The answers given before are all in the sick person's chart, but because the new doctor is assuming responsibility for many people, asking these questions again serves as an efficient way to get to know them a bit in their first meeting. It is common for nurses to accompany the doctor on these visits, and the doctor may direct some questions about the medical situation first to one of the nurses who has already been caring for the sick person. This is normal and should be encouraging. It shows that the doctor is trying to get the most complete picture possible. In a teaching hospital, residents may also be in the room. The doctor may also ask the residents questions. These are usually aimed at teaching the students rather than getting a clearer picture of the situation.

People who stay for only a few days in the hospital—and who are not there during one of these transitions—may never have to adjust to a new attending physician. For people who are nearing the end of life, however, hospital stays of longer than a week are common. Making these transitions as smooth as possible helps to maintain the quality of the medical care and limits the amount of distress and discomfort for everyone. The most important contribution that the sick person and the family can make to a smooth transition is to be welcoming and patient with the process. Asking questions of a nurse practitioner or the nursing supervisor on the hall or unit during the first evening in the hospital can be especially helpful:

- "Who is my attending physician right now?"
- "When is my attending physician likely to visit our room next?"
- "When is the next handoff from one attending physician to another?"
- "Would my attending physician be open to our asking a couple of questions?"
- [If yes:] "Here are the questions that we have. Can you help us word them correctly?"

Although the attending physician likely has many people to see fairly quickly, the nurse practitioners, nursing supervisor, or charge nurse will know the doctor well enough to help you all get off on the right foot with one another.

Problem: The Many Voices

The attending physician is responsible for knowing the big picture and coordinating the care of the sick person, but the attending physician is caring for lots of people and may not have time to answer questions as they arise. In some hospitals, the attending physician may be hard to find at all after making a single daily visit. For most people with grave medical conditions, the challenge of seeing the big picture is complicated by input from all the *other* doctors and specialists who visit during the day. When my father was in the hospital for the last time, he was visited at least once a day by the hospitalist (the attending physician), a pulmonologist (a lung doctor), a cardiologist (a heart doctor), a nephrologist (a kidney doctor), a palliative-care physician (about pain management), a palliative-care advanced-practice nurse, a respiratory therapist (to work on his breathing), and a speech pathologist (to check on his ability to swallow and take food by mouth). The doctors sometimes ordered tests (X-ray, CT scan, blood work), which meant that others would come to draw blood, take the X-ray with a portable machine, or push my dad's bed to another room for a scan.

Every time a new scan, test, or diagnostic procedure was performed, someone—a radiologist or a lab technician, for example—would have to interpret the results and have the new information added to my dad's chart. On a typical day, more than ten different people contributed to the growing pile of data about my dad's condition. Many of these people visited the room. Some of them said very little, but most would offer some assessment of how my dad was doing. Over the course of the day, we were given a lot of information about *aspects* of my dad's condition. What no one gave was an *overall* assessment of his condition.

My dad's experience is now fairly typical: lots of people offering partial perspectives, but almost no one volunteering to explain the big picture. A trained medical professional would know how to add the perspectives together, but without that training it can be bewildering.

Because the sick person and the family are eager to know the big picture, it is tempting to focus on the part they understand best. With my dad, the cardiologist was always upbeat: Dad's heart was strong and getting stronger! Even though the other physicians were justifiably worried about my dad's lungs, it was difficult to see that the good news about his heart was largely irrelevant. A heart event had brought him to the hospital, but his lungs were going to fail him long before his heart did.

Temperament should not be decisive in end-of-life decision-making. I am an optimistic person. If I had not heard similar stories over and over at ethics committee meetings, I would probably have seized on the cardiologist's rosy outlook and treated it as the key to my decision-making. I may even have urged my dad to override his "do not intubate" instructions, hoping that intubation would soon be unnecessary as the rest of his system caught up with his heart. Had I been a pessimist, the discouraging assessment from the pulmonologist might have dominated my sense of the big picture. With my dad's condition, that would have been about right, but it would have been a fluke: even if he was likely to recover and return home, my pessimism would have led me to give him bad advice and make bad decisions for him if needed. It is vital that sick people and their loved ones get a clear *overall* assessment of the medical situation *by someone medically trained and not emotionally entangled in what is happening*. In some cases, getting the big picture will happen only if the sick person or the family is persistent in asking for it.

Solution 1: Palliative-Care Consult

The single most important question I asked during my dad's last hospital stay was, "Is there a palliative-care physician caring for my father?" The first time I spoke with the charge nurse on my dad's floor (see solution 2 below), I learned that my dad was in a fair amount of pain. (He had sounded odd when I spoke to him by phone, but I couldn't tell whether it was from anxiety, exhaustion, or something else. The charge nurse said that it was pain.) Palliative care is a relatively new medical specialty, and one of the most influential members of the ethics committee I'm on is the head of the palliative-care service at the hospital. I knew to ask for a pain-management specialist from listening to him, and the palliative-care doctor who joined the team caring for my dad became my go-to source for the big picture.

When a palliative-care service is available, it is worth asking for that service to be involved. But even in hospitals where the service exists, other physicians can be reluctant to ask the palliative-care team to become involved. Mostly this is just a matter of habit—it takes time to learn to use new options—but sometimes the service is not mentioned because every physician has some training in pain management. Calling in a separate specialist can seem like an admission of failure. For this reason, it is worth saying, "I'm not questioning your expertise, but I would appreciate your ordering a palliative-care consult. I want to make sure I'm doing everything to keep (myself/my loved one) comfortable." Recently, a friend of mine tried this approach to get palliative care involved for her father. The doctor's response was, "He's not dying yet, so we don't need palliative care." She now wishes she had said, "Whether he's dying or not, I want a pain specialist called in." Sometimes it is necessary to insist.

The specialized training in pain management that the palliative-care team members bring is valuable in itself. Probably even more valuable is their access to the sick person's full medical record and their willingness to talk about the medical situation while taking all of it into account. The pain-management team can read all the notes that other doctors and specialists have left in the sick person's chart. They also have the medical training to see how those notes contribute to the big picture. While they are typically empathetic people and good listeners, they are also likely to take the time needed to attend carefully to the sick person's concerns and to the family's need for clarity. The other medical professionals involved are likely to be struggling to keep up with their long task lists for the day. The palliative-care doctors and nurses will be less pressured to move on.

When my dad was dying, the palliative-care physician regularly spent twenty minutes or more two or three times a day, answering my questions about my dad's condition. He had access to the latest lab reports, test results, doctors' orders, and nurses' notes. Between my phone calls, he also sought out the doctors who were caring for my dad to get firsthand accounts of what they were seeing. After my dad decided to discontinue the uncomfortable (and minimally effective) breathing mask, the palliative-care physician stayed in the room for almost an hour, slowly increasing the morphine dosage so that it was not the morphine that killed him. During this time, the specialist taught me how to tell whether my dad was in pain just from his facial expressions and the way he held his body. Even if the palliative-care specialist had been a tenth as thoughtful as he was, his presence would have been a great blessing.

Solution 2: The Charge Nurse or Nurse Practitioner

As helpful as the palliative-care team members can be, they are typically around only during the day. In hospitals without a pain-management service or after business hours, nurses are likely to be the best source for the big picture. In most large hospitals, every sick person has a team of nurses involved. It is common to have a nursing assistant, a primary-care nurse, a charge nurse, a nurse manager, and a hospital supervisor. The primary-care nurse has access to the full medical record, has the training to estimate what the data and notes probably mean, and likely has the willingness and the authority to call a physician for help.[2] In general, nurses are reluctant to offer medical opinions because that is outside their scope of practice. This reluctance is appropriate, since the physician is ultimately responsible for interpreting the medical situation accurately. The primary-care nurse has the experience necessary to clarify the big picture *as the attending physician understands it.* Since decisions about medical care will be based

---

2. In more advanced hospitals, the nurses doing routine care are often highly trained nurse practitioners. They are also an excellent source for conveying the big picture because they know so much about the hour-by-hour changes in what is happening and they also have the authority and the training to review the entire chart. A nurse practitioner will usually know the big picture and have time to explain it. For an overview of the training and responsibilities of nurse practitioners and physician assistants, see http://www.pg2pa.org/PA_NP.html.

on that attending physician's recommendations, this is the big picture that the sick person and family need most.

Some effort and tact may be needed to ask a nurse for help with the big picture. The primary-care nurse is likely to visit the room at least once an hour. Anytime the sick person or the family needs anything, this is the nurse to go looking for, starting at the nurse's station. Although the primary-care nurse may not be comfortable explaining the big picture, this nurse is an excellent resource for understanding what is happening in the moment. Asking one or (at most) two friendly questions on each visit can decrease anxiety and help in preparing for decisions that may be needed later:

- "This number on the monitor for vital signs has been changing. What does it mean? What should I want it to be?"
- "My husband is fidgeting in his sleep more than he does at home. Should I be worried?"
- "I know that things can get hectic during a shift change, and I don't want to be a nuisance. When do the doctors and nurses rotate on and off?"
- "It says here [on the whiteboard] that Karen is the charge nurse. I can't figure out something that the doctor said earlier. Would Karen have time to talk to me in the next couple of hours?"

It is important to ask in a way that makes it clear that you are not aiming to complain about the primary-care nurse. No one benefits when people deal with their anxieties and frustrations by complaining about the way they are being treated. Sadly, it happens a lot, so nurses may hesitate to find the charge nurse when you ask for help.

The charge nurse will be overseeing the work of the primary-care nurse and may not be at the nurse's station. Try to avoid asking for time with the charge nurse in the first or last hour of a shift. Time pressures will undermine the conversation, frustrating both of you. When talking with physicians, it is best to ask directly for the big picture. With the charge nurse, it is best to summarize what you think the big picture is and ask whether you are missing something important. When possible, ask questions that give the charge nurse the option of saying, "Let me check on that," or "I'll be seeing the [attending] physician soon; I'll find out." Questions about the sick person's specific situation may not get an immediate answer, but the charge nurse will make a serious effort to get the answer. On the other hand, questions about what to expect *in general* are likely to be answered right away. Most charge nurses will give an immediate answer to a question such as this: "The doctor is asking us to approve a DNR order. What would happen if we said no and then CPR was needed?" The question does not ask for a medical judgment about any specific person; it is about what happens when CPR is attempted. Most nurses are eager to help people understand how badly television has distorted what really happens in the hospital.

USING THE LONG WAITS WELL

Just as fictional hospital dramas suggest that a hospital stay is packed with exciting, crucial moments, this chapter has focused on times when something important is happening. The reality is much less lively. When someone is sick enough to need hospitalization, most of that person's time is spent sleeping. For the sick person, the long stretches of inactivity between nurse or doctor visits may pass quickly. For loved ones, boredom is a serious problem. When they are possible, conversations between the sick person and family members may be awkward because of anxiety, pain, or simply not knowing what to say. Talking about what is happening in the lives of loved ones not in the hospital is likely to be more encouraging and less tiring than rehashing all that is not known about the immediate health future.[3] Two final words about using the time well may help.

Focus on maximizing the impact of the medical means being

---

3. For helpful, practical advice about hospital visits, see Karen Whitley Bell, *Living at the End of Life: A Hospice Nurse Addresses the Most Common Questions* (New York: Sterling Ethos, 2010), especially 92–95.

used. Be a pleasant person for the hospital staff who visit the room. Be appreciative of their work and treat them like friends rather than hired servants or machines. Remember that they are probably being evaluated on their efficiency, including how quickly they can do all that is needed in your room before moving on to another. Keep a notebook in which you write down questions that occur to you when no one else is there. When you get a chance to talk to a physician or a charge nurse, the notebook will make it easy to ask the most important questions quickly.

Most importantly, pray. Prayer is always the most powerful thing we can do. Pray for peace when you are anxious. Pray for healing. Pray for wisdom, guidance, and clarity. Pray that the doctors will be insightful, careful, and skillful. Pray that pain will be minimized. Pray with thanksgiving when any of these other prayers are answered, even if in a small way. When you run out of your own words, open the book of Psalms and read them aloud. Holy Spirit–inspired prayers are an excellent way to attune your heart to God's will. Whether you are in the hospital for the last time or not, walking through it in step with the Spirit is the way of wisdom and peace.

KEY TERMS

charge nurse
hospitalist
intensivist
interim discharge summary
nurse practitioner (NP)
palliative care
physician assistant (PA)

STUDY AND *DISCUSSION QUESTIONS

1. Describe how fictional portrayals of end-of-life situations might leave people unprepared for the complexity of real-life decisions in the hospital.

2. *Why do fictional hospital dramas *today* typically involve central characters who grow by abandoning long-held moral convictions?

3. What is the most common way that prayer and spiritual seriousness are depicted in fictional hospital dramas today?

4. *What can people (and churches) be doing to prepare to be spiritually serious and ready for the combination of tedium and complexity that is common when a loved one is nearing death in the hospital?

5. How has the role of the family doctor in the care of hospitalized people changed between 2000 and 2017?

6. What advantages come with an expanded role for staff physicians in end-of-life situations?

7. What challenges come with this role expansion?

8. *Assess the claim (now widely accepted in the medical field) that the advantages of expanded use of staff physicians greatly exceed the difficulties involved.

9. Why is it common for many physicians from different specialties to be involved in a person's care?

10. Why can it be difficult to get a single, overall (big) picture of the medical situation that someone is facing?

11. What does a palliative-care service or specialist do?

12. *Why are physicians sometimes reluctant to call in a palliative-care specialist?

13. How can nurses help in getting the big picture (remembering that there are different kinds of nurses)?

14. Give a short summary of the steps that a husband should take in order to get the big picture of the medical situation that his wife is facing.

15. What is the primary task of someone who is visiting a friend or loved one in the hospital?

16. What is the best way to get answers to medical questions when visiting a friend or loved one in the hospital?

17. *How important is it for someone to be in the room with a sick person who is unconscious and not likely to regain consciousness?

FOR FURTHER READING

Bell, Karen Whitley. *Living at the End of Life*. New York: Sterling Ethos, 2010.

Feldman, David B., and S. Andrew Lasher Jr. *The End-of-Life Handbook*. Oakland, CA: New Harbinger Publications, 2012.

Henry, Stella Mora. *The Eldercare Handbook: Difficult Choices, Compassionate Solutions*. New York: HarperCollins, 2006.

Holstege, Henry, and Robert Riekse, eds. *Caring for Aging Loved Ones*. Colorado Springs: Focus on the Family, 2002.

Perry, John J. "The Rise and Impact of Nurse Practitioners and Physician Assistants on Their Own and Cross-Occupation Incomes." *Contemporary Economic Policy* 27, 4 (2009): 491–511.

8

THINGS TO DO NOW

Perplexing choices about life-sustaining medical treatment are still choices. In the midst of the distress of making these decisions, it is easy to forget that nearly *everyone* else in human history had to face death without the options we enjoy. We are able to accept or decline ventilator support or tube-feeding because we are blessed in three important ways. First, we are living after the development of CPR, mechanical respiratory support, and a host of other devices and techniques that have been available for only the last fifty years. Second, we often have access to the material resources to purchase these amazing medical services. Third, we live in a political system that leaves medical decisions in the hands of individuals. If we want hip-replacement surgery or kidney dialysis and have the money to pay for it, no government official will veto our decisions.

Many countries today have the medical means available, but decisions about their use are made by government officials tasked with making the best use of medical resources for society as a whole. I was recently discussing end-of-life decision-making with a church-planter in the Czech Republic. He was mystified by a case I was describing that involved the choice by someone about whether to start using a ventilator. Finally he asked, "Where is the government official who makes these decisions? How is it up to the sick person? How old is the sick person? If she is over 75, there is no way that the government will let the doctors start using the ventilator." This is not how it works in the United States and some other countries. The hard choices described in this book do not arise in other parts of the world. The hard choices were the stuff of fantasy before the development of the medical techniques and devices. The difficulties that come with the choices are the result of being materially rich and economically free.

The blessings of material wealth and economic freedom are great, but they are neither ultimate goods nor ends in themselves. Peace with God in Christ is an infinitely greater good, and all the blessings we enjoy in this life are given to enable us to bless others. For most of us, physical death is still a long way away. Decisions about life-sustaining medical treatment for our parents may be close to us, but not yet in sight. Yet there are important things that we can be doing now to bless our families, our churches, and our communities. This final chapter sketches ways to put the advice in this book to use right away.

BLESSING OUR FAMILIES

Even if our death is still decades away, we can take steps now to limit the distress and increase the peace of our loved ones when that time finally arrives. Most of us are aware that we need to make careful plans to ensure that we have the money to care for ourselves as we age. We know that it is wise to seek the advice of trained and accredited financial counselors and even to make sacrifices now in order to avoid being a great financial burden to our families. We also know that we can spare our loved ones grief and expense by working with an attorney to write a will and by storing the paperwork and passwords where they can be easily found. These steps are a hassle, and it isn't fun to think through what the world will be like when we are dead. We take them because we know how awful it is to add financial and legal worries to the pain of grieving the death of a loved one. Taking these steps allows us to bless our loved ones even after we are dead.

Completing an Advance Directive

The sadness and disorientation surrounding death do not begin at the time of physical death. As death approaches, our loved ones will be distressed by what is coming. If we lose the capacity to make medical decisions, our loved ones will be called on to speak for us. If we have not left instructions about what values we want to guide those choices, their grief over what is happening will be increased by having to make choices with enormous consequences. Not only will they be likely to add to *our* suffering by continuing excessively burdensome treatment, but they will probably exacerbate their own anguish in second-guessing or disagreements as the days add up. We can bless our families now by completing an advance directive:

- Identify and secure the agreement of an agent (such as a spouse) and at least one alternate agent (such as a sibling, child, or friend).
- Talk candidly with the agent and adult family members about the priorities we want honored. Find cases in this book that involve medical challenges that we are likely to face. Talk through what we would want chosen if those situations arose. Talk openly about how we want our resources used if the medical options cannot restore our ability to make decisions and impose great burdens.
- Fill out a state-approved advance directive form that will be honored, including having it witnessed or notarized.
- Give copies of the form to our doctors, agent, and hospital. Put a copy in a safe place, and tell our adult family members where they can find it.

Our families may think we are crazy. Some of them will think that we must have received really bad news about our health from our doctors. Others will ask whether we are dying. (That was the reaction of my 20-year-old daughter when I tried to explain my advance directive to the family.) Our loved ones will not think it is a blessing to be asked to think through our death, but they will be *really* happy that we pushed through it if they ever have to make decisions on our behalf.

Explaining What We Want to Happen to Our Bodies

While you have your family members thinking about your death, tell them what you want to happen to your remains. God's Word assures us that we will be raised together with Christ at the last day. The hope of the resurrection is a certainty, not a fuzzy wish. Just as Christ was raised, we will be resurrected, receiving back our bodies in glorified form.[1] We don't know much about what those bodies will be like, but they will be wonderful. The Bible does not tell us how God will give us our bodies back, but we know that even those who were torn apart by beasts, drowned and eaten by fish, or burned to ashes will all get their bodies back. Whatever happens to our bodies after we die, God will clothe us with our bodies in glorified form when Christ returns.

God's power to do this means that what we ask our loved ones to do with our mortal bodies cannot affect what happens at the resurrection. Burial in a tomb cut out of rock, burial in a casket in the ground, burial at sea, and cremation are all biblically permissible options. Telling our loved ones which of these we want will save them from having to figure it out in a hurry right in the midst of the fog of losing us. It would be even better to take the steps to specify the details involved, setting aside money to pay for it all. We can explain what process we want used and the equipment that will be needed (plot, casket, urn, etc.), and we can make sure that an attorney is ready to handle all the legal documents (such as the many death certificates that are needed). Our loved ones will appreciate the foresight and care that we put into this.

For most Americans, cremation is the least expensive option, but things other than cost are worth considering. What our loved ones do with our dead bodies makes a statement. For many years, pagan rulers tried to mock the Christian hope in the resurrection by burning

---

1. Just how the resurrection will work is unknown. We know that it will happen, but we don't know what our bodies will look like or what powers they will have. We know from Scripture, however, that they will be *our* bodies. Resurrection is not reincarnation. In reincarnation, a soul is given a *different* body. I discuss the difference between resurrection and reincarnation in "Choosing to Die: The Gift of Mortality in Middle-earth," a chapter in *The Lord of the Rings and Philosophy: One Book to Rule Them All*, ed. Gregory Bassham and Eric Bronson (Chicago: Open Court, 2003), 123–36.

Christian bodies. They were effectively saying, "Let's see your God put *that* back together!" For Christian communities whose memories include such taunts, cremation may seem like an act of despair or a denial of the hope of the resurrection. On the positive side, some Puritans carefully buried the bodies of believers with the grave facing east and leaving a pair of shoes at the foot of the plot. They did this to reinforce their expectation that when Christ returned with the rising sun, their loved ones would be able to put their glorified, bodily feet in their shoes and run to Jesus. This would be possible even if their ashes had been buried there, but burying the bodies *showed* their confidence in the resurrection to all who were watching.

Before deciding what we want done with our dead bodies, we should consider what our neighbors and nearby believers would "hear" from our choice. Burying our bodies rather than cremating them might be used to make our confident hope in the resurrection easier to see. But it might not, especially if we cannot explain what we are doing. It is also possible that cremating our bodies will offend fellow believers. Their misgivings are worth taking into account. Along with careful attention to expense and logistics, we should be eager to avoid giving offense. I have told my family that if it would not be a financial burden, I would like to be buried rather than cremated. I want every mention of "burial" to include an explicit mention that I am looking forward to the resurrection of my body at Christ's return. I think this will be best for me, but I do not think the Bible requires that my body be buried.

Drafting the Bulletin for Your Own Memorial Service

Explaining what we want to happen to our bodies will feel creepy. Planning our own memorial services will feel arrogant. We should push through those feelings, accepting that our loved ones will be thankful that they do not have to figure these things out without our input. In both cases, our loved ones will want to do what we would wish, honoring our lives in ways that we would appreciate. Writing out what we want said about us would be inappropriate, but identifying passages of Scripture that we wish read and hymns that we wish sung will answer

questions that planners will certainly have *about what we would want.*
A good time to think through these preferences is when we are attending memorial services for others. We can save the bulletins for services
we like and put notes on them about what worked. We can also list
our favorite hymns and explain them to our loved ones.

Beyond selecting passages and hymns, we can also remove some of
the trouble that will accompany deciding who (if anyone) will speak
about us. Especially in large families, someone has to decide who will
"say a few words" and who will only sit quietly with the family. Feelings
can be hurt easily, and sometimes people with close ties are ineffective
public speakers. Our memorial services are not entertainment events,
but in services aimed at celebrating our going home, speakers who are
comfortable up front make it easier for everyone to rejoice. Expressing
a desire that the program include a specific friend or family member
who knows how to speak will probably be a relief to those planning
our services.

Finally, we can think through what our families might do with
gifts given to honor our lives. When the bulletin at a memorial service
says, "In lieu of flowers, please consider making a donation to the local
crisis pregnancy center," someone had to decide to make the request.
Being able to say that this is what *we* wanted spares the organizers from
explaining it further.

Much of this memorial service planning may seem too obvious
to mention, but it is worth getting right. Some of the most thrilling
and satisfying events I have attended in my life have been memorial services. Celebrating God's faithfulness in and through the life of
one of his children can be profoundly encouraging. Closing a service
by mocking death with James Ward's song "Death Is Ended" brings
heaven very close.

BLESSING OUR CHURCHES

The final recommendation made by the 1988 PCA Report on
Heroic Measures is that churches prepare to deal with the issues surrounding end-of-life decisions:

A person or committee in each church should be designated for special study concerning the terminally ill. The seriousness of the issues and their complexity require more than a casual or wait-until-something-happens approach. Further, virtually everyone will face some facet of these problems with some family members. A resource is needed locally to offer Biblical advice and options to those involved. It is doubtful that every pastor will have the time necessary to devote to this particular area. Formal teaching sessions and distribution of literature for the congregation should also be arranged. Physicians in the congregation should be involved as well.[2]

This book can serve as one of the resources to assist elders and others in giving biblical advice. "Formal teaching sessions" can also be organized. I teach this material as a four-week Sunday school series and as a series of evening events when I am joined by physicians who are members at my church.[3]

The events that involve "physicians in the congregation" are by far the best attended and most successful. Everyone understands that the opportunity to ask physicians questions at no cost should be taken seriously. The physicians do not have to prepare for the meetings. I give them the case studies that we will discuss ahead of time, but the case studies involve situations that they deal with week after week. The moderator/leader mostly tries to stay out of the way. Once the physicians have said what they think matters in the case, the audience will have all sorts of questions. Audience members will also want to tell what it was like when they went through similar situations with

2. 1988 PCA Report on Heroic Measures, § IV.5.

3. The curricula I developed for these events (handouts, leaders' guides, discussion prompts, etc.) are available as free downloads through the P&R website. "Ask the Doctors" (sketched in Appendix B) is a four-session adult education curriculum. It requires the involvement of at least one believing physician (ideally a church member). "Leaving Instructions" (sketched in Appendix C) is a four-week Sunday school curriculum that can be taught by anyone. The lessons highlight key passages of Scripture and drive discussion by asking class members to read parts in a scripted dialogue among people facing an end-of-life treatment choice.

loved ones. By the third forty-five-minute session, most of the participants are interested in completing their own advance directives if they can ask questions as they fill them out. I have since worked with people in my congregation with a parent who was nearing death *but had an advance directive* that had been completed as the result of those meetings. The information about the parent's wishes in those forms has been a great comfort to the family and to the medical personnel involved.

Another way to bless our churches is to let the elders know that we are available to be a "local resource" for people facing difficult choices. We should be eager to answer questions about biblical principles guiding medical decisions. We can join a pastor or elder who visits a family in the hospital. The pastor or elder can ask whether it would be okay for us to be there, joining with the family in prayer and gently seeking to understand the loved one's virtues and joys. Unless specifically asked for help in making a decision, we should focus on grieving with the family over the brokenness of the world and the way in which that brokenness is manifesting itself in what is happening. We can be a welcome presence by letting the family members control the conversation and, when asked what we think, by encouraging them to talk about their loved one and their hope in Christ.

BLESSING OUR COMMUNITIES

Increasing the number of church members with advance directives will make life easier for the doctors and nurses who will care for those members as they approach death. The medical personnel will be spared the task of leading family members through the long process of figuring out what the dying person would want. The doctors and nurses will also be given clear evidence that Christians do not cling to life desperately, accepting or declining medical treatment as part of a lifelong effort to serve Christ with every gift of health, wealth, and time. Having gospel hope expressed in thoughtful planning may be the greatest blessing that we can give to those caring for us or our loved ones as we near death.

Another way in which we can bless our communities is to volunteer our time and moral sensibilities to local hospital ethics committees and hospice services. Anyone who has read this book and is willing to listen more than to speak is ready to be an appreciated member of a hospital ethics committee. And nearly everyone who reads this book will live near a hospital looking for community members willing to serve.

In order to receive federal Medicare or Medicaid funds, a hospital must meet the standards set by the Joint Commission for the Accreditation of Healthcare Organizations (JCAHO).[4] Most insurance providers also require JCAHO accreditation, which means that few hospitals can afford to ignore JCAHO expectations. One of those expectations is that a hospital have a mechanism for considering and educating constituents on "ethical issues in patient care."[5] A functioning ethics committee is the surest way to satisfy this expectation, and the hardest slots to fill on an effective ethics committee are the ones for people who do not have a financial stake in the hospital's work. Community members who are not medically trained count.

The most valued community members are those who can be counted on to attend the meetings and who have some familiarity with ethical decision-making. These committees need people who show up, listen carefully, and are willing to explain what they think is right. Getting started with an ethics committee may be as simple as calling the hospital and asking the person who answers when the ethics committee meets and whether visitors are allowed to sit in. After we have silently observed a couple of meetings, someone is likely to ask us whether we want to join. In other cases, it may be necessary to ask a doctor or nurse at church how to get started.

4. The JCAHO standards are available at https://www.jointcommission.org /standards_information/standards.aspx.

5. A helpful summary of efforts to meet this standard is given in Sharon E. Caulfield's article "Health Care Facility Ethics Committees: New Issues in the Age of Transparency," *Human Rights* (American Bar Association) 34 (Fall 2007), http:// www.americanbar.org/publications/human_rights_magazine_home/human_rights _vol34_2007/fall2007/hr_fall07_caulfi.html.

Serving on a local hospital ethics committee blesses our community by helping the hospital maintain its accreditation and by inserting biblical thinking into the committee's ethical deliberations. Volunteering at a hospice service blesses the community by increasing the number of people who are willing to care for people that the wider culture is passing by. American society values productivity and entertainment. People who cannot make our lives easier or more fun are not valued. Even though people in hospice care often have much to offer others—wisdom, insight, genuine compassion, and morally serious encouragement—the culture is not interested in what they have to give.

Hospice volunteers ride along with nurses or chaplains, visiting those who are nearing death and turning a meeting of two into a party of three. They serve hospice workers by helping them focus on the sick person's specific needs on the drive to the next home. Volunteers serve the sick person by reminding him or her that the person is not forgotten and is valued by people who are not being paid to show up. They give the sick person someone else willing to hear the person's story, and sometimes someone else with whom to pray. (On my last home visit with a hospice chaplain, an older man who was only days from glory prayed for *me*.) What Jesus commands is also for our good. Volunteering with a hospice service will bless our communities as well as blessing us.

PRAYING

It is not trite to end by saying that the most important thing we can do now is to pray. Prayer is one of God's appointed ways of accomplishing his purposes in the world. Those who are physically healthy can both volunteer and pray. Some people have only enough physical strength to pray, and yet their efforts are the most powerful. Because our culture prizes earthly power and influence above spiritual power, it is easy for us to overlook the impact of the faithful prayers of the physically weak. The pastor of a local PCA church showed me how wrong the world is about the physically weak.

This pastor served a flock that included dozens of members who were too frail to leave their houses. These "shut-ins" would ask him what their lives were good for. They didn't see how they could serve anyone, and they wondered whether they had become nothing more than a burden to their families and utterly forgotten by everyone else. While he was praying about how to answer them, it occurred to him that his church also had six marriages that were so deeply in crisis that the elders did not see how the husband and wife could ever be reconciled. The elders had used every approach they could think of, along with praying that God would work in their lives. But the trajectory of these marriages was still downward.

Using different names for the couples in crisis, the pastor asked each of the shut-ins to commit to spending time in prayer every morning and evening for one of the couples. Twelve of the shut-ins made the commitment. For two of the couples, God's answer was to turn the hearts of the husband and wife toward each other. They were reconciled and are growing together. In addition, all the shut-ins who labored for the couples in prayer had their spirits and their health improve. They rejoiced at God's mercy to those in distress and reveled in their ability to serve their brothers and sisters.

We all should be praying for those who are nearing death, and those whose activities are limited by physical challenges should be encouraged to pray for them as well. While it may not often happen that our prayers will lead to surprising physical restoration, we will be able to rejoice when prayer causes estranged family members to come together in peace or difficult medical decisions are easier to make than anyone expected.

We should be praying that God would draw near to those who are facing hard choices about medical options, either for themselves or for loved ones. We should be praying that God would give the medical personnel wisdom and skill. And we should be praying that if God wills, those near to death would be restored to health. We should pray when we are by ourselves, and we should make the time to visit them in the hospital and pray with them there. As we draw near to death, we should draw near to each other, united in love and in our confidence that Christ has defeated death.

KEY TERMS

advance directive
ethics committee
hospice care

STUDY AND *DISCUSSION QUESTIONS

1. Why would someone say that "an advance directive is the greatest *chesed* [blessing/expression of love] that someone can give to their family"?
2. What do you gain for yourself by completing an advance directive, explaining it to your family/agents, and putting it where it will be found if needed?
3. What do you lose by completing all the steps to produce an advance directive?
4. *What should be said to someone who says, "I'm too young to worry about this now"?
5. *What should be said to someone who says, "I trust my family to make the right decisions when the time comes; I don't want to distress them with thoughts of my death now"?
6. *What should be said to someone who says, "I can see that this is important, but I have even more important things to do right now"?
7. What elements should a helpful funeral/memorial service plan include?
8. What passages do you want read at your funeral/memorial service?
9. *Does the Bible forbid cremation as the means of handling your dead body? Why or why not?
10. What should church leaders be doing to prepare church members to handle end-of-life decisions faithfully?
11. What can church members (with oversight from church leaders) do to help fellow members prepare to handle end-of-life decisions faithfully?
12. What should church leaders and members do when fellow believers are in the hospital, close to death? (More than one kind of action should be listed.)

13. *Describe the actions of people you know who blessed fellow believers and their families who were in the hospital.
14. What should be said to someone who says, "Hospice care is a death sentence"?
15. What can believers do to contribute to their local communities' efforts to support people through end-of-life crises?
16. What should a prayer for a sick friend or loved one include if the sick person or the sick person's family are listening?
17. *Is it biblically appropriate to take into account the other people who are listening when we pray?
18. *Whom might we pray for right now?

FOR FURTHER READING

California Coalition for Compassionate Care. "Talking It Over: A Guide for Group Discussions on End-of-Life Decisions" (1999).

Caulfield, Sharon E. "Health Care Facility Ethics Committees: New Issues in the Age of Transparency." *Human Rights* (American Bar Association) 34 (Fall 2007). http://www.americanbar.org /publications/human_rights_magazine_home/human_rights _vol34_2007/fall2007/hr_fall07_caulfi.html.

Connor, Stephen R. "Development of Hospice and Palliative Care in the United States." *Omega: Journal of Death & Dying* 56, 1 (2007): 89–99.

Lucas, Sean Michael. *On Being Presbyterian: Our Beliefs, Practices, and Stories*. Phillipsburg, NJ: P&R Publishing, 2006.

Morhaim, Dan. *The Better End: Surviving (and Dying) on Your Own Terms in Today's Modern Medical World*. Baltimore: Johns Hopkins University Press, 2012.

Roberts, Barbara M. *Helping Those Who Hurt*. Colorado Springs: NavPress, 2009.

Schostak, Zev. "Holding On or Letting Go: Aggressive Treatment or Hospice Care? Making End-of-Life Medical Decisions" (December 4, 2008). http://www.yutorah.org/.

Appendix A

Principles Identified, Defended, and Applied

Note: The Scripture passages listed with each principle are a place to start when searching the Scriptures; they are not offered as sufficient proof of biblical warrant by themselves. The biblical foundation for these principles is explained more fully in the chapters listed for them. The principles are also applied to medical choices in the chapters listed.

- **Permission to Decline Treatment:** God's Word permits us to decline life-sustaining medical treatment that is ineffective or that we, as servants of Christ, judge to be excessively burdensome. [John 10:17–18; chaps. 1, 6]
- **The Duty to Steward Our Resources:** God's Word requires us to make faithful use of all our talents, opportunities, and resources: time, energy, attention, and money. [Matt. 25:14–30; chaps. 2, 6]
- **Protection for the Least of These:** God's Word calls us to seek to defend and protect those who are voiceless and suffering. [Matt. 25:31–46; chap. 2]
- **Servant Authority to Make Medical Choices:** God's Word teaches that every adult has the authority to accept or decline medical attention as part of his or her responsibility as an image-bearer of God. (The authority does not reside in each of us absolutely. The authority is delegated to us by God as his servants.) [Luke 12:35–48; chap. 2]

- **Authority to Make Choices in Advance:** God's Word permits us to accept or decline medical treatment in advance, including leaving an advance directive or other instructions. These instructions are binding if they conform to God's law. [Col. 4:10; chap. 2]
- **Advance Directives Can Be a Blessing:** God's Word encourages us to take steps to remove unnecessary distress from those we love and ought to honor. Legally executed advance directives diminish the burdens of fear and indecision from all those who will have to make medical decisions for us if we cannot make them for ourselves. Advance directives clarify who is to decide if we cannot, and they reduce the need for anyone to guess about our wishes. [Gen. 50:25; Ex. 13:19; chap. 2]
- **Covenant Decision-Making Authority:** God's Word authorizes spouses to speak (give a substituted judgment) for each other. [Matt. 19:4–6; chaps. 2, 6]
- **Family Decision-Making Authority:** God's Word permits our children and parents to make choices for us when we are unable to make them for ourselves as part of the authority structure implicit in the fifth commandment. [Ex. 20:12; chap. 2]
- **Obligation to Accept Care:** God's Word obligates us to accept loving care that is likely to maintain or restore our health. [John 5:2–9; chap. 2]
- **Human Life Is Precious:** God's Word obligates us to protect and nurture human life. [Gen. 9:1–7; chap. 2]
- **Earthly Life Is Not the Highest Good:** God's Word teaches that long physical life is a great good, but it is not the highest biblical good. [1 Kings 3:10–14; chap. 2]
- **A Time to Die:** God's Word permits us to accept death in the Lord as a blessing when our service to Christ is full. [Eccl. 3:1–8; chap. 2]
- **Death Is Defeated:** God's Word assures us that death is

a great evil, but it is not the ultimate evil, and it has been defeated by Christ. [1 Cor. 15:50–57; chap. 2]

- **The Ordinary Means of Grace:** God's Word teaches that the spiritual goods of meditating on God's Word, partaking of the sacraments, prayer, and fellowship with other believers are great goods that we should seek out and not neglect. [Ps. 19:10; 1 Cor. 11:23–26; Eph. 1:18–19; chap. 2]
- **Called to Be Reconciled:** God's Word calls us to be reconciled to others whom we have wronged. [Matt. 5:23–24; chap. 2]
- **Not Obligated to Suffer Only to Stay Alive:** God's Word does not say that we are required to suffer merely in order to live as long as possible. [Phil. 1:19–26; chap. 2]
- **Called to Suffer for Christ's Sake:** God's Word calls us to suffer for the name of Christ if persecuted, or to testify to Christ's lordship. [Matt. 5:11–12; 1 Peter 4:12–19; chap. 2]
- **Prohibition against Taking Life:** God's Word forbids us as private citizens to take steps that intentionally end someone's life. [Ex. 20:13; Num. 35:9–34; chap. 2]
- **Faithful Relief from Pain:** God's Word permits us to seek relief from pain in ways consistent with being a faithful steward of our resources and our witness to the gospel. [Luke 8:43–48; Acts 22:22–28; chap. 2]
- **Declining Ineffective Treatment Is Not Taking Someone's Life:** God's Word permits us to decline ineffective or excessively burdensome treatment, so declining treatment is not forbidden, and thus it is not intentionally ending someone's life. [Luke 2:29–30; chap. 2]
- **Called to Pray for Healing and All Our Other Needs:** God's Word calls us to pray for all that we need, both supernatural—such as wisdom, peace, and healing—and natural—memory, skill, professional judgment, and healing. [Phil. 4:4–7; chap. 2]
- **God Does Not Need Us:** God's Word does not call us

to use medical means to give God time to heal. [Acts 17:24–25; chap. 2]

- **Against Planning on a Miracle:** God's Word calls us to pray when we are sick or in distress, asking God to work a wonder according to his will; but we are called to submit to God's will, making plans that do not depend on God's working a miracle. [2 Sam. 12:15–23; chaps. 2, 6]

- **The Privilege of Being Cared For:** God's Word discourages us from treating dependence on others when we are sick or infirm as a great burden. [Matt. 9:1–8; chap. 3]

- **The Duty to Care for Ourselves:** God's Word does not permit us to reject food that is offered in the ordinary way when we are hungry. [1 Sam. 28:20–25; chap. 3]

- **The Duty to Show Love by Feeding:** God's Word calls us to feed our loved ones when they are hungry and to give them drink when they are thirsty. [Mark 5:43; chap. 3]

- **No Duty to Force-Feed:** God's Word does not require us to force food or water on our loved ones by mechanical means if the burdens of those means greatly exceed the benefits involved. [inferred from other principles in chap. 3]

- **Prohibition against Unpayable Debts:** God's Word forbids accepting medical services for which we cannot reasonably expect to pay out of resources that we possess, that we can expect to earn, or that we have been explicitly promised by reliable people. [Eccl. 5:4–5; chap. 6]

- **Against Presuming on Charity:** God's Word counsels against making promises that depend on the generosity of others. [Matt. 20:1–15; chap. 6]

- **The Goodness of Leaving an Inheritance:** God's Word encourages us to leave an inheritance to our children. [Prov. 13:22; chap. 6]

- **Obligation to Provide and Serve:** God's Word requires us to care for those who depend on us and to use our time and talents to serve others as we are able. [Matt. 7:7–11; 1 Tim. 5:8; chap. 6]

- **Making Prudent Plans:** God's Word encourages us to make reasonable plans about future resources and needs. [Prov. 6:6–11; Luke 14:28; chap. 6]
- **Expectation of Children's Growing to Have Similar Values:** God's Word gives diligent parents confidence that their children will grow up to share their loves and commitments. While the children are young, parents may assume their own biblical priorities when speaking for their children. [Prov. 22:6; chap. 6]

Appendix B

Sketch of the Lesson Plans for "Ask the Doctors"

Church Education Efforts on End-of-Life Decision-Making

The complete lesson plans for the four-session event are available as free downloads through the P&R website.

Objectives for the Four Sessions:
- To acquaint participants with how Christian physicians and other medical professionals think about end-of-life situations and choices.
- To increase participants' knowledge of biblical principles that should inform end-of-life decision-making.
- To encourage participants to complete their own advance directives in a biblically sound way.

Audience: Adults of all ages. People with grown children or aging parents are likely to find the sessions especially engaging and helpful.

Venue: Wednesday night (or similar) church education events. Time chosen to accommodate the schedule of the medical professionals who will volunteer their time to answer questions.

Logistical Details:

- Four sessions, each between forty minutes and one hour.
- The sessions build on each other, but each can be profitable in itself.
- No maximum or minimum class size, but if there are more than sixty participants, accommodating everyone's questions or personal narratives will be difficult. Having doctors and nurses available to answer questions is likely to increase attendance and to increase the pressure to allow people to have their questions answered.

Leader/Expert Qualifications Needed:

- The sessions depend on the presence of at least one Christian medical professional with experience in caring for people near the end of life. One Christian physician or one Christian advanced-practice nurse with ICU experience would be sufficient.
- Medical professionals who are members of the church are the very best experts to involve, since they will be trusted both for their faith and for their expertise.
- A panel of two physicians who are members of the local congregation is ideal. They will agree about most things (raising confidence about their advice), and will disagree in their approach to giving difficult news.
- The leader of the session needs only to be able and willing to review the leaders' guide in advance of each session.
- While not absolutely necessary for success, the presence of a Christian attorney willing to answer questions about legal implications is a big bonus.

A Leaders' Guide Is Provided for Each Session That:

- Suggests a reflection to use with each of the passages of Scripture.
- Expands on the medical and other details in the cases.
- Highlights pastoral challenges likely to arise.

- Proposes lines of discussion for the questions asked after each case.

The real work is done by the medical personnel, but they do not need to prepare for the sessions. They face the issues involved every day.

Handout masters are provided for each session that summarize the cases and list the questions and principles to be discussed.

Note: These plans are ambitious, but devised so that they can work even if time allows for discussion of only the first of the cases in each session. As the participants discover that the medical professionals are going to give helpful answers, it is likely that time will allow for only one case to be discussed in detail.

SESSION HIGHLIGHTS

Session 1: Must We "Do Everything"?
- **Principles proposed** (possible lesson outcomes):
  - Faithful stewardship of our earthly life ordinarily includes using medical means (as feasible) to extend it.
  - But long life is not the only biblical good that we might pursue. It isn't even the most important good.
  - It is biblically permissible to decline or withdraw medical treatment that compromises the honest pursuit of other biblical goods, especially spiritual goods.
- **Biblical reflection** on John 10:1–18.
- **Case 1A** about Mary, a 69-year-old believer with pancreatic cancer.
- **Central question** (among a set of questions): Is Mary biblically obligated to pursue a painful round of experimental treatment?
- **Biblical reflection** on Acts 6:8–7:3; 7:51–60.
- **Case 1B** about Bob, an 86-year-old believer with heart and breathing issues.

- **Central question** for the set: Is Bob biblically obligated to use mechanical breathing assistance until he dies of some other cause?

Session 2: Choosing for Loved Ones
- **Principles proposed** (possible lesson outcomes):
  - A request to authorize a DNR from a doctor we trust to honor life should be presumed to be medically and biblically appropriate.
  - The Bible does not require us to attempt resuscitation when the attempt would impose a great physical burden and is unlikely to restore us to life outside the hospital.
  - It is an act of biblical love to assign an agent regarding our own care.
  - A responsible agent will make choices the way the principal would have made them, as long as the choices are biblically permissible.
- **Biblical reflection** on Genesis 25:7–8; Psalm 116.
- **Case 2A** about Mildred, 70 years old, in the ICU with doctors asking about a DNR order.
- **Central question:** Would it be biblically permissible to approve the DNR order?
- **Biblical reflection** on Ephesians 6:1–4; 1 Peter 2:18–25.
- **Case 2B** about responding to claims that people make about being asked to serve as an agent, making health care decisions for someone when the time comes.
- **Central question:** What is the loving, biblically appropriate thing to say here?

Session 3: Completing an Advance Directive
- **Principles proposed** (possible lesson outcomes):
  - Earthly, natural benefits and burdens are important, but spiritual benefits and burdens should also be considered.
  - Care should be taken, but discontinuing *artificial* nutrition and hydration may be medically and biblically

appropriate if they are not supporting comfort or recovery.

- **Biblical reflection** on Deuteronomy 34:4–7; John 19:28–30.
- **Case 3A** about George, 81, a believer whose advance directive requests that life-sustaining medical treatment not be used if he is unable to enjoy the ordinary means of grace.
- **Central question:** Is George biblically permitted to value the spiritual good of ordinary communion with God more than the physical good of extending his earthly life?
- **Biblical reflection** on Philippians 1:18b–23.
- **Case 3B** about Judy, a 46-year-old believer in a persistent vegetative state.
- **Central question:** Would it be biblically permissible for the family and doctor to discontinue artificially administered nutrition and fluids?

Session 4: Supporting the Sick

- **Principles proposed** (possible lesson outcomes):
  - We should move toward rather than away from those limited by sickness or age.
  - Moving toward those in need in a helpful way involves learning how to do it from those who know how.
- **Biblical reflection** on Matthew 25:31–40; 2 Corinthians 12:7–10.
- **Case 4A** about Marvin, 52, a believer in critical condition in the hospital after a serious accident at work.
- **Central question:** What are the most helpful steps that members of our church can take to support Marvin and his family at this time?
- **Biblical reflection** on Proverbs 23:22–24; Romans 12:9–10.
- **Case 4B** about Hilda, an 84-year-old believer who is no longer strong enough to leave her home, but whose mind is still sharp.
- **Central question:** What are the most helpful ways that the members of our church can care for and support Hilda?

Appendix C

SKETCH OF THE LESSON PLANS FOR "LEAVING INSTRUCTIONS"

ADULT SUNDAY SCHOOL SERIES ON END-OF-LIFE DECISION-MAKING

The complete lesson plans for the four-class series are available as free downloads through the P&R website.

OBJECTIVES FOR THE FOUR SESSIONS

- To increase participants' knowledge of biblical principles that should inform end-of-life decision-making.
- To increase participants' willingness to discuss their own wishes about end-of-life treatment with their families and loved ones.
- To encourage participants to complete their own advance directives in a biblically sound way.

Audience: Adults and older teens.

Venue: Sunday school hour.

Logistical Details:
- Four class sessions, each between 40 minutes and one hour.
- Each class session is driven by a dialogue that is acted out by

members of the class, so encouraging attendance by people who enjoy reading through/acting out a scene is worth the effort.

- The sessions build on each other, but each can be profitable in itself.
- No maximum or minimum class size.

Leader/expert qualifications needed:

- The leader of the session should be willing to read through the Leaders' Guide (at least) and to serve as the "expert" on the material. Familiarity with the contents of this book will help.
- An hour of preparation by the leader is likely necessary: to read through the dialogue and other materials, to imagine the questions that are likely to arise, and to pray for wisdom.

A Leaders' Guide Is Provided for Each Session That:

- Suggests a reflection to use with each of the passages of Scripture.
- Gives an overview of the aims for the lesson/class session.
- Suggests passages of Scripture to read and discuss.
- Gives discussion questions and recommends lines to pursue in discussing them.
- Details "Principles and Applications" to propose and discuss.
- Tells another story that might be read and discussed if time allows.
- Recommends "homework" activities/questions for participants to attempt before the next session.

Handout masters are provided for each session that summarize the cases and list the questions and principles to be discussed. The third and fourth lessons include instructions for "Preludes" that explain technical terminology used by hospital workers and others.

Dialogue/script masters are provided for the actors to use for each of the dialogues.

Note: The sketches of the lessons below give only the first two of the biblical passages, discussion questions, and principles for application in each lesson. The full plans (available as free downloads from the P&R website) include many more.

LESSON/CLASS SESSION HIGHLIGHTS

Lesson 1: What the Bible Says about Life and Death

- **Central question:** What does the Bible teach about the value of living as long as possible?
- **Case study/sketch:** Kathy, 66 with a cancer diagnosis, and Pastor Mike, discussing whether the Bible calls Kathy to join an experimental trial.
- **Biblical reflection** (in part):
  - Genesis 2:7.
  - Psalm 91:1, 16.
- **For discussion** (in part):
  - Is human life *more* valuable than animal or plant life? Why?
  - The Bible refers to "life" over four hundred times. Physical, earthly life in the body is only one of the things that "life" means in the Bible. What else might "life" mean in the Bible?
- **Principles and applications** (proposed and in part):
  - Kathy's life is a gift from God and should be cherished (and not merely thrown away).
  - The Bible does not *require* Kathy to treat living as long as possible as her first priority.
- **For consideration** (homework):
  - What do you most fear regarding your own death?
  - Where do you want to die (if you would be allowed to choose)? In the hospital connected to machines? At home with family nearby?

Lesson 2: Faithfully Saying, "That's Enough"

- **Central question:** What does the Bible teach about declining life-sustaining treatment?

- **Case study/sketch:** Dialogue between Sam, his children, and a friend. Sam wants his family not to call an ambulance if he collapses.
- **Biblical reflection** (in part):
  - Deuteronomy 34:4–7.
  - John 10:17–18.
- **For discussion** (in part):
  - Is Sam asking his children to help him commit suicide?
  - Does Sam's plan violate the sixth commandment?
- **Principles and applications** (proposed and in part):
  - We have the authority to say no in advance to life-sustaining medical care in some circumstances.
  - There is a time to die, and Christ has defeated death for us.
- **For consideration** (homework):
  - Whom do you want to make medical decisions for you if you cannot make them?
  - What activities of your daily life do you value most (and why)?

Lesson 3: Deciding for Others

- **Central question:** What does the Bible teach about deciding for others and about suffering?
- **Case study/sketch:** Dialogue between Miriam, Lucy, and Amanda about what to do about Nora, who becomes uncontrollable during the kidney dialysis she needs.
- **Prelude** on decisional capacity and the biblical basis for surrogate decision-making.
- **Biblical reflection** (in part):
  - Romans 12:9–10.
  - Colossians 3:20.
- **For discussion** (in part):
  - What *goal* should Miriam have for her mother's medical care? (In the hospital, the "goal of care" is either "cure/restore" or "peaceful death." Is one of these the right one, or is there a third?)

- Is it ever biblically permissible to make "peaceful death" our goal?
- **Principles and applications** (proposed and in part):
  - Family members have a covenant responsibility and duty to choose for loved ones who cannot speak for themselves, making biblically permissible choices according to the loved ones' values.
  - We may be called to suffer for the gospel, but we are not required to suffer merely to stay alive.
- **For consideration** (homework):
  - How does your family resolve deep differences about what ought to be *done*? (This is not the same thing as how your family handles differences of opinion when no action is required.)
  - Whom would you want to join the discussion if your family was disagreeing about what to do?
  - Are you willing to leave written instructions for your family about the medical care you would want if you couldn't make the decisions?

Lesson 4: Completing an Advance Directive

- **Central question:** What might a biblically appropriate advance directive for end-of-life care look like?
- **Case study/sketch:** The story of Wilfred, 81, a believer who is comatose, and whose children cannot agree about whether to discontinue the use of a ventilator.
- **Prelude** on technical terminology such as *DNR, POST/ POLST,* and so on.
- **Biblical reflection** (in part):
  - Genesis 48:21–49:33.
  - Deuteronomy 33:1–29.
- **For discussion** (in part):
  - Does it matter for the decisions whether Wilfred is a Christian?
  - The children in this case disagree about what the goal

should be for Wilfred's care. Can you tell from the scenario what *he* would want the goal to be (cure/restoration? a peaceful death?)?

- **Principles and applications** (proposed and in part):
  - We can bless our families by completing advance directives.
  - We should be working to understand what our loved ones would want if we must decide for them.
- **For consideration** (homework): Complete your own advance directive!

GLOSSARY

abortion. The termination of a pregnancy after, accompanied by, resulting in, or closely followed by the death of the baby (embryo or fetus).

advance directive. A legal document (as a living will) signed by a living, competent person in order to provide guidance for medical and health care decisions (as the termination of life support and organ donation) if the person becomes incapable of making such decisions. See also durable power of attorney.

advanced-practice nurse. A nurse who has a post-master's certificate or practice-focused doctor of nursing practice degree. Depending on training, an advanced-practice nurse is a nurse practitioner (NP), clinical nurse specialist (CNS), certified nurse-midwife (CNM), or certified nurse anesthetist (CNA).

AED. Automated external defibrillator; a portable electronic device that attaches to the chest and operates automatically to measure the heart's rhythm to determine whether an electric shock is needed. It is designed to be used by someone without medical training.

agent. One who speaks or acts for a principal.

angina. A disease marked by spasmodic attacks of intense suffocative pain: as (1) a severe inflammatory or ulcerated condition of the mouth or throat (diphtheritic *angina*); (2) a disease marked by brief sudden attacks of chest pain or discomfort caused by deficient oxygenation of the heart muscles usually resulting from impaired blood flow to the heart (angina pectoris).

artificial nutrition and hydration (ANH). Introducing fluids and liquid food into the stomach by way of a flexible tube (as of polyurethane or silicone) passed into the stomach (as by way of the nasal passages or through a surgical opening in the abdominal wall). Also called tube-feeding.

aspiration. A drawing of something in, out, up, or through by or as if by suction: as (1) the act of breathing and especially of breathing in; (2) the withdrawal of fluid or friable tissue from the body; (3) the taking of foreign matter into the lungs with the respiratory current.

benefits and burdens. Any or all of the effects of a course of action or treatment, including physical, psychological, social, financial, and spiritual advantages and disadvantages likely (humanly speaking) to occur. See also excessively burdensome treatment.

BiPap. BiLevel Positive Airway Pressure; a noninvasive form of treatment for people suffering from sleep apnea or other respiratory dysfunction.

bypass. (1) A surgically established shunt. (2) A surgical procedure for the establishment of a shunt.

casuistry. (1) The method of gaining clarity about moral decisions by considering less vexing analogous cases. (2) Moral reasoning by analogy. Because religious groups have used the term to refer to strained reasoning to justify odious actions, it is often used in a negative sense.

charge nurse. A nurse who is in charge of a health care unit (as a hospital ward, emergency room, or nursing home).

chest compressions. The act of applying pressure to someone's chest in order to help blood flow through the heart in an emergency situation.

confusion. The inability to think as clearly or quickly as one normally does. The person may feel disoriented and have difficulty paying attention, remembering, and making decisions. Many times, confusion lasts for a short time and goes away. But see permanent confusion.

CPR. Cardiopulmonary resuscitation; a procedure designed to restore normal breathing after cardiac arrest that includes the clearance of air passages to the lungs, the mouth-to-mouth method of artificial respiration, and cardiac massage by the exertion of pressure on the chest.

decisional capacity. The ability of health care subjects to make their own health care decisions. Questions of capacity sometimes extend to other contexts, such as capacity to stand trial in a court of law and the ability to make decisions that relate to personal care and finances.

deontological. Having to do with duty or obligation; *deontologial ethics* are theories of moral norms based on the notions of obligation, duty, or rights.

diaconal ministry. A church's organized effort to meet temporal needs, typically led by deacons set aside for the task.

dialysis. (1) The separation of substances in solution by means of their unequal diffusion through semipermeable membranes; *especially* such a separation of colloids from soluble substances. (2) Either of two medical procedures to remove wastes or toxins from the blood and adjust fluid and electrolyte imbalances by utilizing rates at which substances diffuse through a semipermeable membrane: (a) the process of removing blood from an artery (as of a person with kidney dysfunction), purifying it by dialysis, adding vital substances, and returning it to a vein—also called *hemodialysis;* (b) a procedure performed in the peritoneal cavity in which the peritoneum acts as the semipermeable membrane—also called *peritoneal dialysis.*

do-not-resuscitate (DNR) order. A legal order written either in the hospital or on a legal form to withhold cardiopulmonary resuscitation (CPR) or advanced cardiac life support (ACLS), in respect of a person's wishes in case his or her heart were to stop or the person were to stop breathing.

durable power of attorney. A type of advance directive in which legal documents provide the power of attorney to another person in the case of an incapacitating medical condition.

ECMO. Extracorporeal membrane oxygenation; essentially, an external lung that filters the blood, removing carbon dioxide and adding oxygen.

electrical defibrillation. A process in which an electrical device called a *defibrillator* sends an electric shock to the heart to stop an arrhythmia, resulting in the return of a productive heart rhythm.

emphysema. A condition characterized by air-filled expansions in interstitial or subcutaneous tissues; *specifically*, a condition of the lung that is marked by distension and eventual rupture of the alveoli with progressive loss of pulmonary elasticity that is accompanied by shortness of breath with or without cough, and that may lead to impairment of heart action.

ethics committee. A group of people gathered by a hospital to meet regularly to review and discuss difficult cases, hospital policies, and programs for education. Ethics committees typically include physicians, nurses, therapists, and administrators employed by the hospital, as well as members of the local community.

excessively burdensome treatment. Medical options for which the burdens foreseeably endured greatly outweigh the benefits foreseeably gained. See also benefits and burdens.

false promise. A promise without the intention or the reasonable expectation of being able to fulfill it.

full code. A hospital designation that means to intercede if a person's heart stops beating or if the person stops breathing. It is the opposite *code* of DNR. Cf. long code.

future earning potential. The total amount that someone is likely to earn over a lifetime of work given current talents if diligently developed and applied.

Glasgow Coma Scale. A scale that is used to assess the severity of a brain injury. It consists of values from 3 to 15 obtained by summing the ratings assigned to three variables depending on whether and how the person responds to certain standard stimuli by opening the eyes, giving an oral response, and giving a motor response. A low score (as 3 to 5) indicates a poor chance of recovery, and a high score (as 8 to 15) indicates a good chance of recovery.

global brain injury. Damage to brain function (reduced neuronal capacity) affecting multiple regions or systems. Also called *global brain abnormality.*

heroic measures. Medical treatments or techniques used to sustain life in a way that defies contemporary expectations about what medical means can accomplish. Heroic measures were first used for CPR and mechanical support for breathing, hydration, or nutrition in the mid-twentieth century, since before then medical means were not available to extend life. The term is no longer in general use, in part because medical means of sustaining life are no longer thought to be amazing.

hospice care. A facility or program designed to provide a caring environment for meeting the physical and emotional needs of the terminally ill.

hospitalist. A licensed staff physician employed by a hospital or other medical institution to oversee medical care for people on a unit, floor, or ward.

image-bearer (of God). A human being, and thus one made in the image of God (Gen. 1:26–27) and worthy of respect and protection.

informed consent. Permission granted in the knowledge of the possible consequences, typically that which is given by a person to a doctor for treatment with full knowledge of the possible risks and benefits.

intensivist. A licensed staff physician employed by a hospital to oversee medical care for people in an intensive care unit.

interim discharge summary. A report—either oral or written—from one staff physician to another transferring oversight of the medical care for all the people on a hospital unit, floor, or ward.

long code. A resuscitation attempt (CPR) that is unusually protracted. Cf. full code.

martyr. A person who suffers or, especially, dies for the sake of bearing witness to the truth of the gospel of Jesus Christ.

1988 PCA Report on Heroic Measures. A report written by the Ad Interim Committee on Heroic Measures appointed by the

15th General Assembly of the Presbyterian Church in America (1987) in response to an overture (#37) from the Presbytery of Illiana. The committee was formed "to study such questions as 'What constitutes heroic measures?', 'At what point do modern medical approaches attempt to usurp the life/death authority of God?', 'When may Christians properly refuse heroic attempts to prolong life?', and to provide helpful Scriptural insight and direction for families finding themselves in this dilemma" (Minutes of the 15th General Assembly, p. 86). The committee consisted of William Hall, James Hurley, Reginald F. McLelland, F. Edward Payne, and John Van Voorhis. The 16th General Assembly (1988) adopted the report, which appears on pages 16–83 of Appendix S of the Minutes of the 16th General Assembly.

nurse practitioner (NP). A registered nurse who through advanced training is qualified to assume some of the duties and responsibilities formerly assumed only by a physician. See also advanced-practice nurse.

ordinary means of grace. Those institutions ordained by God to be the ordinary channels of grace to the souls of men. These are the Word, the sacraments, and prayer.

organ donation. The taking of healthy organs and tissues from one person for transplantation into another. Organs that can be donated include kidneys, heart, liver, pancreas, intestines, lungs, skin, and corneas.

palliative care. Medical and related care provided to a person with a serious, life-threatening, or terminal illness that is not intended to provide curative treatment but rather to manage symptoms, relieve pain and discomfort, improve quality of life, and meet the person's emotional, social, and spiritual needs.

Parkinson's disease. A chronic progressive neurological disease chiefly of later life that is linked to decreased dopamine production in the substantia nigra, is of unknown cause, and is marked especially by tremor of resting muscles, rigidity, slowness of movement, impaired balance, and a shuffling gait.

permanent confusion. Permanent and incurable confusion that may be associated with delirium or dementia.

permanent unconsciousness. An incurable and irreversible condition in which the person is medically assessed as having no reasonable probability of recovery from an irreversible coma or a permanent vegetative state. Also called *persistent vegetative state.*

physician assistant (PA). A specially trained person who is certified to provide basic medical services (as the diagnosis and treatment of common ailments), usually under the supervision of a licensed physician.

physician-assisted suicide. Suicide by a person facilitated by means or information (as a drug prescription or indication of the lethal dosage) provided by a physician aware of the person's intent.

principal. The person for whom an agent or surrogate speaks or acts. See also surrogate decision.

quality of life. Physical, social, psychological, and spiritual well-being.

Schiavo, Terri. The decisionally incapable woman at the center of a 2005 legal dispute about her husband's wish to discontinue artificial nutrition and hydration. See also decisional capacity.

statin. Any of a group of lipid-lowering drugs (as lovastatin and simvastatin) that function by inhibiting a liver enzyme that controls the synthesis of cholesterol and by promoting the production of LDL-binding receptors in the liver, resulting in a usually marked decrease in the level of LDL and a modest increase in the level of HDL circulating in blood plasma.

stewardship. The responsible management of something—resources, talents, time, opportunities—entrusted to one's care, especially by God.

"sticker price" for medical care. The advertised price or the price for service published by a medical provider (hospital, physician, therapist, etc.), usually higher than insurers pay for the service.

substituted judgment. A decision by a surrogate for a now-incompetent person based on indications of what the person's wishes would have been if he or she were able to make the decision required. See also surrogate decision.

suffering. Any experience unpleasant enough that (all things being equal) one would like it to end.[1]

suicide. The intentional taking of one's own life. Cf. physician-assisted suicide.

surrogate decision. A decision made by someone in accordance with the values and wishes of another person; the surrogate chooses what the principal would choose. See also substituted judgment.

suzerain. The great king or lord who enters into a covenant with a subjected/vassal people. A suzerain-vassal covenant gives the historical grounds for the suzerain's claims, the suzerain's laws, the blessings that the vassal people will enjoy if they keep the terms of the covenant, and the punishments that the vassals will receive if they do not keep the terms.

terminal illness. A disease that cannot be cured or adequately treated and that is reasonably expected to result in the death of the person within a short time. This term is more commonly used for progressive diseases such as cancer and advanced heart disease than for trauma.

time-limited trial. A period of treatment to assess the balance of the benefits versus the burdens of therapy for a person when it is not clear whether he or she will benefit from the therapy. Clear parameters and timelines are delineated in advance of the limited trial so that it will be possible to determine at the end whether the therapy should be continued. See benefits and burdens.

tube-feeding. See artificial nutrition and hydration.

unpayable debt. An obligation to repay that exceeds all resources, including likely future earnings and the value of assets that can be sold.

utilitarian. Having to do with what is useful or (in moral theory) productive of pleasure and the absence of pain. Systems of

---

1. Mark Talbot, "On Not Being Beastly: Suffering and the Biblical Narrative" (keynote address, Covenant College Undergraduate Philosophy Conference, Lookout Mountain, GA, March 24, 2017), 13.

utilitarian ethics hold that morally right/good actions are those that maximize the happiness of those affected by the actions.

vascular dementia. Dementia (as multi-infarct dementia) of abrupt or gradual onset that is caused by cerebrovascular disease.

vassal. Relating to the subject or conquered people under the rule or protection of a suzerain.

BIBLIOGRAPHY

Abernathy, Amy, and David C. Currow. "Letters: Time-Limited Trials." *Journal of the American Medical Association* 307, 1 (January 4, 2012): 33–34.

American Heart Association. "Simulated Resuscitation Attempt." https://www.youtube.com/watch?v=eXmAzsRQi9I.

Arias, Jalayne J. "A Time to Step In: Legal Mechanisms for Protecting Those with Declining Capacity." *American Journal of Law & Medicine* 39, 1 (2013): 134–59.

Balaban, Richard B. "A Physician's Guide to Talking about End-of-Life Care." *Journal of General Internal Medicine* 15, 3 (March 2000): 195–200.

Bane, J. Donald, Austin H. Kutscher, Robert E. Neale, and Robert B. Reeves Jr., eds. *Death and Ministry*. New York: Seabury Press, 1975.

Barclay, Laurie. "Guidelines Offer Pointers for Clinicians on End-of-Life Discussions." *Medscape Education Clinical Briefs*. http://www.medscape.org/viewarticle/812161.

Barry, Robert. "The Biblical Teaching on Suicide." *Issues in Law & Medicine* 13, 3 (Winter 1997): 283–99.

Beauchamp, Tom, and James Childress. *Principles of Biomedical Ethics*. New York: Oxford University Press, 1979.

Bell, Karen Whitley. *Living at the End of Life: A Hospice Nurse Addresses the Most Common Questions*. New York: Sterling Ethos, 2010.

Berlinger, Nancy, Bruce Jennings, and Susan M. Wolf. *The Hastings Center Guidelines for Decisions on Life-Sustaining Treatment and*

Care near the End of Life. 2nd ed. New York: Oxford University Press, 2013.

Bingham, John. "Parents Who Believe in Miracles 'Torturing' Dying Children, Doctors Warn." *Telegraph* (UK), August 13, 2012. http://www.telegraph.co.uk/health/healthnews/9473093/.

Biro, David. *The Language of Pain: Finding Words, Compassion, and Relief.* New York: W. W. Norton & Company, 2010.

Blackford, Martin. "Judge Rules Boy's Life Support Can Be Switched Off despite Parents' Hope of Miracle." *Telegraph* (UK), August 13, 2012. http://www.telegraph.co.uk/health/childrens health/9470501/.

California Coalition for Compassionate Care. "Talking It Over: A Guide for Group Discussions on End-of-Life Decisions" (1999).

Calvin, John. *Institutes of the Christian Religion.* Edited by John T. McNeill. Translated by Ford Lewis Battles. Philadelphia: Westminster Press, 1960.

Caplan, Arthur. "Little Hope for Medical Futility." *Mayo Clinic Proceedings* 87 (November 2012): 1040–41.

———. "Not My Turn." *Lancet* 380 (2012): 968–69.

Caring Connections. "Talking with Others about Their End-of-Life Wishes." Subsection of "Planning Ahead: Have You Made a Plan?" http://www.caringinfo.org/i4a/pages/index.cfm?pageid=3282.

Caulfield, Sharon E. "Health Care Facility Ethics Committees: New Issues in the Age of Transparency." *Human Rights* (American Bar Association) 34 (Fall 2007). http://www.americanbar.org /publications/human_rights_magazine_home/human_rights _vol34_2007/fall2007/hr_fall07_caulfi.html.

Childress, James F. "Organ Donation after Circulatory Determination of Death: Lessons and Unresolved Controversies." *Journal of Law, Medicine & Ethics* 36, 4 (Winter 2008): 766–71.

Connor, Stephen R. "Development of Hospice and Palliative Care in the United States." *Omega: Journal of Death & Dying* 56, 1 (2007): 89–99.

The Conversation Project. http://theconversationproject.org.

Crouch, Andy. *Playing God: Redeeming the Gift of Power.* Downers Grove, IL: InterVarsity Press, 2013.

Curtis, J. Randall, Ruth A. Engelberg, Mark E. Bensink, and Scott D. Ramsey. "End-of-Life Care in the Intensive Care Unit: Can We Simultaneously Increase Quality and Reduce Costs?" *American Journal of Respiratory and Critical Care Medicine* 186, 7 (October 1, 2012): 587–92.

Davis, Bill. "Choosing to Die: The Gift of Mortality in Middle-earth." In *The Lord of the Rings and Philosophy: One Book to Rule Them All,* edited by Gregory Bassham and Eric Bronson, 123–36. Chicago: Open Court, 2003.

DeGrazia, David, Thomas Mappes, and Jeffrey Brand-Ballard, eds. *Biomedical Ethics.* 7th ed. New York: McGraw-Hill, 2011.

Delehanty, Hugh, and Elinor Ginzler. *Caring for Your Parents: The Complete Family Guide: Practical Advice You Can Trust from the Experts at AARP.* 2nd ed. New York: Sterling, 2008.

DeLisser, Horace M. "A Practical Approach to the Family That Expects a Miracle." *Chest* 135, 6 (June 2009): 1643–47. http://www.ncbi.nlm.nih.gov/pmc/articles/PMC2821292/.

Douma, Jochem. *The Ten Commandments: Manual for the Christian Life.* Translated by Nelson Kloosterman. Phillipsburg, NJ: P&R Publishing, 1996.

Downie, Robin. "Guest Editorial: A Personal View: Health Care Ethics and Casuistry." *Journal of Medical Ethics* 18, 2 (1992): 61–66.

Eddy, Mary Baker. *Science and Health.* Boston: First Church of Christ, Scientist, 1994.

Edgar, William. "Health: Medical/Ethical Issues." Art. 2.P in *Serving and Challenging Seniors.* N.p.: Presbyterian Church in America, Christian Education and Publications, n.d.

Entwistle, Vikki, et al. "Supporting Patient Autonomy: The Importance of Clinician-Patient Relationships." *Journal of Gastroenterology and Internal Medicine* (March 6, 2010).

Ethical and Religious Directives for Catholic Health Care Services. Washington, DC: United States Conference of Catholic Bishops, 2009.

Feldman, David B., and S. Andrew Lasher Jr. *The End-of-Life Handbook*. Oakland, CA: New Harbinger Publications, 2012.

Ferguson, Sinclair B., David F. Wright, and J. I. Packer. *New Dictionary of Theology*. Downers Grove, IL: InterVarsity Press, 1988.

Fitzpatrick, Jeanne, and Eileen M. Fitzpatrick. *A Better Way of Dying: How to Make Choices at the End of Life*. New York: Penguin, 2010.

Fortunato, John. "'Irreversibility' and the Modern Understanding of Death." *Discussions* 9, 2 (2013). http://www.inquiriesjournal.com /a?id=795.

Foucault, Michel. *The Birth of the Clinic*. London: Routledge, 1963. Reprint, New York: Vintage Books, 1994.

Frame, John M. *The Doctrine of the Christian Life*. A Theology of Lordship. Phillipsburg, NJ: P&R Publishing, 2008.

———. *Medical Ethics: Principles, Persons, and Problems*. Phillipsburg, NJ: Presbyterian and Reformed, 1988.

Garr, W. Randall. *In His Own Image and Likeness: Humanity, Divinity, and Monotheism*. Leiden: Brill, 2003.

Getz, Gene A. *A Biblical Theology of Material Possessions*. Chicago: Moody Press, 1990.

Gomes, Barbara, Natalia Calanzani, Marjolein Gysels, Sue Hall, and Irene J. Higginson. "Heterogeneity and Changes in Preferences for Dying at Home: A Systematic Review." *BMC Palliative Care* 12, 1 (2013): 7–19.

Henry, Stella Mora. *The Eldercare Handbook: Difficult Choices, Compassionate Solutions*. New York: HarperCollins, 2006.

Higgins, James. "Casuistry Revisited." *Heythrop Journal* (2012): 806–36.

Holstege, Henry, and Robert Riekse, eds. *Caring for Aging Loved Ones*. Colorado Springs: Focus on the Family, 2002.

Huntington, Clare, and Elizabeth Scott. "Children's Health in a Legal Framework." *The Future of Children* 25, 1 (2015): 177–97. http:// www.jstor.org.ezproxy.covenant.edu/stable/43267768.

Jones, David Clyde. *Biblical Christian Ethics*. Grand Rapids: Baker, 1994.

Jonsen, Al. *The Abuse of Casuistry: A History of Moral Reasoning.* Berkeley, CA: University of California Press, 1988.

Kaiser, Walter C., Jr. "How Can Christians Derive Principles from Specific Commands of the Law?" In *Readings in Christian Ethics,* ed. David K. Clark and Robert V. Rakestraw, 192–201. Grand Rapids: Baker, 1994.

Keller, Timothy. *Counterfeit Gods: The Empty Promises of Money, Sex, and Power, and the Only Hope That Matters.* New York: Penguin, 2011.

Kleinmann, A. E., et al. "Systems-Level Assessment of Interobserver Agreement (IOA) for Implementation of Protective Holding (Therapeutic Restraint) in a Behavioral Healthcare Setting." *Journal of Developmental and Physical Disabilities* 21, 6 (2009): 473–83.

Koskenniemi, Erkki, Kirsi Nisula, and Jorma Toppari. "Wine Mixed with Myrrh (Mark 15.23) and *Crurifragium* (John 19.31–32): Two Details of the Passion Narratives." *Journal for the Study of the New Testament* 27, 4 (2005): 379–91.

Litwa, M. David. "Self-Sacrifice to Save the Life of Another in Jewish and Christian Traditions." *Heythrop Journal* 50, 6 (November 2009): 912–22.

Lucas, Sean Michael. *On Being Presbyterian: Our Beliefs, Practices, and Stories.* Phillipsburg, NJ: P&R Publishing, 2006.

Maguire, Daniel C. "Ethics: How to Do It." In *Readings in Christian Ethics,* ed. David K. Clark and Robert V. Rakestraw, 284–90. Grand Rapids, Baker, 1994.

McLelland, Reginald, Ed Payne, et al. *Study Committee Report on Heroic Measures,* adopted by the 1988 General Assembly of the Presbyterian Church in America. http://pcahistory.org/pca/2-378.html.

Meilaender, Gilbert. *Bioethics: A Primer for Christians.* 2nd ed. Grand Rapids: Eerdmans, 2005.

———. "I Want to Burden My Loved Ones." *First Things* (March 2010). http://www.firstthings.com/article/2010/03/i-want-to-burden-my-loved-ones.

————. *Neither Beast nor God: The Dignity of the Human Person.* New York: New Atlantis Books, 2009.

Middleton, Richard. *The Liberating Image: The Imago Dei in Genesis 1.* Grand Rapids: Brazos, 2005.

Morhaim, Dan. *The Better End: Surviving (and Dying) on Your Own Terms in Today's Modern Medical World.* Baltimore: Johns Hopkins University Press, 2012.

Mottram, Kenneth P. *Caring for Those in Crisis: Facing Ethical Dilemmas with Patients and Families.* Grand Rapids: Brazos, 2007.

Orr, Robert D. *Medical Ethics and the Faith Factor: A Handbook for Clergy and Health-Care Professionals.* Grand Rapids: Eerdmans, 2009.

Paris, John J. "Terri Schiavo and the Use of Artificial Nutrition and Fluids: Insights from the Catholic Tradition on End-of-Life Care." *Palliative & Supportive Care* 4, 2 (2006): 117–20.

Pence, Gregory. *Classic Cases in Medical Ethics: Accounts of Cases That Have Shaped Medical Ethics, with Philosophical, Legal, and Historical Backgrounds.* Boston: McGraw Hill, 2004.

Perry, John J. "The Rise and Impact of Nurse Practitioners and Physician Assistants on Their Own and Cross-Occupation Incomes." *Contemporary Economic Policy* 27, 4 (2009): 491–511.

Perry, Joshua E., Larry R. Churchill, and Howard S. Kirshner. "The Terri Schiavo Case: Legal, Ethical, and Medical Perspectives." *Annals of Internal Medicine* 143, 10 (November 15, 2005): 744–48.

Plantinga, Cornelius. *Not the Way It's Supposed to Be: A Breviary of Sin.* Grand Rapids: Eerdmans, 1995.

Quill, Timothy E., and Robert Holloway. "Time-Limited Trials near the End of Life." *Journal of the American Medical Association* 306, 13 (October 3, 2011): 1483–84.

Ramsey, Paul. *The Patient as Person.* New Haven, CT: Yale University Press, 1970.

Rawls, John. *A Theory of Justice.* 2nd ed. Cambridge, MA: Harvard University Press, 1999.

Roberts, Barbara M. *Helping Those Who Hurt.* Colorado Springs: NavPress, 2009.

Sabatino, Charles P. "The Evolution of Health Care Advance Planning Law and Policy." *Milbank Quarterly* 88, 2 (2010): 211–39. http://www.jstor.org.ezproxy.covenant.edu/stable/25698387.

Schenker, Yael, Megan Crowley-Matoka, Daniel Dohan, Greer A. Tiver, Robert Arnold, and Douglas B. White. "I Don't Want to Be the One Saying 'We Should Just Let Him Die': Intrapersonal Tensions Experienced by Surrogate Decision Makers in the ICU." *Journal of General Internal Medicine* 27, 12 (December 2012): 1657–65.

Schlissel, Elliot. "History of Living Wills." http://www.schlissellaw firm/com/history-of-living-wills/.

Schostak, Zev. "Holding On or Letting Go: Aggressive Treatment or Hospice Care? Making End-of-Life Medical Decisions" (December 4, 2008). http://www.yutorah.org/.

Siegel, Andrew M., Anna S. Barnwell, and Dominic A. Sisti. "Assessing Decision-Making Capacity: A Primer for the Development of Hospital Practice Guidelines." *HEC Forum: HealthCare Ethics Committee Forum: An Interprofessional Journal on Healthcare Institutions' Ethical and Legal Issues* 26, 2 (2014): 159–68.

Singh, Swati, et al. "Evaluation of Cardiopulmonary Resuscitation (CPR) for Patient Outcomes and Their Predictors." *Journal of Clinical & Diagnostic Research* 10, 1 (2016): 1–4.

Society of Critical Care Medicine. "Resolving End-of-Life Conflicts in the ICU" (August 5, 2010) (podcast).

Stewart, Gary P., et al. *Basic Questions on End of Life Decisions: How Do We Know What's Right?* Grand Rapids: Kregel, 1998.

Talbot, Mark. "On Not Being Beastly: Suffering and the Biblical Narrative." Keynote address at the Covenant College Undergraduate Philosophy Conference, Lookout Mountain, GA, March 24, 2017.

VanDrunen, David. *Bioethics and the Christian Life: A Guide to Making Difficult Decisions.* Wheaton, IL: Crossway, 2009.

Van Pelt, Rich, and Jim Hancock. *The Youth Worker's Guide to Helping Teenagers in Crisis.* Grand Rapids: Zondervan, 2005.

Varelius, Jukka. "The Value of Autonomy in Medical Ethics." *Medicine, Health Care and Philosophy* 9 (2006): 377–88.

Waples, Elaine. "4 Perfect Questions When Facing an End of Life Situation." http://www.kevinmd.com/blog/2012/04/4-perfect -questions-facing-life-situation.html.

Warfield, B. B. *Counterfeit Miracles*. New York: Charles Scribner's Sons, 1918.

The Westminster Confession of Faith and Catechisms as Adopted by the Presbyterian Church in America with Proof Texts. Lawrenceville, GA: Committee on Education & Publication of the PCA, 2007.

Wise, Robert L. *When There Is No Miracle: Finding Hope in Pain and Suffering*. Glendale, CA: G/L Publications, 1977.

Zientek, David M. "Artificial Nutrition and Hydration in Catholic Healthcare: Balancing Tradition, Recent Teaching, and Law." *HEC Forum* 25, 2 (June 2013): 145–59.

Zukerman, Rachelle. *Eldercare for Dummies*. New York: Wiley Publishing, 2003.

INDEX OF SCRIPTURE

INDEX OF SUBJECTS
AND NAMES